Changing Writing

Changing Writing

A Guide with Scenarios

Johndan Johnson-Eilola
Clarkson University

BEDFORD/ST. MARTIN'S

Boston • New York

For Bedford/St. Martin's

Vice President Editorial, Macmillan Higher Education Humanities: Edwin Hill
Editorial Director for English and Music: Karen S. Henry
Publisher for Composition and Business and Technical Writing: Leasa Burton
Senior Developmental Editor: Caroline Thompson
Production Editor: Kendra LeFleur
Production Assistant: Erica Zhang
Senior Production Supervisor: Jennifer Peterson
Marketing Manager: Emily Rowin
Editorial Assistant: Brenna Cleeland
Copy Editor: Lisa Wehrle
Indexer: Jake Kawatski
Photo Researcher: Julie Tesser
Director of Rights and Permissions: Hilary Newman
Senior Art Director: Anna Palchik
Text Design: Jonathan Nix
Cover Design: Billy Boardman
Composition: Graphic World
Printing and Binding: RR Donnelley and Sons

Manufactured in the United States of America.

9   8   7   6   5   4
f   e   d   c   b   a

For information, write: Bedford/St. Martin's, 75 Arlington Street, Boston, MA 02116
   (617-399-4000)

ISBN 978-1-4576-0678-6

Acknowledgments

Preface

Writing, as most of us have realized by now, is changing. Alongside traditional texts like essays and research papers, our students (and we) now create Facebook pages and Tweets, Tumblr posts and text messages. We are constantly adapting to emerging media and technologies. By bringing these new forms of writing into our classrooms, we make composition more relevant and our students more successful. But like older forms of writing, these new forms are also designed to create change—by inspiring action, adding to readers' and writers' knowledge, or altering their attitudes. *Changing Writing* is based on the idea that if students understand that all writing creates change, and that anything can be a text, they can learn how to approach any writing situation in ways that make their communications more successful and rewarding.

By learning to approach any situation through the simple, rhetorical framework of purpose, audience, context, and text, students will discover that the same questions that help them develop strategies for writing an academic paper can help them develop strategies for writing a weblog post, creating a video, or launching a social media campaign to create change. They'll learn how to select genres that most effectively address specific writing situations, choosing the medium most likely to support the change they want to make with their writing. And they'll learn to examine their own writing practices, including the tools they use and the spaces they work in, to develop their own flexible strategies and best practices for writing.

A Portable, Adaptable Framework for Writing

In *Changing Writing,* approaching writing situations always involves the process of working recursively across four aspects of the situation, referred to in the book as PACT: purpose, audience, context and text.

v

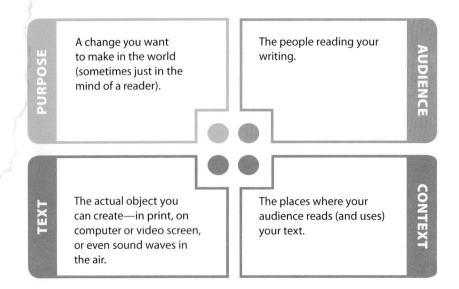

Each of these four aspects motivates questions about the situation that, as they are answered, help students construct texts that create change, using media and genres that work well for their audience and context. In important ways, the framework can be seen as both concrete and abstract depending on the writer's perspective and stage of the writing process: PACT charts throughout *Changing Writing* ask students to take up, recursively, one of four perspectives on the writing situation. Throughout this book students are also provided with suggestions about what questions to ask from those perspectives (a list of illustrative questions can be found in the PACT chart on pages 42–43).

But students are also pushed to see the framework and process as flexible, adaptable to new writing situations and technologies. Like any useful rhetorical framework, *Changing Writing* is a portable system that can be stretched and repositioned to adapt. Will the framework help students learn to write a persuasive essay about a social topic? Of course—they can work through the four aspects, asking questions and drafting a traditional, word-based text. What about creating a weblog that persuades people to become more aware about information privacy? No problem. What happens when text messaging is replaced by a new genre for short, personal communicative texts? The framework and process can easily be applied to this new situation, this new genre, to help students create effective texts.

Scenarios for Writing

Changing Writing is a two-part resource. The first part of the book introduces the PACT framework, showing students how it can be applied to different writing situations. Chapters then move through writing processes in a sequence that will help classes start writing quickly before moving into more advanced topics including graphic design, writing from research, collaborative work, and publishing texts.

The second part of *Changing Writing,* the web-based component in LaunchPad Solo at macmillanhighered.com/changing, lays out specific writing scenarios that challenge students to draw on the chapters of the textbook in relatively complex ways as they work with a range of concrete purposes, audiences, contexts, and texts. Students engage creatively with projects as diverse as tracking and reflecting on their use of mass media, increasing voter registration on campus, podcasting campus life, creating a Facebook page for an organization, designing cover art for digital music, educating high school students about online dangers, helping senior citizens avoid phishing scams, and mapping data to create an argument about a social issue that interests them.

The scenarios live online, taking advantage of the Web to deliver raw material in digital format. A few of the scenarios ask students to draw on existing texts, organizational policies, existing e-mail messages, and other material to be used as raw content for the new text students are asked to write. Support for the scenarios is built in, with suggested strategies, questions to keep in mind, annotated models, and suggested background readings. The online scenarios also include space for students to begin work on their PACT charts and to reflect on completed assignments.

Scenarios offer instructors a resource for managing complexity in assignments: They are more complicated than chapter exercises or discussion prompts but also somewhat limited, giving students a bounded but still complex space to practice what they're learning. Both parts of *Changing Writing* link concretely to each other: the first ten chapters include Scenario Connections, briefer assignments that help students get started on smaller tasks related to the larger scenarios. And each scenario includes Chapter Connections, specific links back to chapters or sections students should refer to as they work.

Instructors can tailor the scenarios to fit their own purposes and students. The instructor's manual includes suggestions for changing the scope or focus of each scenario to suit different types of assignments.

Changing Writing includes five scenarios in its printed pages to give you a sense of how they work. The entire collection of scenarios is located in LaunchPad Solo for *Changing Writing* at macmillanhighered.com/ changing. For more about LaunchPad Solo, see the inside back cover.

Special Features

Changing Writing scaffolds the more complex scenario assignments with several other types of activities.

- **Reflect & Discuss** prompts scattered throughout the chapters can be used for small-group or full-class discussions.
- **Texts for Analysis** Most chapters include one or more real-world texts, providing students with material on which to practice using the PACT framework as a tool for critical reading. The texts represent a wide range of media and genres, including articles, websites, blogs, editorials, images, posters, advertisements, and student papers.
- **Exercises** at the end of each chapter ask students to practice what they've learned in short writing assignments.
- **Scenario Connections** at the end of each chapter help students get started on small chunks of longer scenario assignments.

In addition to the scenarios, LaunchPad Solo for *Changing Writing* includes the following features to support students' learning.

- **Digital writing tutorials** help students use free and common digital tools to support their work on multimodal projects. The tutorials offer basic tips for photo editing with Gimp, audio recording with Audacity, creating presentations with PowerPoint and Prezi, tracking sources with Evernote and Zotero, and more.
- **Tutorials on critical reading and working with sources** help students develop active reading strategies and learn how to document sources in MLA and APA styles.
- **LearningCurve** activities are game-like adaptive quizzes that help students focus on what they need to learn. Topics include critical reading, topic sentences, and common grammar errors.

Acknowledgments

Several people contributed important sample texts that helped illustrate concepts described in *Changing Writing*. Thanks to Zach Durocher, Brien O'Keefe, Dan Mandle, Kyle Pulver, Chris Talbot, Kim Villemaire, Rachel Ramprasad, Rachel Steinhaus, and Linnea Snyder, for sample texts. Jennifer Mitchell was instrumental in helping me recruit samples from her own students—much appreciated.

Many people reviewed various portions of the manuscript over the development process. As anyone who has reviewed textbook draft materials knows, good reviewing involves careful thought, clear thinking, and patience. My thanks to Jared Abraham, Weatherford College; Beth Bensen-Barber, J. Sargeant Reynolds Community College; Julie Myatt Barger, Middle Tennessee State University; Betty Bettachi, Collin County Community College; Carol Ann Britt, San Antonio College; Ron Brooks, Oklahoma State University; Jeffrey Cain, Sacred Heart University; Angie Cook, Cisco College; Dànielle Nicole DeVoss, Michigan State University; Bradley Dilger, Western Illinois University; Erin Flewelling, San Diego State University; Lauren Garcia-DuPlain, The University of Akron; Francesca Gentile, University of Oregon; Risa P. Gorelick, Monmouth University; Letizia Guglielmo, Kennesaw State University; Stephanie Hedge, Ball State University; Will Hochman, Southern Connecticut State University; Susan Kates, University of Oklahoma; Marshall Kitchens, Oakland University; Rita Malenczyk, Eastern Connecticut State University; Ryan Moeller, Utah State University; Randall Monty, University of Texas at El Paso; Courtney Mustoe, University of Nebraska at Omaha; Karin Russell, Keiser University; Steve Smith, University of Louisville; Kathleen Smyth, University of Utah; Kyle Stedman, University of South Florida; Derek Van Ittersum, Kent State University; and several anonymous reviewers.

At Bedford/St. Martin's I was lucky enough to work with a long list of extremely talented and encouraging team members, which include Denise Wydra, Leasa Burton, Anna Palchik, and Kendra LeFleur in addition to copyeditor Lisa Wehrle. I am particularly grateful for Carrie Thompson's help in restructuring and polishing nearly every aspect of the manuscript, from clarifying the structure of the text at the broadest levels to providing elegant phrases to replace my often-awkward constructions.

I would also like to thank Stuart Selber, who talked me into taking on this project many years ago and has continued to encourage me during the long process of completing it. Wooly bully.

As always, I appreciate the support of my wife Kelly and daughter Carolyn, who have had to hear more about the project than nearly anyone involved (possibly including me). Thanks.

Johndan Johnson-Eilola
https://twitter.com/johndan

Get the most out of your course with *Changing Writing: A Guide with Scenarios*

Bedford/St. Martin's offers resources and format choices that help you and your students get even more out of the book and your course. To learn more about or order any of the following products, contact your Bedford/St. Martin's sales representative, e-mail sales support (sales_support@bfwpub.com), or visit the Web site at macmillanhighered.com/changing.

Choose from Alternative Formats of *Changing Writing: A Guide with Scenarios*

Bedford/St. Martin's offers a range of affordable formats, allowing students to choose the one that works for them. For details, visit macmillanhighered.com/changing/formats.

- *Bedford e-Book to Go* A portable, downloadable e-book at about half the price of the print book. To order the Bedford e-Book to Go, use ISBN 978-1-4576-8762-4.

- *Other popular e-book formats* For details, visit macmillanhighered .com/ebooks

Select Value Packages

Add value to your text by packaging one of the following resources with *Changing Writing: A Guide with Scenarios*. To learn more about package options for any of the following products, contact your Bedford/St. Martin's sales representative or visit macmillanhighered .com/changing/catalog.

 LEARNINGCURVE FOR READERS AND WRITERS, Bedford/St. Martin's adaptive quizzing program, quickly learns what students already know and helps them practice what they don't yet understand. Game-like quizzing motivates students to engage with their course, and reporting tools help teachers discern their students' needs. *LearningCurve for Readers and Writers* can be packaged with *Changing Writing: A Guide with Scenarios* at a significant discount. An activation code is required. To order LearningCurve packaged with the print book, use ISBN 1–319–01180–2 or 978–1–319–01180–2. For details, visit bedfordstmartins.com /englishlearningcurve

I-SERIES This popular series presents multimedia tutorials in a flexible format—because there are things you can't do in a book.

- *ix visualizing composition 2.0* helps students put into practice key rhetorical and visual concepts. To order *ix visualizing composition* packaged with the print book, use ISBN 1–319–01183–7 or 978–1–319–01183–3.

- *i-claim: visualizing argument* offers a new way to see argument—with six multimedia tutorials, an illustrated glossary, and a wide array of multimedia arguments. To order *i-claim: visualizing argument* packaged with the print book, use ISBN 1–319–01179–9 or 978–1–319–01179–6.

PORTFOLIO KEEPING, THIRD EDITION, by Nedra Reynolds and Elizabeth Davis provides all the information students need to use the portfolio method successfully in a writing course. *Portfolio Teaching,* a companion guide for instructors, provides the practical information instructors and writing program administrators need to use the portfolio method successfully in a writing course. To order *Portfolio Keeping* packaged with the print book, use ISBN 1–319–01182–9 or 978–1–319–01182–6.

Make Learning Fun with ReWriting 3

bedfordstmartins.com/rewriting
New open online resources with videos and interactive elements engage students in new ways of writing. You'll find tutorials about using common digital writing tools, an interactive peer review game, Extreme Paragraph Makeover, and more—all for free and for fun. Visit bedfordstmartins.com/rewriting.

Instructor Resources

macmillanhighered.com/changing/catalog
You have a lot to do in your course. Bedford/St. Martin's wants to make it easy for you to find the support you need—and to get it quickly.

INSTRUCTOR'S MANUAL FOR *CHANGING WRITING: A GUIDE WITH SCENARIOS* is available as a PDF that can be downloaded from the Bedford/St. Martin's online catalog. The Instructor's Manual, written by Johndan Johnson-Eilola, includes sample syllabi and assignment sequences, tips for adapting the book's scenarios into assignments to suit your particular pedagogical goals, rubrics for evaluating student work, and an index of scenarios that makes it easy for you to find assignments that relate to particular topics, genres, or outcomes.

Sample Syllabi from the Instructor's Manual are available separately for download. The sample syllabi suggest three different ways to combine the readings, exercises, and scenarios in *Changing Writing* during a 15-week course.

TEACHING CENTRAL offers the entire list of Bedford/St. Martin's print and online professional resources in one place. You'll find landmark reference works, sourcebooks on pedagogical issues, award-winning collections, and practical advice for the classroom—all free for instructors.

BITS collects creative ideas for teaching a range of composition topics in an easily searchable blog format. A community of teachers—leading scholars, authors, and editors—discuss revision, research, grammar and style, technology, peer review, and much more. Take, use, adapt, and pass the ideas around. Then, come back to the site to comment or share your own suggestion.

THE BEDFORD COURSEPACK FOR COMPOSITION is available for the most common course management systems—Blackboard, Angel, Desire-2Learn, Web CT, Moodle, and Sakai—and allows you to easily download digital materials from Bedford/St. Martin's for your course. To see what's available in the Bedford Coursepack for Composition, visit bedfordstmartins.com/coursepacks.

How *Changing Writing: A Guide with Scenarios* Supports WPA Outcomes for First-Year Composition

WPA Outcomes	Relevant Features of *Changing Writing*
Rhetorical Knowledge	
Learn & use key rhetorical concepts through analyzing & composing a variety of texts	• The **rhetorical concepts** of **purpose** and **audience** are essential components of the book's PACT (**Purpose, Audience, Context, Text**) framework. • Chapter 1 explains PACT (see above) as a tool for reading, thinking, and writing, with **purpose** as a starting point for writers and an end point for readers. • Chapter 2 shows students how to **analyze** any text and writing situation, discover **purposes,** and recognize **audiences'** motivators and barriers to change. See also the chapter's PACT chart for sample questions for analyzing purpose and audience. • Scenarios (in Pt. II; all are online, and 5 are in print) give students opportunities to **analyze**, practice, and **compose different kinds of texts** for a range of audiences including peers, high school students, senior citizens, instructors, researchers, and general readers.
Gain experience reading & composing in several genres to understand how genre conventions shape and are shaped by readers' & writers' practices & purposes	• The PACT framework (see above) supports students as **readers and composers** of various texts representing **various genres**. As composers, students choose to work in genres that are best for their purposes, audiences, and contexts, and learn that **genres and audiences shape each other.** • The Introduction explains the range of genres that students will read and compose in. • Chapter 1 covers aspects of texts and their genres. • **Examples**, **Texts for Analysis**, and **Background Texts** give students practice in reading and composing in a variety of genres aimed at different audiences.

Note: This chart aligns with the latest WPA Outcomes Statement, ratified in July 2014.

WPA Outcomes	Relevant Features of *Changing Writing*
Develop facility in responding to a variety of situations and contexts, calling for purposeful shifts in voice, tone, level of formality, design, medium, and/or structure	• **Contexts,** and responding to various **reading and composing situations**, are central to the book's PACT framework. • Chapter 2 focuses on analyzing and approaching different **writing situations**. See also the PACT chart for sample questions for considering texts and contexts. • Scenarios (see earlier description) provide diverse settings in which students respond as readers and writers; the scenarios prompt students to be purposeful in their choices of **tone** and level of **formality** when they compose. Chapter 10 gives advice for revising for rhetorical features before publication. • Chapter 4 focuses on **structuring texts** in ways that are appropriate for a writer's purpose, audience, and context.
Understand and use a variety of technologies to address a range of audiences	• Screenshots throughout the book support student composers with a variety of **digital tools** for drafting, designing, researching, revising, sharing, and publishing texts for **different audiences**. • Scenarios require students to **use digital spaces and digital tools** for composing for **diverse viewers/readers**. • **Digital Writing Tutorials** in LaunchPad Solo (see macmillanhighered.com/changing) help students use free and common tools for tasks such as photo editing, audio recording and editing, and creating presentations. • Chapter 10 offers advice for **choosing media** that will work best for the audience and purpose.
Match the capacities of different environments (e.g., print & electronic) to varying rhetorical situations	• **Examples, Texts for Analysis,** and **Background Texts** demonstrate a variety of **rhetorical strategies** in different **formats, media,** and **genres**. Specifically, the Texts for Analysis (in the chapters) provide samples of various formats, while annotated Background Texts (in the scenarios) show conventions at work. • The **Scenarios** help students practice composing **print and digital** texts, and are supported by best practices for working in electronic environments (in the chapters). • Chapter 5 focuses on designing visual texts in ways that are appropriate for the audience and context and that support writers' purposes, in any format.
Critical Thinking, Reading, & Composing	
Use composing & reading for inquiry, learning, thinking, & communicating in various rhetorical contexts	• The PACT framework—especially the PACT charts—make clear the importance of **reading and composing for inquiry,** analysis, critical thinking, idea generation, and communication—in **various rhetorical situations.** • *Changing Writing* emphasizes texts as tools for changing readers' and writers' **knowledge, opinions, feelings,** and **actions**.

WPA Outcomes	Relevant Features of *Changing Writing*
Read a diverse range of texts, attending especially to relationships between assertion and evidence, to patterns of organization, to interplay between verbal and nonverbal elements, and how these features function for different audiences and situations	<ul><li>The Introduction suggests the evolving nature of texts and the **range of genres** that students will be asked to read and compose in.</li><li>Chapter 1 explores the connections among texts, reading, and writing. **Texts**, including aspects of genre, are foundational to the PACT framework—a structure designed to help students read and compose in genres and media that are best for their purposes, audiences, and contexts.</li><li>**Texts for Analysis** (in the chapters) and annotated **Background Texts** (online in **Scenarios**) give students lots of examples. These texts represent a range of **purposes, audiences, genres, media, organization,** and a variety of visual, **verbal,** and **multimodal elements.**</li></ul>
Locate & evaluate primary & secondary research materials, including journal articles, essays, books, databases, & informal Internet sources.	<ul><li>Chapter 7 helps students **develop a research plan**, prioritize research activities, conduct **primary research**, and **find, evaluate,** and use **secondary sources.**</li><li>Chapter 7 gives advice on conducting informal and formal research, including searching the **Web** and working with **scholarly databases.** Students learn how to evaluate sources for their credibility and track and organize them.</li></ul>
Use strategies—such as interpretation, synthesis, response, critique, and design/redesign—to compose texts that integrate the writer's ideas with those from appropriate sources.	<ul><li>See also the "Rhetorical Knowledge" section above and the "Processes" section below.</li><li>Chapter 1 provides coverage of texts that **integrate** other texts.</li><li>Ch. 7 gives advice on **writing with sources**, showing students how to write with sources: how to quote, paraphrase, summarize, and cite them.</li></ul>
Processes	
Develop a writing project through multiple drafts	<ul><li>The Introduction sets up writing as a **messy, non-linear process.** PACT charts emphasize the recursive nature of writing processes and encourage **continual reevaluation** of texts.</li><li>Chapters 3, 4, and 5 look at writing as a **series of drafts** that involve generating, structuring, and designing ideas.</li><li>Chapter 6 helps students **manage their composing projects**, e.g. by breaking large writing projects into smaller tasks, using timelines, and managing information.</li><li>Chapter 9 presents revision as a process involving multiple rounds of review.</li></ul>

WPA Outcomes	Relevant Features of *Changing Writing*
Develop flexible strategies for reading, drafting, reviewing, collaboration, revising, rewriting, rereading, and editing.	• Chapter 3 offers strategies for generating ideas and moving from ideas to a first draft. • Chapter 8 gives advice on **collaborative writing**. **Reflect & Discuss** prompts encourage students to share ideas and listen to others' ideas in class. • Chapter 9 covers strategies for **reviewing** texts, getting **feedback**, creating a revision plan, and developing revision strategies. • **Revision strategies** for publishing are covered in Chapter 10.
Use composing processes and tools as a means to discover and reconsider ideas.	• The PACT framework and charts urge students to continually re-evaluate their own ideas, processes, and texts as they read and compose.
Experience the collaborative and social aspects of writing processes	• **Reflect & Discuss** prompts encourage sharing ideas and listening to others' ideas in class. • Chapter 7 offers strategies for **involving others** through primary research. • Chapter 8 offers advice for **writing with others, building teams**, managing collaborative projects, and sharing materials. • Chapter 9 explains how to give, get, and interpret **useful feedback**.
Learn to give and act on productive feedback to works in progress	• Chapter 8 offers advice on **giving feedback**, while Chapter 9 helps students **incorporate** what's useful and create revision plans.
Adapt composing processes for a variety of technologies and modalities.	• Chapter 6 offers strategies for **managing composing** projects, with an emphasis on how to organize tasks, texts, and information, including **multimodal** materials. • Chapter 8 helps students **manage collaborative projects** and share materials. • Chapter 10 offers advice for **involving technical experts** and volunteers in publishing texts.
Reflect on the development of composing practices and how those practices influence their work.	• The PACT framework supports the relationship between composing practices and writing. This relationship is central to *Changing Writing*: Writing itself (what we do, what our students do) is changing; and, writing creates change. (See the Preface; also, "Processes" above.) • **Scenarios** provide opportunities to practice choosing media and genres that work best for a specific audience and purpose. Chapter 10 supports that practice with advice to help students choose media that will work best for their purposes and audiences.

WPA Outcomes	Relevant Features of *Changing Writing*
Knowledge of Conventions	
Develop knowledge of linguistic structures, including grammar, punctuation, and spelling, through practice in composing and revising.	• Chapter 9 includes strategies for **surface-level revising**. • LearningCurve activities in LaunchPad Solo provide extra help and **practice with common errors**. • *Changing Writing* can be packaged at a discount with a Bedford **handbook** (such as the interactive *Writer's Help*). Such a resource will complement the book's coverage of composing and revising and provide help with **grammar, punctuation, spelling,** and more.
Understand why genre conventions for structure, paragraphing, tone, and mechanics vary.	• See discussion of **texts** and **genres** in "Critical Thinking, Reading, & Composing" section above. • Annotated **Background Texts** in the **Scenarios** (online) point out the conventions of specific genres. • **Texts for Analysis** (in the chapters) represent many genres, including blog posts, articles, editorials, policy statements, advertisements, posters, research papers, and essays. • Chapter 4 offers advice for structuring texts in different genres.
Gain experience negotiating variations in genre conventions.	See above
Learn common formats and/or design features for different kinds of texts.	• **Examples, Texts for Analysis,** and **Background Texts** demonstrate a variety of **rhetorical strategies** in different **formats, media,** and **genres**. Specifically, the Texts for Analysis (in the chapters) provide samples of various formats, while annotated Background Texts (in the Scenarios) show conventions at work. • The **Scenarios** help students practice composing **print and digital** texts, and are supported by best practices for working in electronic environments (in the chapters).
Explore the concepts of intellectual property (such as fair use and copyright) that motivate documentation conventions	• Chapter 7 gives advice for paraphrasing, quoting, and **citing sources**. • **Documentation tutorials** in LaunchPad Solo demonstrate how to determine what needs to be cited and **how to cite sources** in MLA and APA styles.
Practice applying citation conventions systematically in their own work.	See above.

Contents in Brief

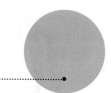

Contents

PART 2: Scenarios for Writing   261

ARGUING A POSITION

Scenario 1. Advocating Voter Registration on Campus   263

Your activist aunt is running for Congress and asks you to devise a campaign to convince college students to register to vote.

 ### Scenario 2. Teamwork Problems

While working on a collaborative project, your team has trouble with a slacker team member. You need to write to the instructor to explain the situation and ask to be graded separately on the project.

ASSIGNMENT: CREATE YOUR PACT CHART

ASSIGNMENT: REFLECT ON THIS SCENARIO

 ### Scenario 3. Arguing for a Handwritten Letter? Or E-mail?

You are asked to settle an argument between your grandparents over whether handwritten letters are more personal than e-mail. You will write a letter to one of them and an e-mail to the other about the benefits of each medium.

Scenario 7. Podcasting Campus Life for Prospective Students

A representative from your school's Admissions Office wants to offer weekly pod-casts about campus life. You will choose an aspect of campus life that you want to describe and create a podcast aimed at prospective students and their families.

Overview

Strategies

Questions to Keep in Mind

Chapter Connections

Background Text

Podcast: University of Kentucky Department of Anthropology, "Choose Your Own Adventure"

ASSIGNMENT: CREATE YOUR PACT CHART

ASSIGNMENT: REFLECT ON THIS SCENARIO

 Scenario 8. Drafting a Poster about Online Privacy

As an intern at a marketing and graphic design agency, you are tasked with creating a poster about online safety and privacy to be displayed in a local high school.

Overview

Strategies

Questions to Keep in Mind

Chapter Connections

Background Text

Report: Mary Madden, Sandra Cortesi, Urs Gasser, Amanda Lenhart, and Maeve Duggan, Summary of Findings from "Parents, Teens, and Online Privacy"

ASSIGNMENT: CREATE YOUR PACT CHART

ASSIGNMENT: REFLECT ON THIS SCENARIO

 Scenario 9. Educating Users about E-mail Scams

As a volunteer at a local senior center, you recently helped a client avoid becoming the victim of a phishing scam. The client asks you to do something to prevent others from falling prey to the same kind of scam—for example, create a brochure or a presentation, or write an article for the center's newsletter.

Overview

Strategies

Questions to Keep in Mind

Chapter Connections

Background Text

E-mail: Phishing E-mail That Purports to Be from PayPal

Part 1

A Guide to Writing

How Writing Is Changing

Effective writing *makes changes*. In most cases, people write to convince others to think or act differently. Good writing usually causes productive changes. A convincing business proposal secures funding for a project. A well-designed website helps users get information they need to file their taxes on time. An encouraging couple of words in a text message or tweet lift a friend's mood on a dark Monday morning. In this sense, writing always changes something.

But the *way we write* also changes constantly. As new tools and processes for writing are developed, new forms and types of texts emerge. Thirty or so years ago, texts produced as part of everyday life tended to be simple in terms of the features they provided to readers. People had little choice because they wrote everything out by hand or by typewriter. Doing research on an issue involved going to the library, looking up the location of books or journals on index cards in enormous sets of drawers, walking across the library or up and down stairs to locate a book, or squinting into special machines to read miniaturized texts on transparent films. (I am not making this up.)

In the early 1980s, researching and writing began migrating into the digital realm. Computers moved out of engineering and science labs and into general-purpose writing labs and dorm rooms. These systems often lacked much in the way of layout capabilities or font choices, but that began to change by the mid-1980s. Newer systems helped people design and print their own newsletters, posters, flyers, zines, and more — even simple interactive multimedia texts with basic audio and video. And where libraries initially introduced computers as digital card catalogs that indexed print books and journals, eventually those texts themselves became available online.

Writing changed again in the mid-to-late 1990s as web-publishing software allowed anyone with an Internet connection and a relatively inexpensive computer (or access to one at a library or school) to publish his or her own texts on the web. As that wave continued, professional-level tools for advanced audio and video production became available to the masses.

● Students researching and writing today
The Star Ledger/Aristide Economopoulos/The Image Works

● Students using a microfilm reader and printer, 1962. People really used these.
Texas A&M University/Cushing Memorial Library and Archives

As our culture became more networked and cellphones morphed into powerful, tiny computers, the growth of social media has altered the terrain of online media, dramatically increasing the amount and type of material people distribute to one another.

Now, people compose queries to access database records, read archival materials scanned into a website at a library on the other side of the world, and take advantage of social tagging features to find useful and interesting texts. As a student, you'll be asked to do more than simply read and analyze existing texts. You'll also do hands-on research, gathering raw data and making new texts that solve real-world problems.

And the sheer volume and diversity of information we have to work with is dramatically larger than was available to earlier writers. When we write today, we frequently find ourselves moving around within large masses of shifting information, rearranging things, filtering data, asking friends or coworkers for input. We e-mail drafts of work back and forth, post files for public comment, collaboratively edit documents in the cloud, coordinate get-togethers by text message, and create data visualizations like the one shown on the next page. Although we haven't completely reinvented writing, the activity today differs from writing a hundred years ago or even ten; it's more dispersed and diverse, more fluid and dynamic.

Composition classrooms, in turn, have opened up to a much wider range of texts. Here's just a sample of texts that you might work on and with in a first-year composition classroom today:

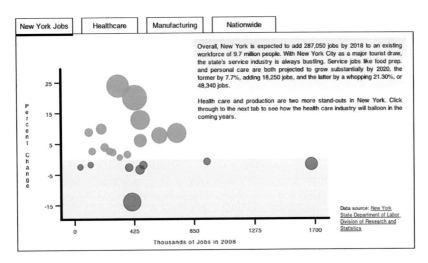

New York Jobs | Healthcare | Manufacturing | Nationwide

Overall, New York is expected to add 287,050 jobs by 2018 to an existing workforce of 9.7 million people. With New York City as a major tourist draw, the state's service industry is always bustling. Service jobs like food prep. and personal care are both projected to grow substantially by 2020, the former by 7.7%, adding 18,250 jobs, and the latter by a whopping 21.30%, or 48,340 jobs.

Health care and production are two more stand-outs in New York. Click through to the next tab to see how the health care industry will balloon in the coming years.

Data source: New York State Department of Labor Division of Research and Statistics

Percent Change

Thousands of Jobs in 2008

● An example of data visualization, one kind of text you might be asked to create
Eliza Ronalds-Hannon and Martin Burch, "Where Will You be Working in 2018?" from
http://datajournalism.2012.cuny.edu. Reprinted by permission.

academic essays	posters	Tumblr
data visualizations	PowerPoint	tweets
e-mail	Prezi	VCasts
graphic novels	research papers	video games
interactive media	songs	videos
letters to the editor	text clouds	weblogs
podcasts	text messages	wikis

You won't cover all of these types of texts in any class, but they suggest the wide range of texts that you might produce in your first-year writing class, in other courses, and in your life outside the classroom. And that range will continue to grow and morph as people create new types of texts.

How This Book Can Help You

You might be asking yourself, *How can I learn to write all these kinds of text?* This sounds like an overwhelming task. But we're going to reframe the question, making it both simpler and farther reaching. The question then becomes: *How can I learn a universal, flexible way to write any kind of text?* In other words, we're going to develop a flexible framework that you can apply to new writing situations as you encounter them.

The general approach is a little like the strategies your mind develops for dealing with new situations by referring to previous experiences: When you approach a new door, you don't sit down with an owner's manual for this specific door to teach yourself how to use it. You've built up simple strategies for knowing, often without even realizing it, where to push or pull or turn to make the door open. You have a couple of general rules about how doors operate: Make the left *or* the right side move toward you or away from you. If there's a knob, you turn the knob and push or pull. If there's no knob, you push or pull the door directly. On rare occasions you'll be baffled by a door — you push on one side only to find out that you're pushing on the side with the hinges, so the door won't budge — but for the most part you've internalized how doors work. You have a flexible framework for how to use a door, and you adapt to each door using that framework. Sometimes your framework fails, but you learn from your mistakes, adapting the framework based on your experiences.

Writing is more complicated than opening doors, but it is not unmanageable. This book gives you a framework for understanding how writing works. You'll work with four key aspects or components of writing:

- **Purpose:** the change you want to make in readers' thinking, feeling, or acting
- **Audience:** people within a context who are making meaning
- **Context:** a location in a space and time or even an online space
- **Text:** a document or other designed object

You'll learn ways to use these four aspects to respond to any writing situation, analyzing the purpose, audience, and context to develop an effective text. You'll look at strategies for generating new ideas and for structuring texts in effective ways. You'll see how to research, manage information, schedule time, and work with others on writing projects.

Because the success of texts you'll be creating will often rely as much on the visual as the alphabetic aspects, you'll even learn some graphic design basics that will help you create texts that have visual impact. You'll learn valuable revision strategies, including ways to get feedback from people who can bring fresh perspectives to your work. Finally, because you'll sometimes be writing for an audience outside the classroom, you'll explore ways for publishing texts in different media.

You'll also have plenty of opportunities to practice what you're learning. In the first part of the book, you'll find short Reflect & Discuss prompts that ask you to think actively about specific issues and discuss them with your classmates. The end of each chapter includes exercises and texts to analyze using material from the chapter. The second part of the book — the writing scenarios at bedfordstmartins .com/changing — includes a variety of writing assignments. These scenarios describe some elements of purpose, audience, context, and text to get you started. You'll then do additional work to create your own texts within the boundaries set up by the assignment.

This Might Get Messy (and That's OK)

Some writing textbooks present writing as a neat, logical, simple process. But we know from looking at real writing situations — in our classes, in dorm rooms, in the workplace — that writing is often very messy. That's not necessarily a bad thing. In fact, once you learn how to work within that chaos, you'll discover that you can become a better writer: better at thinking about writing situations, better at working and communicating with other people, and better at using writing to make change.

Part of accepting that messiness involves accepting that writing (and communication in general) is always an iffy process. The world's a complicated place, and only a tiny portion of it is in your control. Even a well-designed piece of writing may fail to convince readers to change the way you want them to, perhaps because the context has changed in unexpected ways, perhaps because your readers are just having a bad day. But your odds are going to be better if you understand your purpose, audience, context, and text. Once you have a handle on this framework, you'll be able to come up with strategies and tactics for convincing your readers. You'll know what sorts of arguments your readers will be open to, what sorts of information they want, and what types of texts they expect.

Let's get started.

Building a Framework for Reading and Writing

This chapter lays the groundwork for learning how to write effectively by explaining the four-part framework you read about in the introduction. We'll use that framework to analyze texts and how they work with audiences in specific contexts to change things. It might seem odd to start a book on *writing* by looking at *reading*, but looking at reading first simplifies things a little to help get started: You're probably already a little more comfortable as a reader because you've done a lot more reading than writing. You may not have spent a lot of time thinking about your processes of reading, but the four-part framework will help you come to understand how reading works. You'll then leverage that understanding in the remainder of the book to focus on writing.

Purpose + Audience + Context + Text = Rhetoric

Purpose, audience, context, and text, taken together, make up what's called "rhetoric," a field of study that's been around for thousands of years. Although the word sometimes gets used as a negative term ("that's just empty rhetoric"), it's a little more complicated than that. In an important sense, rhetoric is how a writer (or speaker or designer) shapes a text in response to his or her purpose, the audience, and the context. If we were to ignore rhetoric, we would ignore purpose, audience, and context. Our texts would be clumsy, ill-suited to our purposes, and probably not very successful. In most writing, you can't simply tell readers what to think or do. You have to persuade them. In other words, you need to carefully analyze your audience and their context to create a text that makes change.

Even the simplest texts—a stop light at an intersection, for example—persuade us because they are so simple. At first glance, a stop light seems like it's just telling us to stop, so we do. But much more is going on here: As drivers, we're an audience who's been trained over time, through experiences with nearly identical stop lights, how to behave. And a stop light exists in a network of social, legal, and ethical forces ranging from politeness (understanding that people take turns) to traffic laws (getting a ticket for running a red light) to safety (causing an accident by not waiting for a green light).

Shutterstock

8

The effectiveness of a stop light is not accidental. It was written over time by many authors in many contexts for many readers.

All Texts Make Arguments

All texts are arguments for or against change. This is most obvious in strongly stated texts that try to sway someone to make big changes — letters to the editor about things like changing gun laws or tax laws often make strong and obvious rhetorical moves. But even something as seemingly noncontroversial as a recipe works to persuade readers. The recipe from *Cook's Illustrated* magazine on page 10 uses several techniques to convince readers that the magazine is a no-nonsense, objective resource for advice on cooking (a stance *Cook's Illustrated* writers, designers, and editors cultivate in all of their texts, not only in the magazine but also in communications with subscribers).

From the use of black-and-white photography to simple, almost-scientific-sounding text, the writers aim to convince readers that *Cook's Illustrated* is a trusted, valuable source. Nothing about this text is accidental. If you've read other articles in the magazine or seen other texts from the same organization, you'll see a remarkably consistent approach that represents a clear, strong vision of their purpose, audience, and context. One common rhetorical move made by writers in *Cook's Illustrated* is the use of what amount to laboratory experiments:

> Next on my list of ingredients to tinker with was water. The original recipe called for ¾ cup of water to 2 cups of flour. Less water made the crust drier (no surprise) and tougher. More water made the dough chewier, but I soon learned that there was such a thing as too chewy. When I increased the water to 1¼ cups, the crust baked up with huge holes and was as chewy as bubble gum. The crust made with 1 cup of water proved to be a happy medium — chewier than the original pizza crust but not over the top.

So where a traditional recipe would simply tell the reader what to do (mix 1 cup of water and 2 cups of flour), the writer of this article attempts to gain the trust of readers by showing them how methodical she was in testing the recipe to ensure its quality.

The Four Aspects of Writing Situations

Although it's perfectly fine to analyze texts just by looking at them and thinking about how they work, a more structured approach will advance your understanding of what's involved in reading, writing, and using texts. The four aspects of writing situations — purpose, audience, context, and text — provide that structure. Throughout this book,

Reflect & Discuss

What other rhetorical moves does the "Provençal Pizza" article use to convince readers to read and try out the recipes? Can you guess what type of people would be most likely to purchase, read, and use this magazine?

Provençal Pizza

Pissaladière, the classic olive, anchovy, and onion pizza from Provence, is easy enough to prepare, but each ingredient must be handled just so.

> BY JULIA COLLIN DAVISON

Pissaladière is Provençal street food, a fragrant, pizzalike tart prized for its contrast of salty black olives and anchovies against a backdrop of sweet caramelized onions and thyme. Supporting this rough and rustic flavor combination is a wheaty crust with a texture that is part chewy pizza and part crisp cracker. Commonly eaten as an appetizer or even a light supper alongside a salad, this classic French favorite is still something of a foreigner to most Americans—darkly handsome, but a bit difficult to understand.

I had to start with a series of "get acquainted" tests to fully comprehend the range of possibilities. Most recipes produced a crust in the style of a pizza, others called for savory pie dough fit into a fluted tart pan, and I even found a few that used squares of store-bought puff pastry. All of them called for caramelized onions, black olives, thyme, and anchovies, but additional sources of flavor, such as Parmesan, sun-dried tomatoes, basil, and oregano, were not uncommon. As for the basic flavor ingredients, almost all of the caramelized onions were underdone, while the bullish flavor of anchovies overran the olives and thyme. Anchovies, I thought, should not rule out but rather act as a counterpoint to the sweet onions, briny olives, and fragrant thyme.

As for the crust, the test kitchen quickly eliminated puff pastry and pie dough. Unfortunately, the more authentic pizzalike crusts weren't very good, either. Textures were too short (think shortbread) and crackery or overly soft and doughy. Like me, tasters thought that good pissaladière should have a dual-textured crust that is crisp on the outside (like a cracker) and chewy on the inside.

This pizza captures the flavors of Provence—caramelized onions, black olives, anchovies, and fresh thyme—in every bite.

The Crust

Although pizza crusts aren't exactly right for pissaladière, I whipped up three different *Cook's* pizza crusts to see if any could be used as a jumping-off point. The thin crust wasn't sturdy enough and the deep-dish was much too doughy, but the traditional crust was the right thickness (about ½ inch) and had about the right flavor. Knowing that I wanted it to be chewier, with a more crackerlike exterior, I took a closer look at each of its four

major ingredients—bread flour, oil, water, and yeast—to see where I could make adjustments.

I replaced various amounts of bread flour with all-purpose but made zero headway. Bread flour has more protein than all-purpose, and that translates into a more substantial chew. Testing amounts of olive oil ranging from none at all up to 6 tablespoons, I again found that the original recipe (which called for 1 tablespoon) produced the best balance of crisp to tender without causing the dough to be brittle (a problem when the amount of oil dropped below 1 tablespoon) or greasy (a problem when the amount of oil exceeded 1 tablespoon).

Next on my list of ingredients to tinker with was water. The original recipe called for ¾ cup of water to 2 cups of flour. Less water made the crust drier (no surprise) and tougher. More water made the dough chewier, but I soon learned that there was such a thing as too chewy. When I increased the water to 1¼ cups, the crust baked up with huge holes and was as chewy as bubble gum. The crust made with 1 cup of water proved to be a happy medium—chewier than the original pizza crust but not over the top.

When I varied the amount of yeast, the flavor changed (as did the rising time), but not the texture. Less yeast and an overnight rise—a common flavor-enhancing technique—did produce a crust with a slightly more complex flavor, but it was awfully hard to detect once it came up against the onions, olives, and anchovies. One teaspoon of yeast pumped the dough through the first rise in a convenient 75 minutes (give or take 15 minutes, depending on the humidity and the

Understanding the Dough

We found that the same basic ingredients—flour, water, yeast, salt, and oil—can yield doughs that bake up quite differently, depending on the ratio of ingredients as well as the shaping technique and baking temperature. Here are the characteristics and differences of four of our dough recipes.

FOCACCIA DOUGH	**THIN-CRUST PIZZA DOUGH**	**DEEP-DISH DOUGH**	**PISSALADIÈRE DOUGH**
Focaccia is made with a lot of olive oil and is baked in a pan in a moderate oven. As a result, it bakes up thick, chewy, and very soft.	This dough is rolled with a pin until very thin and baked directly on a heated stone in a superhot oven. It bakes up crisp and brittle.	This dough is baked in a pan set on a preheated stone. (Adding olive oil to the pan ensures a crisp bottom.) However, because the dough is so thick, the top and interior are fairly soft.	This recipe combines attributes of all the other doughs. A moderate amount of olive oil is rubbed into the exterior to crisp the crust, and, because the dough is not stretched thin, the interior remains chewy.

● Provençal Pizza recipe from *Cook's Illustrated* magazine
Julia Collin Davison, "Provençal Pizza," *Cook's Illustrated*, March-April 2004, p. 13. Copyright © Cook's Illustrated. Reprinted by permission.

these four aspects are labeled the PACT framework. We'll visualize the framework in a chart like the one shown here.

Aspect 1: Purpose

Writing without purpose is pointless. Even though texts aren't alive in a biological sense, good texts have a sense of purpose, a need to make specific changes, small or large. A text does not need to make all of its purposes obvious to readers. Educational software, for example, often promotes one purpose (fun) to address another, much more subtle purpose (learning). But texts without purpose are likely to fail.

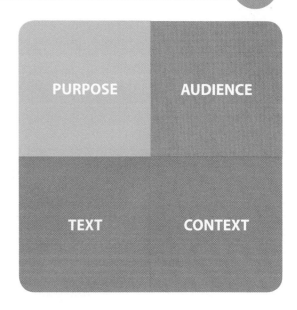

You may have one or more purposes, things that you want to change within a context. But you're not the only actor within that context. Your audience is active; they have their own purposes. And other people may have purposes that involve your audience as well. Your job is to figure out, within this swirling mass of things, which specific changes you want to push at to achieve your goals. As you create texts, you'll need to move back and forth between purpose and the other three aspects to see how they can be used to help reach those goals.

Aspect 2: Audience

The people who read, view, or use your text are your audience. Your audience engages with texts. They don't simply receive your text and obey it. They process it actively, sometimes understanding and using it in ways you didn't predict or for reasons you didn't expect.

WHAT DO READERS WANT? You need to work hard at understanding the needs and motivations of your readers: What are their concerns? What are their goals? Are they already inclined to participate in the change you want them to make, or are you going to be fighting an uphill battle? You need to understand a lot about your readers, the people who will eventually use your document. Without that knowledge you won't be able to write in ways that make productive changes.

HOW DO YOU FIND OUT WHAT READERS WANT? In some cases, learning about your readers will involve research. You might look at other texts that they read, particularly ones that seem especially effective: What makes those texts effective? What aspects or approaches can you adapt for your own text? You might also look at research people have done about your audience: Is it a target market? Is it an audience that others have written about?

In some cases, you'll even contact readers directly, asking them for their opinions about topics, or watching them read and use your document, taking note of places where they struggle so that you can improve the text in a subsequent draft (a practice called usability testing in the software industry).

Aspect 3: Context

In a way, context is the overarching aspect: Everything that happens with the purposes and audiences of texts happens within contexts. Contexts are where the actions of reading, writing, and communicating take place.

CONTEXTS INVOLVE READERS, WRITERS, AND TEXTS Contexts are not neutral: They affect the readers, writers, and texts within them. For example, a stop sign on a street corner means one thing, but a stop sign on a dorm room wall means something else. Readers read text on a website differently than they do a printed version, even if it's exactly the same content. For a variety of reasons, web texts are designed to encourage skimming. Because we're used to being able to jump around within a web text, if the website doesn't support that jumping around — say, by offering short chunks of clearly labeled content — readers tend to lose interest. Readers can force themselves to slow down and read more carefully — more print-like — but it's an effort.

CONTEXTS ARE MESSY A letter to the editor of a local newspaper that criticizes a retail conglomerate's plans to open a new megastore just outside of town might be composed of only a few hundred words. But the context in which that letter appears — a small, somewhat economically challenged semirural community — includes a wide range of powerful forces and varied readers. Local business owners, for example, may be inclined to agree with the letter writer, given their own stake in the issue. Some average citizens may welcome what they see as increased choice, while others may worry about the decline of an already depressed local business district. And into that mix throw numerous other issues on both sides of the debate, discussions at the family dinner table, reports in the local news media, and more. In a context like this, there are no single isolated texts or readers.

Aspect 4: Text

Texts are where information — data, words, images (even audio, motion graphics, and video) — comes together. They are the agents that a writer draws on in an attempt to make changes. Readers engage with texts, attempting to understand and use the information in some way.

ANYTHING CAN BE A TEXT   Texts come in an extremely wide range of sizes and types: not just conventional, typed essays or reports but also weblogs, short films, magazine advertisements, emoticons sent by smartphone, and many other forms. This very broad usage of the term "texts" can be difficult to get used to. If everything is a text, is the term meaningless? Not at all: Considering texts in this way means learning one powerful method for creating and understanding objects and how we relate to them.

Postmodern architects are fond of saying buildings should be read as texts. By this, they suggest that all artifacts — movies, buildings, cellphones, tweets, whatever — are not neutral, isolated objects but things with authors (designers with purposes), readers (users actively engaging with objects), and contexts (scenarios in which people work).

TEXTS ARE OFTEN MADE OF OTHER TEXTS   You might think of writing as the act of creating unique essays or reports or text messages. But texts are increasingly built from preexisting material — quotations from sources, stock art from online photo sites, tables of information generated by third parties. Writing becomes editing and filtering material for readers. Tumblr and Pinterest sites, for example, are often composed primarily of preexisting content, material the writer sifted out from the immense streams and pools of information on the web.

This isn't to say that people don't write "original" text — they certainly do. A lot of writing situations call for both preexisting content and new content that writers develop. You may need to quote some existing texts that support an argument you're making. You may need to reply to an e-mail by quoting the sender's text, framing your response around their questions. You may need to use some preapproved "boilerplate" text that your company requires for legal reasons and add your own writing to it.

YOU WORK ON TEXTS WITH TOOLS   Even though some people still think of writing as emerging, magically and fully formed, from the isolated mind of an author, in most cases writing is closer to architecture and construction than it is to pure creation. Just as good architects and builders carefully consider before beginning construction what site to build on, who the eventual inhabitants and users of a building will be, and what purposes a building will serve, good writers work carefully with context and audience as they construct a text that will achieve their purposes.

When you're writing, you're always using tools: You compose text using a word processor, you flag important websites with a bookmark in your browser, you send messages to a classmate requesting information in an e-mail program. Good writing relies on a whole array of tools.

Sometimes you'll use only a single tool when you write: If you want to see whether a friend will meet you for dinner tonight, you might fire off a short text message. At other times, you'll rely on a wide range of tools to get the job done. A research paper for your class might call for handwritten notes taken at the library; a folder full of PDFs downloaded from online journals; bookmarked pages on the web; a graphics program on your computer for brainstorming, gathering, and arranging notes; a different graphics program for designing figures you're using in the paper; a word processor for working on drafts; an e-mail client to send drafts to your peer review group . . . well, you get the picture.

Good toolboxes are assembled over time. Every writer uses tools differently; writers all have different ways of working. Only through trying out different tools can you figure out which tools work best for you in different writing situations.

Putting It All Together

When we write and when we read we're moving back and forth among purpose, audience, context, and text, making connections among all of these things. Writers often start with a purpose and then do research on their audience and the context to create the text. They may also decide, after thinking about their audience a little or doing some research on the context, to back up and change their purpose. Writing anything but the simplest texts is a process of jumping among these different aspects, sometimes doubling back as work in one aspect shakes things up or adds new information to the mix that requires changes in the other aspects of writing.

Readers often start with a text and work to understand what that text means by making connections between the text, the context, and their own experiences. And, like writers, readers often double back during

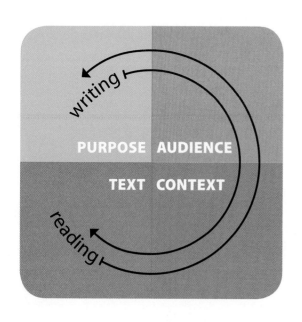

these processes, rereading passages of the text, reconsidering meanings based on the context, attempting to figure out the writer's goals, and more. Working to understand a text always affects the reader in some way. If the text is effective, it will achieve its purpose with the reader. If the text is *not* effective, it will still make some change in the reader simply due to the experience of reading it.

Reading usually starts with texts, and writing usually starts with purposes, as shown in this chart. But there are many exceptions: Readers sometimes know a text's purpose even before they start reading. Or writers trying to solve a problem may spend time doing background research in a context before they decide on a purpose. Reading and writing processes have general tendencies, but none of these processes is set in stone.

Applying the Framework as a Reader

Now that you have a basic understanding of a general framework that includes purpose, context, audience, and text, you can see how this PACT framework can help you analyze texts.

Asking Questions

Quick question: What is this?

If you said *flower*, you'd be correct. You win bonus points if you said it was *a drawing of a flower.* You'd also be correct if you said fleur, květina, בלום, kukka, fiore, or 花—each of which is the word for "flower" in another language.

These answers are all correct because meaning depends partly on **context** and on **audience**. Even though all of these answers are technically correct, the answer that works best will depend on the audience and context.

The flower drawing is actually taken from a more complicated context. Like many interesting texts, people can disagree about what it means.

The PACT framework can help us analyze this text because it gives a simple structure for asking questions about each of the four interrelated aspects of writing. We do this recursively—moving back and

● The flower drawing in its original context
Chris Jackson/Getty Images

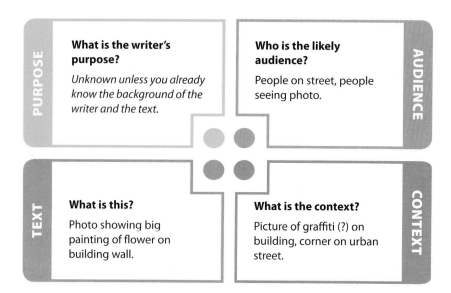

PURPOSE — **What is the writer's purpose?** *Unknown unless you already know the background of the writer and the text.*	**AUDIENCE** — **Who is the likely audience?** People on street, people seeing photo.
TEXT — **What is this?** Photo showing big painting of flower on building wall.	**CONTEXT** — **What is the context?** Picture of graffiti (?) on building, corner on urban street.

forth, over and over, until we're satisfied with the answers. To start, we ask easy questions, in this case starting with what we have — the text, context, and audience — to try to figure out things about purpose.

For readers, assessing a writer's purpose is often difficult. So we'll continue cycling through the other three aspects, asking questions and making connections among them, to see whether eventually a likely purpose emerges.

Making Connections

The diagram on page 17, called a network map, offers one possible (and very simplified) version of some connections we might make when we try to figure out the meaning of the painting. We're using the network map to represent the internal dialogue that readers might engage in as they try to understand the text. (In Chapter 3, you'll see how to use a similar technique, mind mapping, for generating ideas for texts.)

If you track key terms in the internal dialogue, you can see how the network map expands as one term or concept is answered with another. "Photo" connects to "flower" and "lines in street," which become linked to one another and to "painter." This path of questioning and connecting is the heart of actively reading texts.

As readers of this text, we'd probably start with the words in the upper right and then spread out, adding in new words and connections as we thought more about the picture. Connections would spread out from the most obvious ones (flower, painter, building wall) to less obvious but possibly more important ones (graffiti, protest, Banksy). And

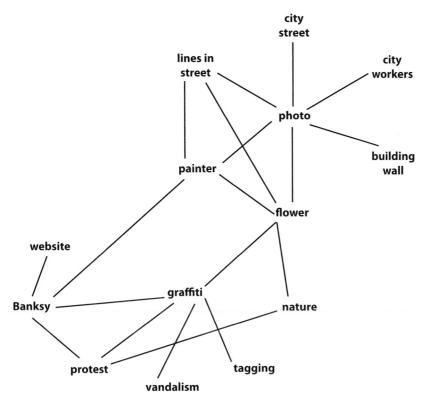

● Network map of one viewer's responses to the flower painting

notice that, in this diagram, what's important isn't just the concepts or objects — it's the connections among them. Words that are more important or "active" have more connections to other words.

Every person's reading process is going to be at least a little bit different. For example, if you're not feeling very motivated, you might not have even really paused to consider the picture beyond saying to yourself, "Weird" or "That's stupid," and then moving on.

Or you might have recognized this as an example of graffiti artist Banksy's work and have skipped pretty quickly to the "protest" idea (because it's a theme he hits on pretty regularly). As you can see in the lower-left corner of the network map, readers in some cases make connections from one text (the graffiti flower) to another (a website) based on their own experiences.

As a reader, you try to make connections between the text and your own context. One big context for the graffiti picture is the very broad Western culture you're probably part of if you're reading this textbook. You recognize the objects in the picture (building wall, street, city workers, and so on) not because of some built-in, genetic ability but because you've *learned* to recognize those things. And you recognize that the picture of the flower is something like graffiti because you've learned what graffiti looks like. As you're going along in your meaning making, you're probably not thinking much about these automatic recognitions until they start to conflict: The picture of the flower seems to be connected to the concept "graffiti," but what's actually been painted — the flower and especially the image of the painter on the wall — aren't typical graffiti images. Returning to your PACT chart and asking new questions based on your previous responses can help you with this process of making meaning.

PURPOSE

What is the writer's purpose?

Unknown unless you already know the background of the writer and the text.

Why would the writer/ artist put this painting on a building?

The writer wants me to connect the flower image to the street. And to graffiti . . .

AUDIENCE

Who is the likely audience?

People on street, people seeing photo.

Am I part of the intended audience?

Maybe I'm not the main audience.

TEXT

What is this?

Photo showing big painting of flower on building wall.

What is significant about the painting?

Wait. The stem of the flower is tied into the lines in the road.

CONTEXT

What is the context?

Picture of graffiti (?) on building, corner on urban street.

Is this really graffiti?

This looks like graffiti, but it's also not: It's not a typical graffiti image. They're usually cartoon figures, words, or simple symbols.

Part of understanding Banksy's work involves knowing who Banksy is and seeing some of the other texts he has created. Without that knowledge, you're left with mild amusement, possibly never making the important connections between protest, graffiti, and nature vs. city street.

Texts like the graffiti flower engage readers because they challenge them: If Banksy had merely spray-painted the words "I wish there were flowers instead of so much asphalt and brick" on the wall, you might have gotten the message more quickly, but it would lack impact. Part of the strength of this message is the work you have to do to understand it. When you "get" the text's meaning, you feel like you've accomplished something.

Applying the Framework as a Writer

What about the flip side of this? How do we get from applying the framework as readers to applying the framework as writers?

As said before, reading usually starts with text, and writing usually starts with purpose.

With this in mind, let's go back to the earlier PACT chart that summarized how we might interpret Banksy's flower graffiti:

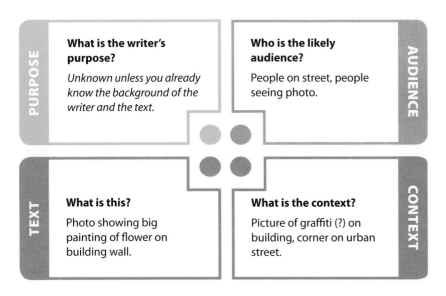

PURPOSE

What is the writer's purpose?

Unknown unless you already know the background of the writer and the text.

AUDIENCE

Who is the likely audience?

People on street, people seeing photo.

TEXT

What is this?

Photo showing big painting of flower on building wall.

CONTEXT

What is the context?

Picture of graffiti (?) on building, corner on urban street.

If we switched things around and asked ourselves how Banksy might have worked, we can imagine him *starting* at the "purpose" area (as writers often do) and moving in the opposite direction from his readers — see the chart on page 20.

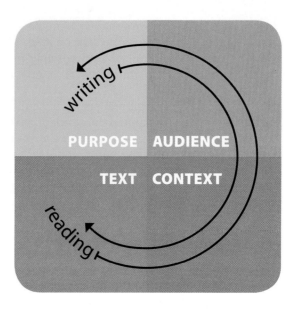

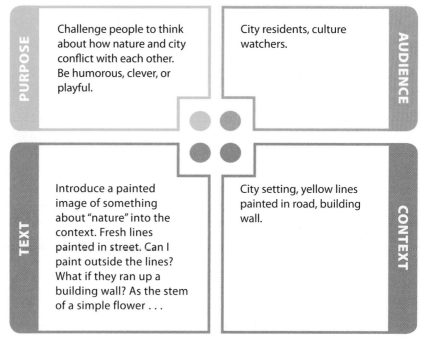

All of this, of course, seems very simple when it's written out after the fact. But it's not really that simple. Banksy probably had to work to make connections among the four aspects as he worked with aspects of the context (*What surfaces do I have available to write on?*), audience (*Who will be seeing this text? What do they know and care about?*), and text

(What image will change my readers' minds and help them think in new ways?). We'll begin exploring how to do that in the next chapter.

Texts for Analysis

Each of the texts below uses different strategies for convincing readers to change their beliefs or actions. As you read through and look at the texts, think about what concepts each one connects to in its readers' contexts. (You may want to sketch out a key word network map while you work or just brainstorm lists of terms and questions.)

Remember that you may not be the intended reader or be present in the ad's intended context, but you can probably put yourself in the shoes of those intended readers.

BLOG POST
Lisa Kalner Williams, "Twitter Etiquette to Use Right Away"

This blog post, written in 2013, provides advice for understanding the cultural and social rules of Twitter. The writer is the founder of Sierra Tierra Marketing, a social media marketing company.

Like learning a new language, mastering Twitter isn't just a matter of learning key terms. It's also about understanding the culture in which these terms are used.

I am often asked the following four questions about Twitter culture and etiquette. Take my answers and apply them to what you and your business do when you tweet.

1. Should I follow everyone who follows me?

Think of Twitter "follows" as valentine cards at grade school. You don't want to be the person who gets all the valentines but gives none in return. Know why? Because it isn't social — and you're engaging on *social* media when you're on Twitter. Being "cool" was fine in school — but on Twitter it really only works for celebrities. (I'm still waiting in vain for Lenny Kravitz to follow me back.)

Take a moment to look at the follower's profile. Does she have a profile photo? Is it PG rated? Does she have a seemingly normal bio? Then show her your "social side" and follow her back.

When I tell this to my students and clients they bristle with, "But I don't really want to read what she has to say."

Ouch. Here's the deal: you're on Twitter, the greatest social listening tool on the planet. Want to know who loves vegan cupcakes? Buys purple eye shadow? Is renting a one bedroom apartment in Boston? Your answers can be had by listening to and searching for appropriate discussions. The best way to systematically look for these relevant discussions is to create saved searches and Twitter lists.

● PURPOSE

What is the main purpose of the text? What other purposes does it serve?

● AUDIENCE

What type of audience do you think this text is intended for?

● CONTEXT

This text was first published on Social Media Today, a website for marketing professionals. Which aspects of the text still work outside of that context? Which do not?

● TEXT

What specific strategies does the writer use to convince the readers to follow the text's advice?

If your business is on a hunt for those vegan cupcake lovers, saved searches will help you wade through Justin Bieber squeals and reflections on coffee to concentrate on the terms that are most meaningful to you.

With Twitter lists, you can divide your listening of followers by categories. A real estate agent on Twitter might divide his followers up by "local folks," "vendors and contractors," "former clients," "coworkers," and "competitors." When he needs to engage with former clients, he can simply click on that respective list and begin listening—without interference from coworkers, contractors, or anyone else he's followed or established a list for on Twitter.

So yes—in most cases, give a reciprocal "follow" to be social. Then use saved searches and Twitter lists to listen to them only when appropriate. (I've created tutorials on <u>searches</u> and <u>lists</u> on YouTube to get you started.)

2. When I follow a new person, I often get a direct message from that person that tells me to follow them on Facebook or go to their blog. What's that? Should I do that with my Twitter account?

That message is called an automatic direct message (an "auto DM"). Many Twitter apps provide this functionality so that users can tell their new followers about their other online channels.

This type of automation <u>flies in the face of social etiquette</u>. If I just met you at a conference, I wouldn't immediately ask you to come with me to my office or home. That invitation would most likely happen once we got to know each other and mutual trust and respect were established.

The same rule applies on Twitter. Let your tweets gently hint at the great content you have on your Facebook page, blog, or other social channel. If your new follower finds the content there of value, he will check it out on his own accord.

3. Do I have to answer every reply or mention I get?

My sweet Lenny Kravitz has over four million followers. It would be nearly impossible for him to answer all the tweets that include @lennykravitz.

If your follower base is in the millions, I'd say it's not worth your time to reply each time your username is mentioned on Twitter. If your base is substantially smaller, chances are mentions of you will be correspondingly fewer. So take the time to be *social* and engage with those who've taken the time to find your username and put it in their tweet.

4. If someone retweets something I posted, how should I respond?

If your posts are getting retweeted, congrats! That means that you are sharing messages of value on Twitter.

Try these two ways to give thanks to those who've taken the time to share your tweet (and thus give you extra exposure). The quickest way to give someone thanks is to "favorite" their retweet of your message. The favorite function is usually indicated with a star icon either underneath or to the right of a particular tweet.

If you wish to give a more personal thanks, send a direct message to that person. Again, don't use the DM to tell the retweeter to check out your other stuff. Just use the message to send a meaningful thanks for the extra legs that person gave your tweet.

What other Twitter culture questions would you like me to answer for you? Ask me in the comments section!

GOVERNMENT DOCUMENT

Executive Office of the President, "Statement of Administration Policy: Lilly Ledbetter Fair Pay Act of 2007"

This text is the official White House statement on the Lilly Ledbetter Fair Pay Act. The bill proposed lengthening the amount of time that employees had to file discrimination suits against employers. The bill was named after Lilly Ledbetter, a woman who had sued her employer for purported discrimination, even though the contested discrimination took place outside of the time frame then allowed to file lawsuits.

● PURPOSE

What effects might this document have? Why name it after Lilly Ledbetter?

● AUDIENCE

Who will use this document? Will some of them have different feelings about the document (more inclined to agree or more inclined to disagree)?

● CONTEXT

What are the important parts of the context?

● TEXT

A pretty dull-looking text from a visual perspective — why is it formatted so simply? Why didn't the writer make it more interesting with splashier fonts or more color? Why is the little circular seal in the upper-left corner important?

EXECUTIVE OFFICE OF THE PRESIDENT
OFFICE OF MANAGEMENT AND BUDGET
WASHINGTON, D.C. 20503

April 22, 2008
(Senate)

STATEMENT OF ADMINISTRATION POLICY

H.R. 2831 – Lilly Ledbetter Fair Pay Act of 2007

(Rep. Miller (D) CA and 93 cosponsors)

The Administration supports our Nation's anti-discrimination laws and is committed to the timely resolution of discrimination claims. For this and other reasons, the Administration strongly opposes the Ledbetter Fair Pay Act of 2007. H.R. 2831 would allow employees to bring a claim of pay or other employment-related discrimination years or even decades after the alleged discrimination occurred. H.R. 2831 constitutes a major change in, and expanded application of, employment discrimination law. The change would serve to impede justice and undermine the important goal of having allegations of discrimination expeditiously resolved. Furthermore, the effective elimination of any statute of limitations in this area would be contrary to the centuries-old notion of a limitations period for all lawsuits. If <u>H.R. 2831 were presented to the President, his senior advisors would recommend that he veto the bill.</u>

Meaningful statutes of limitations in these sorts of fact-intensive cases are crucial to the fair administration of justice. The prompt assertion of employment discrimination permits employers to defend against — and allows employees to prove — claims that arise from employment decisions instead of having to litigate claims that are long past. In such cases, evidence often will have been lost, memories will have faded, and witnesses will have moved on. Moreover, effective statutes of limitations benefit employees by encouraging the prompt discovery, assertion, and resolution of employment discrimination claims so that workplace discrimination can be remedied without delay.

H.R. 2831 purports to undo the Supreme Court's decision of May 29, 2007, in *Ledbetter v. Goodyear Tire & Rubber Co.* by permitting pay discrimination claims to be brought within 180 days not of a discriminatory pay decision, which is the rule under current law, but rather within 180 days of receiving any paycheck affected by such a decision, no matter how far in the past the underlying act of discrimination allegedly occurred. As a result, this legislation effectively eliminates any time requirement for filing a claim involving compensation discrimination. Allegations from 30 years ago or more could be resurrected and filed in federal courts.

Moreover, the bill far exceeds the stated purpose of undoing the Court's decision in *Ledbetter* by extending the expanded statute of limitations to any "other practice" that remotely affects an individual's wages, benefits, or other compensation in the future. This could effectively waive the statute of limitations for a wide variety of claims (such as promotion and arguably even termination decisions) traditionally regarded as actionable only when they occur.

This legislation does not appear to be based on evidence that the current statute of limitations principles have caused any systemic prejudice to the interests of employees, but it is reasonable to expect the bill's vastly expanded statute of limitations would exacerbate the existing heavy burden on the courts by encouraging the filing of stale claims.

ARTICLE

Holly Kruse, "'An Organization of Impersonal Relations': The Internet and Networked Markets" (excerpt)

This article was published in *First Monday,* a web-based academic journal about the Internet.

● PURPOSE

Is this an article about racetrack betting systems? If not, why does the article start with them?

● AUDIENCE

Who reads *First Monday*? Why?

● CONTEXT

Look at *First Monday's* website (firstmonday .org). What other publications is it like?

● TEXT

Why is this document so bland looking compared to other online magazines like *Slate* (slate.com) or *Wired* (wired.com)? In terms of the words and sentences themselves, what "tone" does it have? Formal? Informal?

Introduction

In the first decades of the twentieth century, Australian George Julius perfected a kind of intranet. His totalizator was initially created as a voting machine, but when it didn't well serve that purpose, Julius adapted it to total wagers and calculate odds at racetracks. The first crude totalizator was installed at a racetrack in Auckland, New Zealand in 1913, and by 1930 the machine had been improved and was widely adopted in Australia, the United States, and Europe. Prior to the totalizator's invention, tickets for each race were printed in advance, and human clerks had to manually record bets (Conlon, 2002).

With the arrival of the totalizator, which was electrically connected to clerks' selling machines, tickets issued for each horse in a race and for all horses in a race were automatically totaled. A bet placed with any clerk at any ticket-selling machine was instantly and automatically entered into the pool, which allowed quick calculation of pre-race odds and post-race payouts. Moreover, each "horse counter" on the totalizator machine had a trip switch that could be thrown if a horse was a late scratch in a race so that all betting on that horse would immediately stop at every selling machine. After betting closed on a race, the counters on the totalizator were quickly re-set to zero to enable it to be ready to take bets on the next race soon after the previous one had ended. Preparation for the next race was simple: merely change the paper roll on ticket-issuing machines because a different color was used for each race (Conlon, 2002).

This description of the new totalizator machine at Hialeah Park racetrack in a 1932 edition of the *Miami Herald* illustrates how problematic the previous system had been:

> When the windows open there isn't a printed ticket in the plant. Each [selling] machine is threaded with a roll of blank paper. When you make a bet and the operator presses his lever point, the machine pulls the strip of paper over the printing device, stamps it with the number of your horse, the number of the race, and the amount wagered.
>
> This you see, eliminates printing thousands of extra tickets each day, enables the operators to throw open their windows immediately after the race, ready for the next race. And of course the use of the totalizator gives the bettors the chance to place their money right up to the minute the horses are ready to leave the post. [Quoted in Conlon, 2002]

Obviously, the introduction of the totalizator made processing bets on horse races a vastly more efficient process than it previously had been. One machine in Sydney in the early 1930s could record up to 250,000 bets each minute, a rate quite impossible to achieve with humans recording and totaling bets at a racetrack (Conlon, 2002).

We have become used to a world in which market transactions, like those handled by the totalizator, are mechanized and ultimately automated. Today, many transactions take place via the Internet. And indeed, as the example of the totalizator indicates, parimutuel horse race betting, which can now legally take place online in many states in the United States, as well as across Canada and Australia and many countries in Europe, has much to tell us about the development of communication technologies and how they influence the nature of information flows within countries and across continents.

In the United States and elsewhere, parimutuel wagering on horse racing traditionally took place in the public spaces of racetracks and urban and suburban off-track betting (OTB) facilities where prices have been and still are determined by the actions of others who are also participating in the market. Today, however, with communication and information networks allowing individuals to buy, sell, and bet in semi-public and private spaces, the sensitivity of participants to others in the marketplace — indeed to those who will affect their actions in a particular market at a particular time — has changed. What are we to make of the shift away from the embodied markets — those enacted largely in person, in face-to-face gathering places — that have existed on trading floors and at racetracks and OTBs, and the significance of the types of presence they help to create?

In the case of parimutuel wagering, for instance, network technology, especially the Internet, enables the near-instantaneous transmission of bets from bettors to wagering hubs and of odds information from tote systems to bettors, and the Internet allows bettors to quickly receive data on particular horses in upcoming races. These elements create an environment, characterized by its advantages and its risks, instantly available in virtual space across state, provincial, and national boundaries, expanding its presence to infiltrate new private and public sites, and thus creating new and different forms of connection among participants.

VINTAGE ADVERTISEMENT
Lucky Strike Cigarettes, "You Need This Throat Protection Too!"

This magazine ad, from the first half of the twentieth century, contains content that seems laughable to us today but probably seemed believable to many readers at the time.

PURPOSE

What response is this ad trying to provoke? Sales of cigarettes, obviously, but how is the ad making those sales? How is it persuading readers? What are the implied connections between the visual elements of the ad and the text?

AUDIENCE

Who were the intended readers? What important beliefs did they have (and that the ad played on)?

CONTEXT

Where might readers have seen this? Why were the particular elements chosen? For this specific time, why would the radio microphone have been significant? (What technology might be shown today?)

TEXT

What parts of this advertisement catch your eye? What graphic and textual elements are most prominent? What did the designer do to make them catch your eye? What are the purposes of the different fonts used?

Culture Club/Getty Images

Exercises

1. In your local (community or campus) newspaper, find a letter to the editor or an editorial you disagree with. Create a PACT chart to help you analyze how the text is working. Why did the letter fail to change your opinion? What would the letter writer need to do to really convince you?

2. Find something you wrote five or more years ago that involves a personal belief. How has your context changed? Are your purposes different? Write a short (approximately 500 words) summary of those changes and revise the text to reflect those changes.

3. Go to a fine art or modern art website such as moma.org and locate an image that interests you. Create a network map similar to the one in this chapter that explores ideas and topics you think about while looking at the image. After you've generated twenty nodes on your map, write a brief reflection (500 words or so) on the process of creating the map. Did the act of creating the map affect your understanding of the text? Do you think your classmates would have similar maps, or do your experiences give you a unique perspective? Do you think the artist would agree with your interpretation? Does that matter?

4. Open your e-mail inbox and copy the subject lines of the first ten messages into a new e-mail message addressed to a classmate (skip any messages that are too personal). In the e-mail, ask your classmate to guess at the purpose, audience, and context of each e-mail in a reply to you.

   Analyze the accuracy of your partner's guesses (with three to five sentences each): Was he or she able to guess correctly? Was the problem with the subject line itself or was it only because your partner lacked information that you had (about context, audience, and purpose)? Or did some of the subject lines also puzzle you a little when you received them (before you read the actual messages)? Forward the whole thread, including your analysis, to your instructor.

Scenario Connections

1. In Scenario 14, "Designing Cover Art for Digital Music" (see p. 292), you'll have the opportunity to design cover art for digital albums. Cover art usually provides some factual information (band or musician and title of album) but primarily attempts to create connotations for the viewer — emotions, connections, suggestions. Locate the art for an album you don't know very much about and create a network diagram like the one shown on page 17 that tracks your thought processes as you look at the album cover. Include at least ten terms in your diagram.

2. Scenario 11, "A Story from Your Digital Life," asks you to write a personal narrative about the first time you used a communication technology that was new to you. Read the background text in the scenario and analyze it by

creating a PACT chart. What do you think was the writer's purpose for creating the text? Who was the likely audience? What context was the text written for? Then create a PACT chart that you will use to write your own text for the scenario.

3. Read through Scenario 13, "A Day in Your Online Life." The scenario asks you to keep a log of all of the types of online media you use in a day and reflect on that use. As an exercise, take a single instance of one communication (a Facebook status update, a tweet, e-mail message, and so on) and create a PACT chart. What does the chart tell you about that communication? About your life?

4. Scenario 18, "Creating a Facebook Page for an Organization," asks you to develop a mockup of a Facebook page for a new campus organization that you want to form. To prepare for this scenario, write a brief description of this organization. Where in the context of your campus do you see a need for change? What kinds of changes would you like your organization to create? What will be the purpose and audience of your organization's activities?

Approaching Writing Situations

In Chapter 1, we looked at how to analyze texts using the framework of purpose, audience, context, and text. In this chapter, we'll begin applying this framework to writing situations you encounter when creating new texts.

We deal with a wide range of writing situations every day: Texting a friend back home to see whether he wants to go to a concert over winter break. E-mailing team members to see whether they can meet to work on a project tonight. Working on a résumé to apply for an internship. Creating a poster for your sorority's spring charity event. Most of the time, you might not think a lot about these *as* writing situations: They're just things you do. But thinking systematically about them as writing situations can help make you more effective by helping you understand what rhetorical moves will work best in that specific situation.

Understanding a writing situation involves analyzing a context and the people within it, considering both the current state (the situation as it is now) and a future state (the situation as you would like it to be). More important, understanding a writing situation involves figuring out ways to move from the current state to the future state: What forces will cause that movement? How do you argue for that change?

In many writing situations, we're dealing with one specific problem: How do we convince readers to do something? What argument can we make to convince readers to do something? In some situations, merely asking is enough. A teacher asks a student to solve a problem on the whiteboard at the front of the room, or you send your best friend a text message inviting him to lunch. In those situations, the people in the situation are already inclined to change in ways that the communicator wants, so the communication is likely to succeed.

In more complex situations, though, we need to understand the audience, understand what their world is like, and then provide them with reasons they might want to take some specific action. Thinking of writing as an argument reminds us that we're attempting to get real people, in their own contexts, to align themselves with our purpose.

Reflect & Discuss

Think about a recent disagreement you had with other people in your household, dorm room, or apartment. What were the forces that influenced your opinion and/or statements? What things contributed to how you thought and acted? Consider both local and distant things (people, groups, organizations, situations). List as many of these forces as you can in a word-processing document. Adjust the size of the font to make the strongest forces larger and the weakest forces smaller. What would it take for you to change your position in the disagreement?

Breaking Down the Writing Situation

Any writing situation involves a mix of four primary aspects: purpose, audience, context, and text. It's not always easy to figure out where to start your writing process or what type of text to write. Sometimes asking questions about the context provides the most traction, but other times thinking about audience or purpose is more helpful. In some cases (like some class assignments), the text is your starting point. So rather than artificially constrain yourself to considering these aspects in a set order, you might have the most luck by simply brainstorming ideas across all four

PURPOSE
- What is the problem?
- What, specifically, needs to change?
- What will be required to achieve the change?

AUDIENCE
- What are your readers' positions within their institutions or groups?
- Are readers inclined to agree with the purpose, to oppose it, or to be ambivalent?
- What are the barriers to change in this audience?
- What are this audience's motivations?

TEXT
- What kinds of evidence will persuade the audience?
- How much effort will readers need to put into reading the text?
- What kind of text would best accomplish the purpose?

CONTEXT
- Where is the problem?
- What institutions or groups are your readers in?
- What institutions or groups are you in?
- What are the barriers to change in this context?

areas. You might even decide to work back and forth across more than one aspect. There's not one "correct" way to unravel a writing situation, so it's good to keep yourself open to emerging opportunities.

Below we'll go over the four areas separately, but in practice (as we'll see later) writing is usually much messier. Separating these four aspects of writing is a little artificial but useful in helping us analyze writing processes and situations.

A Writing Scenario

Let's break down a specific writing scenario so we can see how this process and framework can help us begin creating texts. Take a look at Scenario 1, "Advocating Voter Registration on Campus" (p. 263), which asks you to take on the role of a college student during the time of a national election. One of your favorite aunts, herself running for political office, is on a mission to get college students to be more politically active. You agree to work on getting students in your own college to vote in the upcoming election. For the scenario your main goal is to increase student voter registration on your campus.

At this point, you don't know much beyond that general goal: To figure out specifics, you'll need to analyze this writing scenario by asking questions about your context, audience, purpose, and text. You might begin with the questions shown on page 32.

Purpose

Consider the purpose questions first for the voter registration example:

PURPOSE ● ● ●	
What is the problem?	• Not enough students vote in national elections.
What, specifically, needs to change?	• Voter registration rates need to increase. More specifically, readers need to go to the voter registration organization and register. • Do I need to prove an increase? If so, how am I gathering data about previous participation? How will I see whether my campaign is successful?
What will be required to achieve the change?	• Convince students that voting (and therefore, registering to vote) is important. • Convince students that registering is worth the effort. • Idea: Maybe show students that registering is easier than they think.

You can see already how considering purpose raises issues in both audience and context. When you consider what will be required to achieve change, for example, you notice that students might have misconceptions about how much work is involved — maybe if you show them how easy registering is they'll be inclined to do it. Cross-pollination among the four aspects is a good thing. Analyzing writing situations always involves making connections.

Context

So let's leave the purpose questions for a moment and go to the context questions. The specific answers will likely be different for your campus — this is just an example.

CONTEXT ● ● ●

Where is the problem?	• On my campus.
What institutions or groups are your readers in?	• College students at a Big 10 university in the Midwest, average age 21. • Possibly also members (officially or unofficially) of a political party, although those readers are probably already planning to vote.
What institutions or groups are you in?	• College students on my campus. • My sorority. • Students in my major.
What are the barriers to change in this context?	• Not clear to students (or to me) where students can register to vote. Are absentee ballots necessary? Or can students use their dorm or apartment addresses, even if their original homes are downstate or in another state? • Readers have many other contextual demands on time/attention.

You can see here a gap in your own knowledge. You don't actually know the size of the barrier to registration: What's involved in registering to vote? Are absentee ballots necessary? You'll need to do some research on these questions.

Audience

And you may have noticed that you're still left with another big gap: You don't yet know *why* students aren't registering to vote. You can probably come up with some reasons off the top of your head — students are busy, for example, or maybe they (like you) just don't know how or where to register. Turning to the audience questions might help.

AUDIENCE

What are your readers' positions within their institutions or groups?	• Strong identification with university at sporting events (football, basketball) or extracurricular activities (intramural sports, clubs, fraternities or sororities).
Are readers inclined to agree with the purpose, to oppose it, or to be ambivalent?	• Slightly in favor but more uninterested (registering to vote doesn't require a lot of time or effort, so it's likely that most who don't register aren't that motivated).
What are the barriers to change in this audience?	• Readers are probably unfamiliar with voting process (because of inexperience). • Readers have hectic schedules. • Readers may not believe that their votes matter (one voice lost in the crowd).
What are this audience's motivations?	• Various, but typically *not* highly interested in politics. Interests are in getting work done for classes, possibly working part-time to pay for school, having fun in their scarce free time. • Other students who are part of the groups that I'm in may be more likely to agree to register if I make this personal. Idea: Recruit them to create or distribute the texts? • Longer term, they're interested in getting good jobs and starting families.

This is a case where you may actually be a part of the audience you're going to be writing to — maybe you don't register to vote either. You may have quick answers to the "why aren't students registering?" question, but don't fall into the trap of thinking that *your* reasons for not registering are the same as everyone else's.

Text

Let's turn now to the text questions.

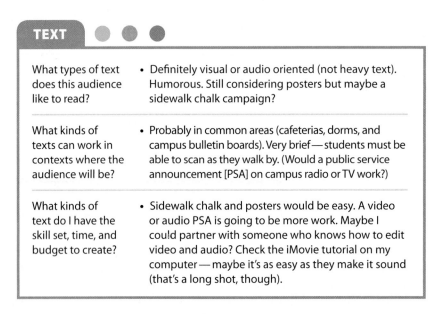

TEXT ● ● ●	
What kinds of evidence will persuade the audience?	• Tangible benefits? Patriotic duty? I need to know more about why they're not registering to decide what will persuade them.
How much effort will readers need to put into reading the text?	• I know from the answers to other questions that these readers won't want to read a lot. The text will need to be simple and straightforward.
What kind of text would best accomplish the purpose?	• Because they won't put in much effort, it needs to be somewhere they already look. Posters on bulletin boards. Banner ad on local website. Satirical political ad? Something surprising, like a horror movie poster about the perils of not voting?

The bottom row highlights one of the most difficult tasks of a purpose-driven project like this: What type of text will work the best? You'll want to ask — and answer — some additional questions about this.

TEXT ● ● ●	
What types of text does this audience like to read?	• Definitely visual or audio oriented (not heavy text). Humorous. Still considering posters but maybe a sidewalk chalk campaign?
What kinds of texts can work in contexts where the audience will be?	• Probably in common areas (cafeterias, dorms, and campus bulletin boards). Very brief — students must be able to scan as they walk by. (Would a public service announcement [PSA] on campus radio or TV work?)
What kinds of text do I have the skill set, time, and budget to create?	• Sidewalk chalk and posters would be easy. A video or audio PSA is going to be more work. Maybe I could partner with someone who knows how to edit video and audio? Check the iMovie tutorial on my computer — maybe it's as easy as they make it sound (that's a long shot, though).

By breaking the situation down, you've been able to look at aspects of purpose, context, audience, and text that will help you create a successful document.

As with many writing situations, the current context involves a lack of action. The change you want is for people to undertake a specific action: register to vote. Your main goal, based on your research about reasons why people don't register, says that whatever communication you design will be primarily informational (people apparently just need information). But people don't automatically read everything put in front of them, especially during election season when they're bombarded with messages. Your message will need to stand out. This suggests the need to play with genre a little as a way to surprise people. Options to explore include satire (along the lines, maybe, of *The Daily Show*), comic book superheroes, horror movie posters, or something similar.

Considering Motivators and Barriers to Change

In one way of thinking, all writing has change as its central purpose. Getting your audience to change, though, is also often the most complicated thing to figure out. Once you've worked through some of the details involved in all four aspects, it's useful to step back and think about what types of things might convince your audience to change in the way you're suggesting. You'll also want to think about what things might be preventing them from changing — what are the barriers to change?

From a psychological standpoint, change is always stressful. We feel stress not only with bad changes (the death of a family member, being fired from a job) but also when good changes take place (getting married, starting a new job). Change of any sort puts us on alert and heightens tension.

So not surprisingly, it's often hard to get people to change. When you write something that intends to cause change, you need to convince people that change is in their best interests.

Identifying Motivators

When you write, you're making an argument about something readers should do — you're looking for things that will motivate readers to change. That motivation can be located in different places: regulations and guidelines that suggest appropriate behavior (and punish inappropriateness), social expectations about politeness, expectations from friends and family, and (most powerfully) internal motivations to succeed and be happy. Effective writing identifies key motivators and connects them to changes you'd like to make in a context: *Doing this will keep*

> **Reflect & Discuss**
>
> Major changes, even positive ones, can be stressful. One common list of stressful events, the Holmes-Rahe Social Adjustment Scale, ranks life events with how much stress they commonly cause. What events are you surprised to see on the list? Why? What events would you add?
>
> Death of spouse: 100
>
> Jail sentence: 63
>
> Marriage: 50
>
> Fired from job: 47
>
> Retirement: 43
>
> New family member: 39
>
> Outstanding personal achievement: 28
>
> Trouble with boss: 23
>
> Christmas: 12
>
> Traffic ticket: 11

you in line with rules you're obliged to follow. Doing this will improve a situation you're in. Doing this will make you happier.

You can encourage people to change by relying on a single motivator, but the most effective writing uses multiple forces for change: *Follow this law not just because it's a law, but because doing so will benefit society and because doing so will make you feel better or be more successful.*

Here's a real-world example. An organization called Creative Commons wants to encourage people who create things—such as music, artwork, and writing—to allow other people to reuse and remix that work without paying royalties or getting permission. Creative Commons is a form of copyright that creators can apply to their work that basically says, "Go ahead and reuse my work."

The main barrier for such reuse and remix is traditional copyright. When people reuse or remix work someone else has created, they are often open to charges of violating copyright, which prohibits freely reusing or remixing someone else's work without their explicit permission in most cases. So even though many content creators would be glad to see other people making use of their work, the implied threat of copyright violation is often a force that keeps that from happening.

Creative Commons had the purpose of remaking copyright to encourage creativity. The founders of the organization analyzed the context and audience and came up with a way to flip copyright on its head, making it more open rather than automatically restrictive. They created several texts to motivate people to change their behaviors. First, legal experts in the organization drafted a set of easy-to-use and easy-to-understand copyright agreements that encourage creative artists to allow other people to use their work without breaking copyright laws. A Creative Commons license specifies how creative work can be used without additional permission. Second, they identified a spectrum of motivators for change that they used to develop texts for their website.

The Creative Commons website (see page 39) highlights several motivators:

- Monetary: Users get free permission to use copyrighted material in their own work.
- Entertainment: Users get increased access to creative materials.
- Social: Users participate in a rising technocultural movement.
- Legal: Average people can avoid minor copyright infringements more easily, thereby avoiding expensive lawsuits.
- Cultural: Users are encouraged to give as well as take materials from the commons.

The table on page 40 can help you consider motivators in most writing situations. The goal in using the table is not to fill in every space—some areas will remain empty—but simply to identify key

About

- Want to let people share and use your photographs, but not allow companies to sell them?
- Looking for access to course materials from the world's top universities?
- Want to encourage readers to re-publish your blog posts, as long as they give you credit?
- Looking for songs that you can use and remix, royalty-free?

If you answered *yes* to any of the questions above, then you should learn more about Creative Commons. Probably the quickest and easiest introduction to CC is to watch the following short **video**.

What is Creative Commons?

Creative Commons is a nonprofit organization that enables the sharing and use of creativity and knowledge through free legal tools.

Our free, easy-to-use **copyright licenses** provide a simple, standardized way to give the public permission to share and use your creative work — on conditions of your choice. CC licenses let you easily change your copyright terms from the default of "all rights reserved" to "**some rights reserved**."

Creative Commons licenses are not an alternative to copyright. **They work alongside copyright** and enable you to modify your copyright terms to best suit your needs.

What can Creative Commons do for me?

If you want to give people the right to share, use, and even build upon a work you've created, you should consider publishing it under a Creative Commons license. CC gives you flexibility (for example, you can choose to allow only non-commercial uses) and protects the people who use your work, so they don't have to worry about copyright infringement, as long as they abide by the conditions you have specified.

If you're looking for content that you can freely and legally use, there is a giant pool of CC-licensed creativity available. . . .

● From the Creative Commons website

benefits for your readers and for other people in the readers' contexts, such as their families, friends, institutions, and societies. The Creative Commons website, for example, argues that negotiating the complex terrain of intellectual property law will be simpler if users elect to participate in the Creative Commons process.

	Readers	Readers' Families	Readers' Friends	Readers' Institutions	Readers' Societies
Motivators »	• Feel good about contributing to society		• Collaborate using readers' materials	• Increase innovation	• Increase innovation
	• See their work being used/ appreciated		• Belong to a group of users (including readers)		

● Some motivators on the Creative Commons website

Not surprisingly, the benefits to readers (who are being encouraged to license their own work to be used freely by people in some situations) are largely intangible — they get nothing tangible back. But they do get to feel good about contributing to society and about seeing their work being appreciated by others. In cases such as this, the motivators listed in the other columns do not benefit only those groups (families, friends, institutions, societies). Instead, elements in those columns also benefit readers — part of what readers feel good about is providing those benefits to friends, institutions, and culture. Some elements remain blank because they don't seem as important in this case. That's not necessarily a problem because not every document or situation deals with every possible factor.

Identifying Barriers

Even when readers are motivated to make the change that you have in mind, there still may be some barriers to overcome. Sometimes identifying (and then addressing) barriers to change is relatively simple. A text message to your best friend telling him what time to meet you at the gym, for example, merely needs to supply a piece of information to get your friend to act. Other changes or situations may require more careful thinking and writing. Applying for a job, for example, often involves considering barriers such as time and attention constraints on the person reviewing letters of application and résumés (yours might be one among hundreds) or mismatches or gaps between your qualifications and those listed as job requirements (you might need to argue that your internship and extensive and relevant volunteer work are equivalent to the two years of job experience listed). And even something as seemingly simple as the text message mentioned above might face challenges, ranging from scheduling conflicts to negative feelings about exercise that you would need to negotiate to achieve your goal.

The table we used for thinking about motivators can also be used for thinking about barriers (see page 41). How might you fill in the table for

(see page 41)

Reflect & Discuss

Consider one text you recently read that you weren't inclined to agree with. What reasons did you have for not wanting to act in the way the communication suggested? How did the communication try to convince you to act anyway? Did the communication succeed?

	Readers	Readers' Families	Readers' Friends	Readers' Institutions	Readers' Societies
Motivators 》					
Barriers 》					

● A table for thinking about motivators and barriers

a campaign designed to convince people to switch from using a Windows platform to using Macs? Or from using either of those to using Linux?

You'll often need to work on multiple, interconnected motivators and barriers when you're dealing with complex situations. A letter to the editor urging your city to adopt new recycling policies might convince a city council member that recycling is a good thing, but the council member might also already be convinced that the city's budget cannot support the expense of ramping up recycling efforts (staff, equipment, transport, and publicity cost money). Change, in that case, would need to include additional arguments — that recycling would not add significant expense, for example, or that the additional expense would be worth the benefit. Audiences have inertia: Bodies in motion tend to stay in motion, and those at rest tend to stay at rest. They might agree with you in principle but in practice think that the change is not worth the effort.

You can think of change as something that goes on in a network of opposing forces, with motivators pushing in the direction of the change you want to make and barriers pushing in other directions. A teacher providing guidance on a draft of a paper is, in a sense, pushing in the same direction as the social and personal forces that encourage a student to do well in the class — motivators. But even in this case, other forces act as barriers — like a party that the writer wants to go to instead of working on revisions to the paper. The outcome of the situation, the change, will depend on the strengths and configuration of all of these forces.

Using PACT throughout the Writing Process

The PACT framework and process provide you with a way to approach complex writing situations. PACT is not simply a form to fill out; it's a toolkit that's useful throughout the writing process. You can create a PACT chart for each project and return to it over and over as you work on your texts. With PACT, you can continually analyze and reanalyze writing situations to respond with texts that are appropriate and effective.

You can use the sample questions below to stimulate your thinking as you work on your own writing projects. You won't need to answer all of these questions for every writing situation or at every stage of your writing process, but you can look at them as starting points and refer back to this list if you get stuck. You'll eventually have to move beyond these questions to develop questions that are specific to your project. Every writing project is different, so this is not an exhaustive list.

PURPOSE

- What is the problem or situation?
- Are there multiple problems?
- What needs to happen?
- What, specifically, needs to change?
- How do you want readers to feel?
- What do you want readers to do?
- What do you want readers to know?
- What do you want readers to believe?
- What will be required to achieve this change?
- What do you already know about the problem or situation?
- What do you need to know?
- How can you find out more about the problem or situation?
- What do other writers say about this problem or situation?
- What effect do you want to have on the audience?
- What effect do you want to have on the context?

AUDIENCE

- Who will see this text?
- Who will use this text?
- What are this audience's motivations?
- What are your readers' concerns?
- What are their goals?
- What do you already know about this audience?
- What do you need to know about them?
- How can you find out more about this audience?
- Have other writers done research on this audience?
- Is the audience interested in the problem or situation?
- Are readers inclined to agree with your purpose, to oppose it, or to be ambivalent?
- What are the barriers to change in this audience?
- What are your readers' positions within their institutions or groups?
- What do readers already know or believe about the problem or situation?
- What experiences have readers already had with the problem or situation?
- How will this change affect readers?
- How can this change benefit readers?
- How can this change benefit readers' families, friends, institutions, and societies?
- What does the audience expect from a text?
- What media can this audience access?

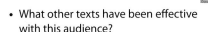

TEXT

- What other texts have been effective with this audience?
- What types of text can work in this context?
- What do similar texts look like? How are they designed and structured?
- What media work best for your audience and purpose?
- How can you motivate readers to respond favorably to your purpose?
- How can you help readers understand what you want them to know?
- How can you encourage readers to do what you want them to do?
- What kinds of information or evidence will persuade the audience?
- How can you establish common ground with this audience?
- What kinds of images or text will evoke a response in readers?
- What kind of visual design will help readers understand your purpose?
- What kind of structure will help readers understand your purpose?
- How much effort will readers need to put into reading the text?
- What kind of text would best accomplish the purpose?
- What types of text does this audience like to read?
- What kinds of text do you have the skill set, time, and budget to create?
- What tools are best for creating this text?
- What strategies will help you create this text?
- What specific tasks are involved in creating this text?
- What strategies will help you revise this text?
- What publication guidelines must your text adhere to?

CONTEXT

- Where is the problem or situation?
- Where are your readers?
- Where and when will readers see your text?
- Where and when will readers use your text?
- What institutions or groups are your readers in?
- What institutions or groups are you in?
- What are the barriers to change in this context?
- What do you already know about this context?
- What do you need to know about this context?
- How can you find out more about this context?
- Have other writers done research on this context?
- What social forces are at work in this context?
- What legal and ethical forces are at work in this context?
- What regulations must you adhere to in this context?
- What other texts exist in this context?
- What media are used in this context?
- What other texts are you responding to?
- Would it help to work with other writers on the text?
- How much time do you have to create the text?
- Who can you ask for feedback on the text?
- Where will your text be published, posted, or distributed?

Texts for Analysis

Compare the two texts below, both written about credit cards for college students. The context and audience for each will be very different, but you'll see that each has an opposing purpose. What techniques does each use to make its argument? You can list the features in a table or highlight or annotate them directly. Write a short summary of the key rhetorical moves that each text makes.

WEB PAGE

Discover Card, "Get the Card for College and Beyond"

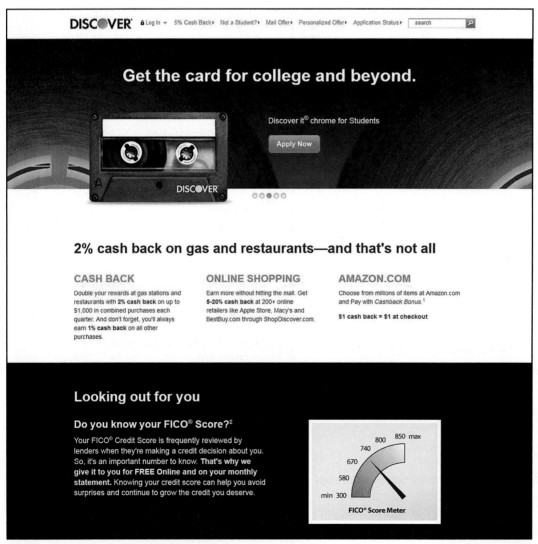

Reproduced by permission of DFS Services LLC.

ONLINE NEWSLETTER ARTICLE
FDIC, "Five Things You Should Know about . . . Credit Cards"

1. **Use them carefully.** Credit cards offer great benefits, especially the ability to buy now and pay later. But you've got to keep the debt levels manageable. If you don't, the costs in terms of fees and interest, or the damage to your credit record, could be significant.

2. **Choose them carefully.** Don't choose a credit card just to get freebies (T-shirts or sports items) or because there's no annual fee. Look for a card that's best for your borrowing habits.

   Example: If you expect to carry a balance on your card from month to month, which means you'll be charged interest, it's more important to look for a card with a low interest rate or a generous "grace period" (more time before your payments are due).

3. **Pay as much as you can to avoid or minimize interest charges.** If possible, pay your bill in full each month. Remember, paying only the minimum due each month means you'll be paying a lot of interest for many years, and those costs could far exceed the amount of your original purchase.

4. **Pay on time.** You'll avoid a late fee of about $35 or more. But more importantly, continued late payments on your credit card may be reported to the major credit bureaus as a sign that you have problems handling your finances.

   And if your credit rating gets downgraded, your card company could raise the interest rate on your credit card, reduce your credit limit (the maximum amount you can borrow) or even cancel your card.

   Late payment on your credit card also can be a mark against you the next time you apply for an apartment or a job.

5. **Protect your credit card numbers from thieves.** Never provide your credit card numbers — both the account numbers and expiration date on the front and the security code on the back — in response to an unsolicited phone call, e-mail or other communication you didn't originate.

   When using your credit card online make sure you're dealing with a legitimate Web site and that your information will be encrypted (scrambled for security purposes) during transmission.

   Major credit card companies also are offering more protection by providing "zero-liability" programs that protect consumers from the unauthorized use of their card.

   In general, only give your credit card or card numbers to reputable merchants or other organizations.

Exercises

1. View several television commercials that you have recorded or can find on YouTube. Write a short essay (750 words) describing which one you like best. Why do you like it? Do you consider that commercial successful in terms of getting you to consider changing your behavior by purchasing the product or service being advertised?

2. Pick a favorite movie, one you know very well. If possible, get a copy of the movie and the working script (sites such as www.imsdb.com or www .movie-page.com/movie_scripts.htm might be starting points). Read some reviews of movies written by professional critics at a site such as www .rottentomatoes.com and write a short (1,000 words or so) critique that analyzes how the film attempts to change the audiences' opinions, feelings, or emotions.

3. Write a letter (of one to two pages) to yourself at some point in the past that attempts to convince yourself to do something different. You can try to correct a mistake you made. Or you could convince your past self to explore an opportunity that might have been interesting or rewarding. Or you could just make your past self think differently. Before you write the letter, work with the PACT framework to think about the writing situation: What aspects of the context will be important? What aspects of the audience — yourself at that point in your life — will be useful to use in your argument? What are the barriers to change, and how can you overcome them?

Scenario Connections

1. Review the PACT charts on pages 33–36, which respond to Scenario 1, "Advocating Voter Registration on Campus" (p. 263). Create your own PACT chart for this scenario. If you were creating a poster to encourage voter registration on campus, what might it say? What would the words and images be?

2. In Scenario 5, "Creating a Parody Ad," you're asked to create an ad that pokes fun at a product or service. You can see an example of a parody ad in the Background Text section of the scenario. The goal of the parody is not to simply criticize but to change the beliefs or behaviors of the people who currently buy that product or service. Pick a product or service that you think has negative effects on people. Create a motivators and barriers table like the one shown on page 41 to help you understand why people currently pay for that product or service. Then create a PACT chart to help you think about a parody ad that might change people's minds or behaviors.

3. Scenario 8, "Drafting a Poster about Online Privacy," involves creating a poster encouraging high school students to be aware of online privacy issues (sharing too much information, sending something private to a person who then redistributes it, and so on). Create a motivators and barriers table like the one shown on page 41 for this high school audience.

4. Scenario 9, "Educating Users about E-mail Scams," asks you to create a text that will help senior citizens avoid falling prey to phishing scams. Read the scenario and analyze the sample phishing e-mail that is included as a Background Text. Mark parts of the e-mail that are motivators with an M and parts that acknowledge barriers with a B. Write a short (one- to three-paragraph) analysis of why this e-mail might be successful in fooling a recipient.

Starting to Write

We're approaching writing here as a process involving multiple drafts; in all but the simplest situations, you should assume that you'll be revising at least once (and often more than once). With few exceptions, people who write for a living draft and redraft frequently. Don't assume you're going to get it right the first time. That may seem depressing at first, but it's actually liberating: If you haven't waited until the last minute, you have the luxury of stepping back from what you're working on, looking at it objectively, and asking yourself, *What can I do next to make this stronger?*

In Chapter 2 we looked at how to analyze writing situations, breaking them into PACT charts and understanding how to motivate readers. In this chapter, we'll explore ways to step from analysis to production, creating texts that address the situations you analyzed.

Analyzing Your Writing Processes

Writing normally involves at least a little preparation, from functional aspects such as getting out your laptop and opening a new document in your word processor to little rituals or habits like getting a glass of iced tea or putting on a favorite playlist in your mp3 player. We generally develop these procedures based on previous experience, often without really thinking about them. If you learn to think about and analyze your writing environment, you can become a more effective writer.

Begin by asking yourself what you need to do to help you focus on writing. Most people need to be free from interruptions, so the living room of the apartment you share with four roommates may not necessarily be the best choice. The table on the next page poses some questions to consider before you actually start working.

As you're analyzing your writing processes, it's often a good idea to keep track of what's going on. For example, you can note each time you stop writing to answer an e-mail or send a text message, adding up the results at the end of your writing session to see how much time these events cost you (not forgetting that each time you go back to writing it will take you a little bit of time to get focused again).

Two writing spaces
Left: Thinkstock; Right: Craig Joiner/agefotostock/Superstock

Your Writing Space

- Is the space free from distractions?
- Should you turn off your cellphone?
- Should you log out of any social networking programs?
- Do you need to hide out or find a location where friends are unlikely to find you?
- Is looking out a window going to make you want to go outside?
- Is it likely you'll need a large table so you can spread out materials (notes, other texts to refer to, etc.)?

Your Writing Tools

- If you're going to be writing from sources, how can you arrange them so that they're easy to access?
- Would you write better if you had a larger monitor (or multiple monitors) so you could look at several things on screen at the same time?
- Do you need to print out materials?
- If you're writing or marking up printouts by hand, do you need something to write with?

Your Writing Habits

- Would putting on headphones or earbuds to listen to music (and block outside noise) be helpful?
- Would it help to get feedback on a draft before revising?
- Do you work best with a neat workspace, or do you like things a little messy?
- Is cleaning your entire workspace just another way to procrastinate? Or will that actually make writing easier?

Your Writing Mind

- Do you write better in the morning, during the day, or at night?
- Do you understand the assignment?
- Do you need to create an outline, or are you going to just start writing?
- Do you work better under pressure? (Are you sure?)
- Are there other important things you know are issues for your writing processes?

Starting Out: An Example

Getting those first words out — for many people, this is one of the most difficult parts of writing. One way to ease slowly into the task is to understand that writing does not start with the act of putting down the first word and sentence of your text. Instead, think of writing as everything you do in relationship to creating a text: gathering research materials, taking notes, reading the description of the assignment, talking to peers, attending class. All of these acts are, in real ways, part of the writing process. When you sit down and begin putting words down, you're already well into the writing process.

Before we dive into techniques for getting started, let's look at an example of one writer, Korrina, beginning a new assignment in her first-year writing class.

Korrina prints out the assignment sheet from the course website and reviews the material, which her teacher discussed in class earlier this week. In this section of the course, the class is examining the ways that advertisements address viewers and try to influence consumers. The first assignment in this module asks Korrina to develop some sort of document or text that will help 9- to 12-year-old children understand how advertisements influence them. The specifics of the assignment — including the type of document — are left up to Korrina.

Project 3: "Start 'Em Early" Creating Consumers

Overview

As we've seen this semester, advertisements are powerful agents that encourage us to take positions and adopt relationships to commercial products. Although they usually are attempting to get us to purchase something, in doing so they structure and change how we see ourselves in the world. Ads work to create new wants or turn wants into needs. And they start in our childhoods, showing us what sorts of activities are appropriate for us based on our gender (even down to the color — pink for girls and blue for boys!).

● Korrina's assignment sheet

For this project, you're going to design a counter-advertisement that attempts to help preteens (children aged 9 through 12) to think critically about advertisements. For simplicity's sake, we're going to limit this to static, visual media, but within that domain you're free to choose what type of text to create (magazine ad, banner ad for the web, even a mockup of a billboard).

Begin by taking a first swing at completing a PACT chart. I'd suggest starting with the P quadrant given that I've already provided a general purpose. Then cycle through the other quadrants a few more times as you think more concretely about the four quadrants.

Important sources for inspiration: advertisements and your own observations. Concrete examples of real ads for children in this age range will be useful. How do they work? What things do they do to persuade children to want the products and activities being advertised? Think about your own experiences—what ads do you remember from your childhood? Why were they compelling to you? If you have younger relatives or family friends in this age range, can you see how ads work on them?

Grading Criteria

Engagement with Process (25%): Engaged with all aspects of drafting, critique, and revision

Effective Approach (25%): Seems to be an effective approach for this audience

● Korrina's assignment sheet (continued)

Visual Design (25%): Layout and use of color work well

Self-Analysis (25%): Explanation of your process and rationale

adequately explains the text

Due Dates

Monday, 10/15: Five sample ads + 1 PACT chart

Friday, 10/18: Very rough sketch or description of ad

Wednesday, 10/24: Workable draft 2 (all major components

present)

Monday, 10/29: Final draft

● Korrina's assignment sheet (continued)

Korrina highlights terms on the assignment sheet to help her begin gathering ideas and thinking about options. After she reads over the material, she opens a blank document in her word-processing program and begins by listing out important terms — ideas that have stuck in her head after reading the sheet and thinking about the teacher's discussion of the project in class.

concrete examples

consumerism

layout

visual design

create wants/needs

example ads

in ad, people who have things (that you want/need)

● Korrina's initial list of important terms

Not much in Korrina's initial list, but it's a starting point, certainly better than a blank page. She saves the file to a new folder she's created to store anything she generates for this assignment. She realizes, though, that this isn't going to get her far. She looks back at her notes. "Example ads. In ad, people who have things (that you want/need)."

Her class has discussed the ways that images in advertising construct visual arguments about ways of living. In class, they've analyzed how things like magazine ads are constructed to focus the viewer's eye on specific parts of an image, often the product or the people within the scene whose lives are apparently made way better because they bought something. In some cases, like perfume or beer ads, the product itself is associated loosely with shiny, happy people in colorful, attractive settings — but the qualities of the product itself aren't even discussed. Korrina has started to notice similar things in many of the advertisements she sees on TV and in magazines, but she hasn't thought much about media that children view. Thinking back to her own childhood, she can recall begging her mother to buy her toys she saw on TV in flashy, fun commercials. In the few cases where her beleaguered mother gave in, Korrina remembers that actually playing with the toys wasn't nearly as much fun as it looked on television.

With these memories swirling around in her head, she heads to the store where she buys several magazines aimed at children: a comic book, a magazine spawned by a popular kids' television channel, and another magazine on popular video games. Back in her dorm room, she uses sticky notes to tag interesting ads. She opens a new document in her word processor and begins taking notes about seven ads from the magazines. (Her notes on Halo 4 and Madden NFL 10 are shown on the following page.) She inserts scanned versions of the ads into her notes so that she can refer to specifics in the ads; she's also saved higher-resolution versions to disk, which she may use later in drafting her document.

Alongside each advertisement she also adds notes about the children whom the ads appear to target, including specific needs or desires that the images seem to answer: happiness, friends, sunshine, action. In thinking about the children who might view the ads, she thinks about her cousin, Cameron, who turned 11 earlier this month. She recognizes Cameron as someone who might be influenced by the ads, particularly the ones for video games. Whenever she visits, Cameron shows her the newest cheats he's discovered for whatever game currently has his attention, talking a hundred miles an hour and rapidly working the controller. The video-game world he lives in expands briefly to include her, as he hopes she'll enjoy the game along with him.

Cool/blue color scheme.

Dark and light contrasts organize the image.

Menacing. Big Freaking Gun (BFG).

Strong lines in background and the BFG lead eyes into the scene.

● Korrina's notes on Halo 4
Robyn Beck/AFP/Getty Images/Newscom

Bright, simple (not subtle) color scheme.

Centered composition aimed square at viewer.

PlayStation 2 cover on left is different than the Wii version on the right. Are the differences important/ intentional?

● Korrina's notes on Madden NFL 10
AP Photo/Paul Sakuma, File

Korrina then starts thinking about what type of document she'll need to develop. She thinks about the other things she's written for classes but quickly discards that idea — Cameron wouldn't get through the first page of a standard college essay. He doesn't read. Actually, that's not true: He reads video-game magazines. And comic books and graphic novels. And websites about video games. She enters some of these options into her brainstorming file. She flips back through some of the magazines, looking at the articles rather than the ads this time. The writing is action packed, punchy even. Very active language. Very short paragraphs. There are lots of images in the articles, screen shots captured from video games and pictures of controllers and consoles. There are lots of brightly colored headlines and quotes taken from the articles, blown up to a larger size and set into the text to grab readers' attention. The sentences are short, but with lots of verbs and action words. Kids do read, she realizes — they just have a different way of reading, different approaches to texts.

She starts working on her PACT chart, putting in material that she's already been thinking about.

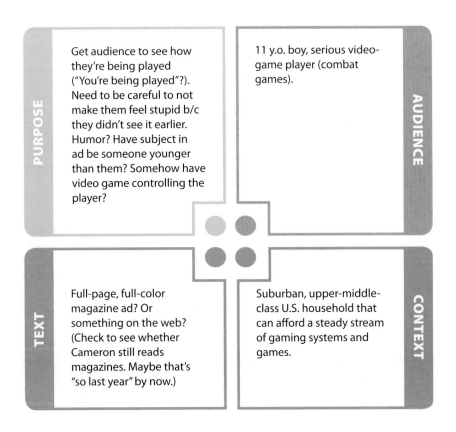

PURPOSE
Get audience to see how they're being played ("You're being played"?). Need to be careful to not make them feel stupid b/c they didn't see it earlier. Humor? Have subject in ad be someone younger than them? Somehow have video game controlling the player?

AUDIENCE
11 y.o. boy, serious video-game player (combat games).

TEXT
Full-page, full-color magazine ad? Or something on the web? (Check to see whether Cameron still reads magazines. Maybe that's "so last year" by now.)

CONTEXT
Suburban, upper-middle-class U.S. household that can afford a steady stream of gaming systems and games.

Maybe she'll take a cue from the magazine articles: She could write a short article (probably no longer than a single page, she thinks) in the style of one of these. As she takes notes about one of the ads, she also begins thinking about how she's going to translate the language of her analysis — which is based on classroom discussions of weighty topics like "design" and "aesthetics" and "desire" — into language that her audience will understand (and want to read). In fact, she starts to realize her whole approach will be different: Korrina has the benefit of a little distance from the topic and knowledge about how advertisements work on people. These things are starting to seem obvious to her, but they won't be obvious (or even welcome) to the preteen boys who read the magazines — her main audience for the project.

Your approach to writing situations will likely be a little different than Korrina's — if nothing else, your writing assignments will likely be different. But some aspects of Korrina's experience can inform your own approaches to writing, ranging from her decision to start with a review of the assignment sheet to her brainstorming activities and drawing on other texts as she worked. In the next section, we'll look at some of the strategies Korrina used as well as a range of additional approaches you can draw on as you begin to write.

Ideas and How to Have Them

As with most things involved in writing, there's no single, correct strategy for coming up with ideas. Different people approach idea generation in different ways. In fact, individual writers usually draw on several strategies, even within a single writing situation. The key thing is to have a toolkit of different strategies that you're comfortable using.

Think about Your Purpose, Audience, Context, and Text

Ask yourself, *What do I need to know to deal with this situation?* Good writing is also good reading. And good reading exists only in the context of people doing that reading. So unless you learn to think like your readers, you'll be limiting what your writing can achieve. Put yourself in your readers' or users' shoes. Readers and users are never mindless robots: They process information (sometimes hastily) and filter it through their own experiences, interests, and opinions. Refer back to your PACT chart, asking new questions and changing your responses if necessary as you generate more ideas. The PACT chart is a way to keep you anchored to the writing situation. Asking yourself questions such as the following can be helpful.

Reflect & Discuss

As you get used to different strategies for generating ideas, occasionally step back and take stock of how the strategies are working. Do some work better than others? Do some seem better matched to certain types of writing problems? If you're really stumped with a writing situation, does a free-form activity like brainstorming work better than outlining? Talk with your classmates to see which strategies they like best and why.

- What do your readers already know about the problem or situation? What else do they need to know?

- How can you convince them to respond positively to your writing? Will you need to provide them with some evidence to convince them of your points? Will you need to explain certain aspects of the situation or define key terms?

- What context will they be in when they read your document?

- How can you help them understand what to do? How can you help them *want* to do it?

Review the Assignment

In many cases, your writing will spring from an assignment you're given. This is true of much writing you'll do in school (essays, technical papers, lab reports, presentations), and it is true of much of the writing you'll do later in the workplace (memos, quarterly reports, webpage and website materials). In some cases and contexts, you'll have freer reign over your assignments, but when you're given an assignment to work from, that's a normal starting point for getting ideas. You can, as Korrina did, use the assignment to help you think about key requirements for the writing project and to set some ground rules for your work.

Review Your Own Notes

As she read through the assignment sheet, Korrina also started taking notes so that she could reference important issues — she highlighted key terms on the page and took notes on her computer for later reference. She also made notes as she analyzed some of the ads she gathered and referred back to notes from class periodically when she was looking at the ads. This interim note taking is a crucial step for many types of writing, especially in complex situations, because it allows you to capture important ideas, concepts, and key terms that you'll need to work with later. Note taking also functions as a vehicle for information, allowing you to move useful information into a new space so you can begin working with it. Notes like this are also crucial in keeping you from forgetting things as you work.

Your memory isn't as good as you think it is. Develop a system for capturing, organizing, and tagging notes. If you don't already have a system, start with the container approach. A simple manila folder can gather all your written materials in one physical location. A folder or directory on your computer can collect electronic files. Although there's some value to the physical act of writing something down, being able to find it later is even more important. Consider apps for note taking such as Evernote (see p. 58), which offers free versions for

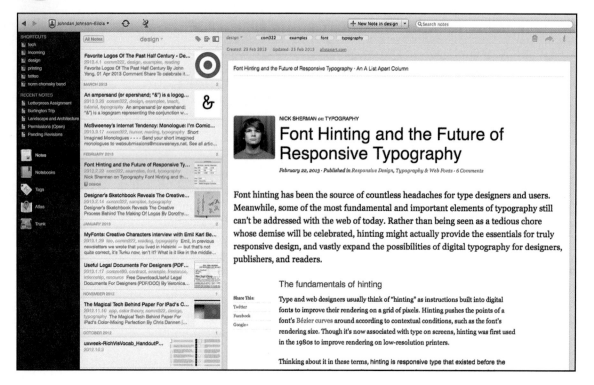

● Programs like Evernote can help capture, organize, and tag your notes for later use
  Nick Sherman, "Font Hinting and the Future of Responsive Typography," February 22, 2013. Reprinted by permission of Evernote and Nick Sherman.

Windows, Mac, iOS, and the web, all of which automatically synchro-nize with one another to keep your notes updated on all platforms.

Talk It Through

Even though a lot of writing is solitary work, talking to other people will often be a crucial part of your writing processes. Think about Kor-rina's conversations with her cousin about his video games. Without the information she gathered, she probably wouldn't have had a good sense of her audience or what strategies to use.

Experienced writers rely heavily on conversations with other people to help them think about their work: They show each other drafts of work, they talk about ideas they've had, they sort out ideas and they come up with new ones by tossing them back and forth with other people. So even though in many cases people work by them-selves when they're putting words to paper or screen, working with other people is a crucial aspect of writing even for individual writing projects.

Read Other Texts

Depending on the writing situation, you'll need to read other things to inform your writing: texts that you'll directly analyze as part of writing (perhaps a short story that you're writing about) as well as texts that help you analyze things (such as commentaries about a political speech you're responding to). Gathering information, reading it, taking notes on it, filtering out the grain from the chaff, and combining it with other information are all extremely useful activities when you're trying to get started with a new writing project. Korrina relied heavily on reading magazines about video games to help her flesh out her understanding of her audience and get a better idea of what drew people into playing these games.

Search Your Memories and Experiences

As Korrina found out from her interactions with Cameron, personal experiences can also provide an important resource for your writing. Obviously, if you're writing about those experiences you're going to draw on your memories. Writing from memory can be a way of making sense of your own experiences, for yourself and for others.

Autobiography is one form of writing from memory, but there are others. Drawing from your own experiences can help you think of topics for research essays, engage in social action, or design posters. Something as mundane as noticing the overflowing dumpsters near your dorm might lead you to research recycling and reuse programs, create surveys on why people choose to or refuse to recycle, or engage in social activism by creating posters or short public service announcements.

Do Research

Writers don't just passively receive new information; they go out and find new information. Korrina used this strategy when she started looking at video-game magazines. But sometimes this involves *conducting* research — asking people to take a survey or participate in an interview, for example; even something as simple as sending someone a text message can be useful in research. Although at some point you'll have to stop gathering new material and actually start drafting a document, doing research before you start is an excellent way to help generate (and test) ideas. As with other strategies we'll discuss, you may also discover that you need to return to research mode after you've begun working on your document — writing itself often generates new ideas, some of them requiring additional research.

Consider interviewing or polling people about key issues related to your project as a way to get a better idea for how people feel about your topic. In some cases, research will confirm your own instincts; in other cases, it will help you reframe issues or rethink an approach.

You can find more strategies for doing research in Chapter 7, which is devoted to the topic.

Freewrite

Freewriting is one of the simplest methods for generating ideas: Just write. Set a time limit — even a few minutes — and identify a problem or topic to write about. You can use a pad of paper and pen or pencil or you can use a computer. Start your timer and begin writing. Stay on topic if you can, but the ultimate goal is to just keep writing. If your mind blanks, write the word "blank" or "nothing" until something related to your topic comes to you.

After you're done, read back through what you've written. Highlight ideas that seem worth coming back to (on paper you can circle them; onscreen you could change the color of promising text). If the strategy seemed useful but you don't have enough material yet, you can try freewriting again on the same topic (or any of the ideas that you highlighted), or you can move on to another technique to continue developing your ideas.

Brainstorm

If you want to generate a lot of ideas quickly, brainstorming is a good bet. Brainstorming is similar to freewriting, but it involves multiple people working simultaneously. Begin by setting up a specific problem to solve and select one person to write down the ideas being generated. It's helpful if the ideas are written out on a whiteboard or projected on a screen so that everyone can see them. Then start the process by having people call out ideas as they have them. One key rule for brainstorming is that there's no room for critique during the production stages — your main goal is to keep ideas coming, without judgment.

After you've finished generating ideas (either with a set time limit or until the ideas stop flowing), you can step back and consider the usefulness of each idea. You may have a set of criteria to use in evaluating the ideas — cost, simplicity, or stability, for example — or you may just consider each to see whether one leaps out as better than the rest. You could even pick the top five for further consideration (possibly using a different strategy for generating ideas).

The brainstorming diagram on page 61 contains ideas generated in response to this question: How can we encourage people to recycle paper on campus?

The diversity of these ideas illustrates one of brainstorming's hallmarks: The results are all over the map. By posing a general problem (not too specific), we've started generating ideas that are technical, informational, economical, and psychological. In the brainstorming session, a writer poses a high-level question ("How can we encourage

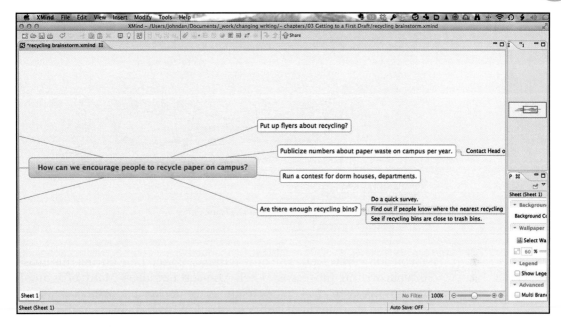

● Brainstorming in XMind, a free program (www.xmind.net)
  Reproduced by permission of Xmind Ltd.

people to recycle paper on campus?"), which she then breaks down into lower-level questions ("Put up flyers about recycling?") and ideas ("Publicize numbers about paper waste on campus per year"). Each question or idea then sparks new ideas ("Contact Head of Facilities for an estimate.") Not every idea is great — putting up flyers could be criticized itself for wasting paper. But some seem worth following up on. We'll come back to the ideas in this diagram as we explore other methods of creating ideas.

Give It a Rest

Sometimes you just need to step away from a project. You might have been working on it too hard for too many hours and be unable to think straight about it. You might need to sleep on the problem so you can come back to it after you're rested. Or if you're the opposite of tired — jittery and jumpy — spend some time doing something that calms you — listening to music, taking a walk outside, or hanging out with your pet.

Sketch It Out

Sketching provides a two-dimensional way of exploring ideas, sort of like mind mapping but with fewer constraints. As an idea-generation technique, sketching doesn't need to be formal or neat, so don't worry

● Planning sketch for Guggenheim Bilbao by Frank Gehry
Courtesy Everett Collection

if you don't draw well. The only purpose of sketching during this phase of your writing process is to help you sort out ideas. Many of "starchitect" Frank Gehry's sketches might strike you as just plain *bad*.

But the sketches help Gehry map out the overall forms of the spaces he is constructing. He did the sketch above while designing the Guggenheim museum in Bilbao, Spain, one of the most famous buildings constructed in the last century.

There are no rules for using sketching as a thinking technique. You might want to work just by tossing terms out on the page or screen, grouping them, drawing lines to connect or divide as you go. Page 63 shows two more examples of sketches.

● Completed Guggenheim Bilbao
Ben Pipe/Getty Images

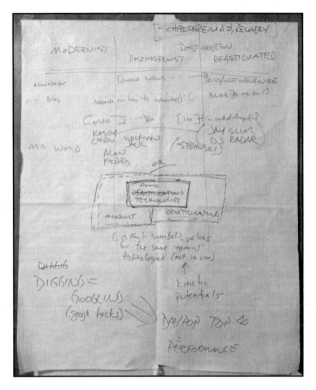

● Planning notes for a book chapter on disk jockeys showing shift
in techniques between 1950s–1960s DJs and 1990s–2000s DJs
Johndan Johnson-Eilola

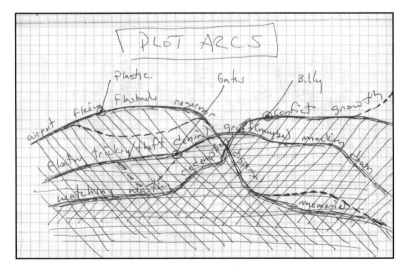

● Interwoven plot lines in a novel showing prominence of each over time, along with
character and location positions
Johndan Johnson-Eilola

Moving from Ideas to a Draft

Once you have ideas, you have a couple of options for creating a first draft. As with idea-generation strategies, there are both unstructured and structured approaches. You should try both out to see what works for you.

Free Draft

Free drafting is freewriting with slightly more focus: Instead of simply writing down whatever pops into your head, free drafting asks you to stay on your general topic. You're not too worried about coherence, logical progression, or transitions: You're focused only on writing about your general topic. Depending on your own preferences, you might start with a rough sequence of topics to cover, or you might do something closer to freewriting.

Unlike freewriting, free drafting is an attempt to actually create a draft. Where freewriting asked you to simply keep generating text — any text — without stopping, free drafting often includes stops and starts, periods where you're *not* putting words on the screen or page. You will probably pause occasionally to reread what you've written and to think about what's coming next. Because you have a lot of leeway in what you write about that topic, you shouldn't feel as much intimidation as you would if you were trying to draft a formal text.

You may find this strategy most productive if you begin by going over your notes or reviewing the assignment, thinking (but not yet writing) about your topic and different approaches to it you might try. But you can also free draft cold, just heading into it without much preparation.

If you're feeling particularly uncreative and resistant to getting started, come up with strategies for forcing yourself to sit: Set a manageable time or page limit that you need to get through and then reward yourself somehow when you meet that goal.

After you've completed a draft, take a short break and then review what you've written. Make notes and begin developing the draft. As you read, flag text that seems useful, copying it to a new file (keep your old file and add "scrap" to the file name because you may decide to use some of it later). Begin organizing your ideas into related groups and into logical orderings. Add notes to yourself about material that needs to be added. This is the start of your first draft. From here, you can simply begin rewriting what you have started, developing key points and revising rough sections.

Mind Map

Mind mapping is a way both to classify concepts and to generate new ideas. Like free drafting, mind mapping is similar to an idea-generation technique, in this case brainstorming. But mind maps are more structured and are usually (but not necessarily) individual rather than team based.

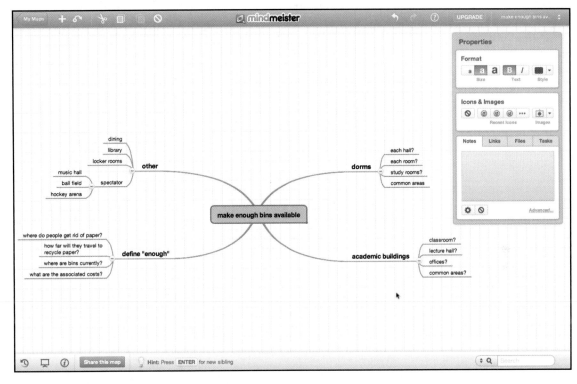

● Mind map constructed using MindMeister, an online program (www.mindmeister.com)
  Reproduced by permission of MindMeister

Mind maps usually begin with a central core idea and then break that concept down in different ways. The map above, which could be expanded greatly with a little more work, takes one of the items from our brainstormed list ("make enough bins available") and teases out what this phrase might mean. Four branches take one aspect of the initial question and break it down into parts. The "academic buildings" branch is broken down into "classroom," "lecture hall," "offices," and "common areas."

There's no single correct way to create a mind map, but the general goal is to get ideas out in a structured way. The central node can be a problem, a concept, an action, or nearly anything. The other nodes connected to the main node then break the central idea down and dig deeper into your issues. In the map above, three of the second-level categories are types of space (dorms, academic buildings, or other spaces), while the fourth category holds related questions. The fourth category might bother some mind map purists — some say that a "miscellaneous" category is a sign of weak structure — but keeping a space for "miscellaneous" items ensures that you don't forget them. For example, deciding whether every room needs a recycling bin will depend on issues such as how far people are willing to travel to recycle paper — can there be recycling bins in the common areas of dorms, or are students willing to recycle only if the bins are in their own rooms? How much extra time will it cost maintenance to empty (and keep separate) the paper being recycled? How much does each bin cost? These issues help us evaluate the mind map we're building.

One variation on mind mapping involves working with sticky notes and a blank wall or whiteboard. The benefit of this approach over a computer-based strategy is that your walls are probably much larger than your computer's display, making it easy to work with larger structures. Sticky notes on a wall also work better for team projects because multiple people can work on the diagram at the same time.

If you're working in your own room, you can leave the sticky notes up and return to them later. If you need to take them down, transfer the notes to a more portable format (copy the notes into a notebook or computer file, maintaining the categories) or take a digital picture of the notes on the wall.

After you've generated the mind map, go over it and think about how you might "flatten" the map into a linear structure while reviewing your PACT chart: What ideas seem to address the writing situation? What will convince your reader? You might consider working your flattened mind map into an outline (described in the following section).

Outline

Outlining is a more traditional approach to writing, but it's also a very successful one for many people. Outlines are typically lists of topics covered in order, arranged in a hierarchy so that overarching topics contain smaller points. An essay on recycling might grow out of an outline such as this:

---

1. Introduction: Short narrative about lack of recycling and local impact on environment
2. State statistics on recycling rates
3. Informal surveys/anecdotes
    a. Sharon's reasons for not recycling
    b. Tyrone's reasons for not recycling
    c. Aaron's reasons for recycling
4. Interview with Andrea Moore, Grounds Supervisor in charge of waste management on campus
    a. Amount of trash taken to landfill per week

---

b. Amount of recycling processed

    i. Glass

    ii. Paper

    iii. Plastic

    iv. Metal

c. Results of efforts to increase recycling

5. Conclusion: Follow-up interviews with Sharon and Tyrone to discuss data from Moore

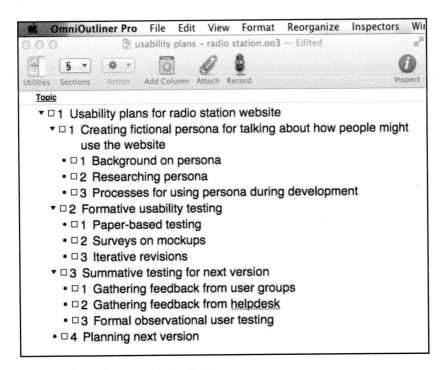

● Section of an outline created in OmniOutliner

Reproduced by permission of the Omni Group

Outlines look neat and orderly compared to freewrites. But while "orderly" is an end goal, the process of writing an outline can actually be as messy as you want it to be: You can start in the middle or by just tossing out a bunch of loose ideas. You can take down the ideas you brainstormed or put up as sticky notes on the wall, or pull ideas from

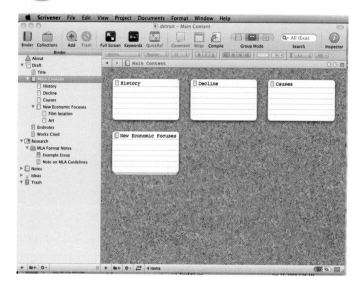

● Notecards view in Scrivener, a program designed to support writing
Reprinted by permission of Scrivener

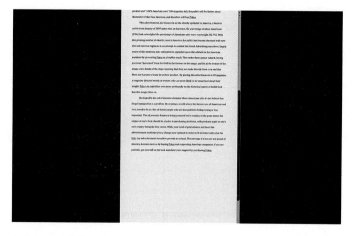

● Scrivener's full-screen mode
Reprinted by permission of Scrivener

your free drafted text, and then begin reordering the topics or main points you find. You could also use the strategy writing students have been using for decades, writing each main idea on an index card, sorting the index cards into piles, one for each major section of the paper, and finally sorting the section piles into a workable order. The stack of index cards is a version of an outline you use to create your first draft.

There's no single best format for an outline: For simple projects, your outline may include only a single level of main points. For more complex projects, you may have many, many hierarchical levels, almost to the point of having one outline entry per paragraph of finished text. Usually you'll be somewhere in the middle, with a few levels of detail. The key (as with much about writing) is to find out what works for you.

Most word processors offer an outline mode. Specialized applications such as OmniOutliner and Scrivener, shown above, provide even stronger support for the organizational work you do when you begin writing. In addition to onscreen index cards and outline tools, Scrivener provides a full-screen mode that blocks other potentially distracting programs from view.

You can also build an outline from a free draft or a mind map, reorganizing the raw text into sections of related material, creating entries in the outline for the sections, and then developing them as needed. This combination of strategies gives you a way to bring order to chaos.

As you order your ideas, you'll need to step back and think of your eventual readers: What are their concerns? Are they inclined to agree

Tips for Keeping the Momentum

Many strategies can help you when drafting to avoid getting bogged down in details or brought to a complete standstill by a thorny problem. Here's a sampling:

- *Don't be tied to the linear order of your outline or free draft.* Start working on the section that you feel most confident in, coming back later to the more complex ones. If you start to lose momentum in a section, jump to another section. In most cases, you'll want to wait to work on the introduction or conclusion. Readers don't care what order you write in — to them, the only thing that matters is the finished text.

- *Be willing to leave notes to yourself about material to work on later.* If you need an example of something but can't think of a good one, just write "{add example here}" and move on. Sometimes the solution will come to you after you've let the problem sit for a while (even suddenly, out of the blue, when you're working on something else).

  Likewise, sometimes you'll find yourself discovering that you need to do some additional research to complete a section. Interrupting your drafting, even just to search the web for a resource, can break the momentum you've built up. You might be better off leaving yourself a note in your draft that describes what research you need to do after you get that first draft finished.

- *Leave time for revising, including some time for your rough draft to just sit while you work on something else.* Although it's possible to finish a draft and immediately start revising it, you're going to be more effective if you schedule some time between finishing a draft and returning to it, at least a few hours (if not a few days). The exception might be for those sections you skipped because you were getting slowed down for some reason. Because you're working nonlinearly, you should feel free to return to those sections to see whether you're able to complete them now.

- *Allow yourself occasional breaks.* Walk across campus to get dinner or a late-night snack, watch a (short) show on TV, or play a video game for a half hour. You'll come back to the draft feeling fresher — just don't let that brief break turn into a four-hour session and don't overdo the number of interruptions. After each break it will take you a little while to get back into drafting; taking breaks too frequently will cause that "restart" time to accumulate.

- *Ignore or turn off automatic spelling and grammar checking in your word processor for the first couple of drafts.* Stopping to puzzle over a sentence flagged for grammatical problems is time wasted during your first draft. You can pay attention to them once you have a solid, readable draft and want to begin focusing on polishing the text.

- *Track your sources.* Although it's important to not get bogged down in details while you're drafting, be sure to keep track of your sources. Attach URLs or author, title, and page number information to any quotations or paraphrases so that you can attribute them formally in your final draft. Losing citation information during your drafting process might cost you the ability to use an important quote. See Chapter 7 for more on tracking sources.

with you, or will you have to convince them? What arguments seem likely to gain traction? What counterarguments will they raise? Assume your readers have two texts in front of them: the text you wrote arguing for one position and another text that argues the opposite position. What points would that opposing text make? What weakness in your position would they go for? How might you argue against them? What aspects of the readers' own positions are most in line with yours?

Continue to refer back to (and revise if necessary) your PACT chart and reread the assignment. Are there ideas in your draft that don't seem to address the assignment? Are there gaps in your PACT chart that will prevent readers from being convinced by your text? Are there obvious counterarguments that readers will make? You'll also continue to analyze and work on your structure using techniques discussed above and in Chapter 4, Structuring Your Texts.

Text for Analysis

BOOK EXCERPT
Anne Lamott, "Shitty First Drafts"

In this excerpt from her book *Bird by Bird: Some Instructions on Writing and Life* (1994), writer Anne Lamott describes her first-hand experiences of her writing processes. Although Lamott has authored well over a dozen books, you may be surprised to find that writing does not come easily to her. Despite popular images of writing as a joyous and natural activity, Lamott says the only way she can write is to "write really, really shitty first drafts." When you write, do you feel like your first drafts need to be complete? Or are you used to having to make several cycles through a draft, slowly revising to arrive at a polished, final draft?

Now, practically even better news than that of short assignments is the idea of shitty first drafts. All good writers write them. This is how they end up with good second drafts and terrific third drafts. People tend to look at successful writers who are getting their books published and maybe even doing well financially and think that they sit down at their desks every morning feeling like a million dollars, feeling great about who they are and how much talent they have and what a great story they have to tell; that they take in a few deep breaths, push back their sleeves, roll their necks a few times to get all the cricks out, and dive in, typing fully formed passages as fast as a court reporter. But this is just the fantasy of the uninitiated. I know some very great writers, writers you love who write beautifully and have made a great deal of money, and not one of them sits down routinely feeling wildly enthusiastic and confident. Not one of them writes elegant first drafts. All right, one of them does, but we do not like her very much. We do not think that she has a rich inner life or that God likes her or can even stand her. (Although when I mentioned this to my priest friend Tom, he said you can safely assume you've created God in your own image when it turns out that God hates all the same people you do.)

Very few writers really know what they are doing until they've done it. Nor do they go about their business feeling dewy and thrilled. They do not type a few stiff warm-up sentences and then find themselves bounding along like huskies across the snow. One writer I know tells me that he sits down every morning and says to himself nicely, "It's not like you don't have a choice, because you do — you can either type, or kill yourself." We all often feel like we are pulling teeth, even those writers whose prose ends up being the most natural and fluid. The right words and sentences just do not come pouring out like ticker tape most of the time. Now, Muriel Spark is said to have felt that she was taking dictation from God every morning — sitting there, one supposes, plugged into a Dictaphone, typing away, humming. But this is a very hostile and aggressive position. One might hope for bad things to rain down on a person like this.

For me and most of the other writers I know, writing is not rapturous. In fact, the only way I can get anything written at all is to write really, really shitty first drafts.

The first draft is the child's draft, where you let it all pour out and then let it romp all over the place, knowing that no one is going to see it and that you can shape it later. You just let this childlike part of you channel whatever voices and visions come through and onto the page. If one of the characters wants to say, "Well, so what, Mr. Poopy Pants?," you let her. No one is going to see it. If the kid wants to get into really sentimental, weepy, emotional territory, you let him. Just get it all down on paper because there may be something great in those six crazy pages that you would never have gotten to by more rational, grown-up means. There may be something in the very last line of the very last paragraph on page six that you just love, that is so beautiful or wild that you now know what you're supposed to be writing about, more or less, or in what direction you might go — but there was no way to get to this without first getting through the first five and a half pages.

I used to write food reviews for *California* magazine before it folded. (My writing food reviews had nothing to do with the magazine folding, although every single review did cause a couple of canceled subscriptions. Some readers took umbrage at my comparing mounds of vegetable puree with various ex-presidents' brains.) These reviews always took two days to write. First I'd go to a restaurant several times with a few opinionated, articulate friends in tow. I'd sit there writing down everything anyone said that was at all interesting or funny. Then on the following Monday I'd sit down at my desk with my notes and try to write the review. Even after I'd been doing this for years, panic would set in. I'd try to write a lead, but instead I'd write a couple of dreadful sentences, xx them out, try again, xx everything out, and then feel despair and worry settle on my chest like an x-ray apron. It's over, I'd think calmly. I'm not going to be able to get the magic to work this time. I'm ruined. I'm through. I'm toast. Maybe, I'd think, I can get my old job back as a clerk-typist. But probably not. I'd get up and study my teeth in the mirror for a while. Then I'd stop, remember to breathe, make a few phone calls, hit the kitchen and chow down. Eventually I'd go back and sit down at my desk, and sigh for the next ten minutes.

Finally I would pick up my one-inch picture frame, stare into it as if for the answer, and every time the answer would come: all I had to do was to write a really shitty first draft of, say, the opening paragraph. And no one was going to see it.

So I'd start writing without reining myself in. It was almost just typing, just making my fingers move. And the writing would be terrible. I'd write a lead paragraph that was a whole page, even though the entire review could only be three pages long, and then I'd start writing up descriptions of the food, one dish at a time, bird by bird, and the critics would be sitting on my shoulders, commenting like cartoon characters. They'd be pretending to snore, or rolling their eyes at my overwrought descriptions, no matter how hard I tried to tone those descriptions down, no matter how conscious I was of what a friend said to me gently in my early days of restaurant reviewing. "Annie," she said, "it is just a piece of *chicken*. It is just a bit of *cake*."

But because by then I had been writing for so long, I would eventually let myself trust the process — sort of, more or less. I'd write a first draft that was maybe twice as long as it should be, with a self-indulgent and boring beginning, stupefying descriptions of the meal, lots of quotes from my black-humored friends that made them sound more like the Manson girls than food lovers, and no ending to speak of. The whole thing would be so long and incoherent and hideous that for the rest of the day I'd obsess about getting creamed by a car before I could write a decent second draft. I'd worry that people would read what I'd written and believe that the accident had really been a suicide, that I had panicked because my talent was waning and my mind was shot.

The next day, I'd sit down, go through it all with a colored pen, take out everything I possibly could, find a new lead somewhere on the second page, figure out a kicky place to end it, and then write a second draft. It always turned out fine, sometimes even funny and weird and helpful. I'd go over it one more time and mail it in.

Then, a month later, when it was time for another review, the whole process would start again, complete with the fears that people would find my first draft before I could rewrite it.

Almost all good writing begins with terrible first efforts. You need to start somewhere. Start by getting something — anything — down on paper. A friend of mine says that the first draft is the down draft — you just get it down. The second draft is the up draft — you fix it up. You try to say what you have to say more accurately. And the third draft is the dental draft, where you check every tooth, to see if it's loose or cramped or decayed, or even, God help us, healthy.

Exercises

1. Take a picture of your own writing space — your desk in your dorm room, a study carrel at the library, your kitchen table covered in books and notes. Describe the key components of the space, including their relationship to one another and why things are where they are. How do this space and the things in it affect your ability to work with information? Are there strategies in this chapter that would work better for you than others? Are there strategies that would be difficult for you to use? Annotate the picture (either on paper or in a graphics program), showing relationships and labeling items that you discuss in a short (1,000-word) essay describing your writing space.

2. For the space you described in exercise 1, write a short essay describing what you like and dislike about this space. Could you change this space to more effectively support your work?

3. Write a 1,000-word, first-person narrative (a story told from your own perspective) along with pictures (a camera phone is fine) in which you describe your writing process. Talk about your normal process for writing. What space works best and why? What strategies do you use? Do you think there are things you could do that would make you a more effective writer?

4. Share your notes from exercise 1, 2, or 3 with classmates. What similarities do you see among writers? Do other people's experiences give you ideas to try out with your own writing?

5. You've been asked to write an editorial for your school's newspaper on the question, "Should laptop computers be required for all students?" You can take either position. Complete a rough PACT chart and generate five or six

ideas by brainstorming or freewriting. Then create a rough outline using mind mapping, sticky notes, or index cards. What are the topics, and what order did you put them in? How will readers perceive them?

Scenario Connections

1. For Scenario 8, "Drafting a Poster about Online Privacy," you'll need to narrow the topic of online privacy to some specific aspects you want to focus on. Read through the scenario and then use one of the strategies in the "Ideas and How to Have Them" section (pp. 56–63) to generate some ideas for your poster. Note: Choose a strategy that involves producing something (brainstorming, sketching, etc.), not one that asks you to review, read, or reflect.

2. In Scenario 11, "A Story from Your Digital Life," you'll have the opportunity to write about your experiences learning a new communication technology (e-mail, Twitter, etc.). Choose a technology you want to write about and then create a PACT chart and a first draft of your story using the free drafting or outlining techniques described on page 64 and pages 66–68.

3. Many of the scenarios give you some space to pick your own topic. For example, Scenario 4, "Making Invisible Things Visible: Mapping Data," requires you to take statistical data about some population and put that data on a map to reveal relationships. For example, you might make a map of a community that shows average household income in relationship to hospitals to see whether there's a possible connection between the two. Nearly any sort of data can be mapped in this way, so one challenge you'll face is deciding what to map. Use mind mapping (pp. 64–66) or brainstorming (pp. 60–61) techniques to create a list of at least 10 topics you might look at.

4. Follow the instructions in Scenario 12, "Analyzing Your Media Diet," for keeping a diary of all the media you encounter during a 24-hour period. Then use mind mapping, outlining, or index cards (see pp. 64–68) to begin to analyze and classify the concepts you note in your diary entries. Develop an outline of points you will want to cover in the analysis you'll write for the scenario.

Structuring Your Texts

You might have noticed that a lot of the early stages of writing ask you to work at a very broad level, creating and arranging sections rather than crafting individual sentences. In fact, in your early drafts, you probably shouldn't spend much time worrying about individual words or sentences, transitions between sections, or even introductions and conclusions (write those last).

Why should you avoid working on details in the early stages? Because pretty words that go nowhere aren't going to do anything for readers except pass time. To use the obvious metaphor, you don't put up your curtains before you've built the walls of your house. In the end, you want both sound structure *and* well-written sentences, but structural work is best undertaken earlier in the process.

Another reason to work on large items first is because working on structure often reveals large-scale issues with your text, including things that may make you delete a whole section or combine two sections into one or swap the ordering of sections. If you spend a great deal of time polishing your sentences or crafting careful transitions too early in the process, you'll find yourself having to cut out or extensively revise large sections of prose, a painful process.

You'll find yourself moving items around in your text because the order of elements is crucial to how readers interpret texts. Knowing how common structures work — and what structures tend to work for what purposes — is key to creating effective texts. There are nearly as many ways to order or structure your text as there are texts themselves. Your writing situation, your readers, the text you're creating, and the change you want to make in the world are unique. The structures you use will necessarily change from one writing project to the next. Still, there are some common overall strategies that you can adapt (or combine) as necessary. These are methods for taking the raw material you have created and ordering it in some way that addresses the specific situation you and your readers are in.

In this chapter, we'll be dealing primarily with structuring alphabetic aspects of texts — paragraphs and sections. In Chapter 5, we'll focus explicitly on structuring texts with visual design. In many cases, you'll need to work with both types of structure to create effective texts.

Considering Your Audience

Think carefully about your audience as you organize your ideas. You don't want to simply dump a bunch of raw data on them. Instead, you'll want to think about your readers' mindset:

- Are they interested in your topic already?
- How much do they know about it?
- Are they inclined to agree with you? Or are they disinterested or even opposed?
- Given their perspective, what key points does the text need to make?
- If they currently disagree with you, how can you establish a common ground where you can make your points?

Working on your PACT chart can help you answer these questions.

For example, this editorial from the *Des Moines Register* shifts the debate about wind energy away from ecological issues, framing it instead as a story about jobs during a harsh economy, an issue that more of its readers are likely to identify with:

> Iowa has enjoyed tremendous economic benefits by being a leader in both wind power development and wind manufacturing. It is puzzling, then, to see Thomas Pyle of the Koch-funded American Energy Alliance attack an industry that pumps billions into our state's economy ["Hand-outs for 'Green' Projects Hurt Iowans," Jan. 23].
>
> Iowa is a longtime pioneer in wind power, and that heritage is reflected every day in the more than 7,000 wind jobs that are creating value for Iowa manufacturing.
>
> The production tax credit for wind fosters economic development not only in Iowa, but in all 50 states. From farmers to autoworkers, Americans everywhere are benefiting from wind energy.

When you write, you have a lot of power to create texts that adapt to (and even change) the contexts where your readers engage with your text. Readers obviously bring a lot to a text. They actively construct meanings using the raw materials of their own experiences and the text itself. But the writer of a well-constructed text understands what readers bring to the text, anticipates the counterarguments readers will make, and knows what will convince readers to make targeted changes.

Developing a Thesis

In a traditional, persuasive text such as an essay, an editorial, or a research paper, you usually have a main point you want to prove — the "thesis." The thesis is usually a short direct statement near the start of your text (traditionally at the end of an introduction) that you will spend the rest of your text making a case for. The purpose of your text is getting your audience to agree with your thesis even if they didn't start out with that opinion. Here are some simple examples:

- Learning a foreign language is an ethical necessity for people in the twenty-first century.
- Network neutrality spurs innovation, economic growth, and freedom of speech.
- Some video games should be considered artistic work.
- The flood of information we face distracts us from real issues.
- Vegetarian diets can provide as much nutrition as omnivorous diets.

In a lot of cases, your thesis statement will grow out of the purpose you listed in your PACT chart. But a thesis needs to also take into account context and audience. For example, if your purpose is "Get people to appreciate the complexities of the show *The Walking Dead*," your thesis statement probably should not be something as clumsy as "You! Start appreciating the complexities of *The Walking Dead*!" You'll be more successful if, after analyzing your context and audience (as well as the show itself), you come up with something like "Although on the surface *The Walking Dead* appears to be just another show about zombies, a close analysis reveals a complex, multithreaded critique of modern culture."

Think of your thesis as a variant of a scientific hypothesis: a tentative statement that you're going to test. In the case of a hypothesis, you might run a series of controlled experiments to see whether your hypothesis holds up in light of the data generated. A thesis is tested by your research and thinking about your context, audience, and text. As you work, you may find that your thesis needs to be modified or changed. Clinging too tightly to your thesis can result in a text that's weak and fails to achieve its purpose.

Not every text requires a formal thesis. Narrative forms like short stories, movies, video games, or songs don't normally state a thesis (although they could). And some texts that have a thesis might hold off on spelling it out until the end, after slowly and carefully building up to it. The decision on whether to use one should be informed by the work you do with your PACT chart.

Don't settle firmly on your thesis too early. A strong, interesting text rarely turns out the way you thought it would at the start. As you move back and forth in your PACT chart, revising sections as you continue to think about your project, you'll likely find that your ideas about your thesis are shifting. As you begin drafting, you'll probably also discover that arguments that seemed simple at first glance are actually more complicated. After rereading or getting feedback on a draft, you might discover some of your arguments don't work out. You might even decide to change your mind completely about your thesis. A good writer is open to change, alert to the ways the text may need to shift in response to new information and thought.

Once you have a tentative thesis, cycle through your PACT chart and develop material that supports your thesis, trying to understand what things will convince your audience that your thesis is believable. Return to your PACT chart throughout your writing process, asking more questions and refining your answers to see whether your ideas about your purpose, audience, context, or text are changing. (If you get stuck, try some of the questions in the PACT chart in Chapter 2 on pages 42–43.) How long you continue looking at and revising the PACT chart varies from project to project, but it's a good idea to continue working with it until you've developed a full, fairly solid draft of your text. You might want to return to it even after you've got a full draft to make sure you're not drifting in unintentional ways.

Writing an Introduction and Conclusion: Wait

A lot of people believe they have to write their introduction before they get to the body of the text and that they have to write a conclusion when they get to the end of the first draft. That's usually a mistake. Spending a lot of time on the introduction at the very start is a bad idea for two reasons: If you change your thesis, you'll probably need to change your introduction. Even worse, you might find that your main argument has shifted during drafting and revising. If you've spent time polishing an introduction, you might resist changing your thesis because you don't want to change your introduction.

Hold off working on your introduction and conclusion until you have a pretty solid draft. We'll return to discussing these sections of your text later in the chapter.

Deciding on a Structure for Your Text

You might be wondering how to decide what order to put your ideas in. The structures that follow are different ways to present your arguments. You can experiment with them as you work on a first draft, fitting them to your audience and text. Sometimes the type of text will determine the structure. For example, scientific journal articles, feasibility studies, and pop songs each have a limited number of acceptable structures. Using an unconventional structure may confuse or annoy readers.

In other types of texts, you may have more freedom — personal essays can follow many different formats. And don't be afraid to consider working against the grain, breaking the conventions of the text to intrigue the reader.

Structure Overview

There are a nearly infinite number of ways to structure a text, especially when you realize multiple structures are often combined in single texts. Jennifer Egan's Pulitzer Prize–winning *A Visit from the Goon Squad*, a traditional novel about people working in the music industry, included a chapter composed completely of PowerPoint slides (see p. 80). The descriptions and examples in the table that follows are just a starting point; be open to the possibility that you might be able to create a more effective text by mixing things up or using an unfamiliar structure.

If you're considering mixing these structures up to create interesting hybrids or using a structure that's not common for the type of text you're working on, think carefully about your readers and their context. Will readers be impressed by your ingenuity? Or will they be annoyed? Will your chemistry teacher be awed by your interpretive dance lab report? What are the consequences if you guess wrong? What are the rewards if you're right?

If	Use	Examples
drama or entertainment is » the goal	thesis last (p. 80)	detective stories, theatrical plays
your readers want to see the » big picture early on	thesis first (p. 81)	academic essays, proposals, memos
you're writing a story or time » is important	time based (p. 82)	biographies, instructions for doing something
the spatial elements of the » context are important	context based (p. 83)	descriptions of places, overviews of something physical or visual
readers will seize on an » obvious reason to disagree	weakness first (p. 84)	political speeches and ads, proposals
your main point is » very strong and the weak points are insignificant or absent (or you hope your readers won't see them)	strength first (p. 85)	advertisements, testimonials, obituaries

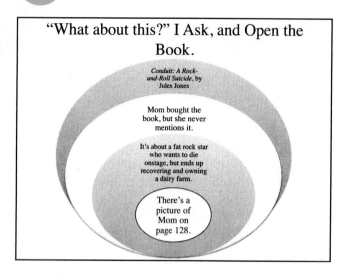

"What about this?" I Ask, and Open the Book.

Conduit: A Rock-and-Roll Suicide, by Jules Jones

Mom bought the book, but she never mentions it.

It's about a fat rock star who wants to die onstage, but ends up recovering and owning a dairy farm.

There's a picture of Mom on page 128.

● A slide from a PowerPoint presentation in Jennifer Egan's novel *A Visit from the Goon Squad*

Thesis Last

Let's start with a structure that places the thesis or main point at the end of your argument. This structure is not used in traditional research papers where you usually state your thesis at the outset. But often texts that have entertainment as their purpose will increase the dramatic tension by putting their main point at the end, gradually and carefully leading readers to that point.

In a thesis-last textual structure, you lay out your main points as evidence and use them to lead readers to your thesis: *We see that in all of these cases,* x *happens at the same time that* y *happens. Therefore,* x *and* y *must be somehow connected.*

Stories that have a moral at the end also use thesis-last structures.

Note that when you structure a text as thesis last, it's *readers* who come to the thesis last. Your actual writing process may have also come to the thesis after a series of observations, but it also could have come early in the writing process.

Thesis-last structures also allow you to lay out a series of observations or pieces of data on two sides (or more) of an argument and then examine the "big picture" before arriving at a conclusion. Ethically speaking, you should work to explain both sides of an argument and not set up what's called a straw man argument, an unbalanced viewpoint with all the strongest points from your preferred side but only the weakest points from the opposite side. An unbalanced viewpoint might succeed in fooling some readers, but if they notice your bias, they're much less likely to trust you in the future.

In an article about sportscaster John Madden, Matthew Futterman assembles a long list of individual facts about John Madden, including many negative observations:

> In statements made during several recent NBC broadcasts, Mr. Madden, who is 72, has misjudged the number of times NFL teams execute running plays from the shotgun formation, attributed two offensive strategies to a team whose players deny using them and misstated how often the San Diego Chargers call pass plays.

> In a recent playoff game, Mr. Madden said the New York Giants, who faced a third down with 10 yards to go, had not performed well in those

situations. Seconds later, Mr. Madden's NBC booth partner, Al Michaels, called his attention to a graphic on the screen which noted that the Giants were tops in the NFL in third-and-long situations. "That was just some buttoning up that we needed to do," Mr. Michaels said, "Third and 10 isn't a good situation for anyone."

Over the course of the article, the author moves back and forth, positive and negative, before coming down on the side of Madden's continued importance to football coverage:

With three more years on his contract at NBC, Mr. Madden is scheduled to call at least one more Super Bowl. No matter how well he masters the facts, it's clear that many people will be happy to see him.

"I know there's talk he's lost a step," said Mr. Pilson. "I'm still very, very comfortable with John Madden."

The thesis-last structure allows you to lay out evidence in a way that seems (and, ideally, is) impartial, constructing a full, clear picture that is judged only once it's complete. Thesis-last structures are useful in contexts where the issues are complicated; they allow you to acknowledge counterarguments and gray areas that readers might already know — you're displaying your fairness and honesty by bringing them up instead of hiding them.

Thesis First

Thesis-first structures are the flip side of thesis-last structures: start from your thesis and then present pieces of evidence or make logical points in support of the thesis.

In an article from *Psychology Today*, Loretta Graziano Bruening begins with a short piece of deductive reasoning to demonstrate why people allow themselves to be bullied:

Bullies thrive because mammals tend to stick with the herd. Your mammal brain knows the herd could turn on you when you oppose a bully. A mammal without a herd soon lands in the jaws of a predator. That's why people fear losing the safety of social alliances — and appease bullies instead of opposing them.

In the first two sentences, Bruening walks through this deductive argument:

1. Bullies thrive because mammals tend to stick to the herd.
2. You are a mammal.
3. Therefore, you tend to stick to the herd.

The opening paragraph of Linnea Snyder's essay "Memorializing September 11, 2001" takes a slightly more complex tack as it signals a two-part structure in which she will analyze the different responses to two highly visible 9/11 memorials:

> Choosing the right way to commemorate a special event is not easy. Choosing the right way to commemorate a traumatic terrorist attack is even harder. September 11, 2001, left people around the world shocked and devastated. As time passed, it was clear that memorials needed to be created for those who lost their lives in the attacks in order to remember them and in order for their families, friends, and the general public to move on from the tragedy. Two important and interesting memorials came about in the months and years following 9/11: composer John Adams's opus *On the Transmigration of Souls* and architect Daniel Libeskind's Freedom Tower. Although the objectives of these memorials were the same — to relieve the pain of September 11th — they were received in opposite manners. One is a piece of music — something to listen to, absorb, and then move away from — while the other is a building: something that will be present for many generations. The political implications, over-the-top tone, and permanent quality of Libeskind's tower caused it to be more negatively received by the public, and ultimately rejected, while Adams's *On the Transmigration of Souls* was appreciated for its temporary quality and theme of healing.

You can see here the way Snyder begins with a general observation: "Choosing the right way to commemorate a special event is not easy. Choosing the right way to commemorate a traumatic terrorist attack is even harder." She provides some additional detail to focus her argument on two 9/11 memorials before stating her thesis: "The political implications, over-the-top tone, and permanent quality of Libeskind's tower caused it to be more negatively received by the public, and ultimately rejected, while Adams's *On the Transmigration of Souls* was appreciated for its temporary quality and theme of healing." The rest of the paper provides evidence to support this statement. (For the complete paper, see Chapter 7, pages 185–97.)

Time Based

Time-based structures obviously work well for situations in which time is an important factor, for example, stories that involve gradually unfolding experiences or timelines recounting historical events, legal proceedings, and so forth. In many cases, a time-based structure is used along with other structures, with the other structures reflecting on or analyzing the time-based content. A lab report, for example, often includes "methods" and "results" sections that describe the sequence of an actual experiment; these sections are invariably followed by some sort of "discussion" section that analyzes or tries to explain the time-based sections.

Narratives and biographies often adopt time-based structures because they grow out of lived experiences. A biography of film director David Lynch, for example, begins as many biographies do, with the person's birth:

> David Lynch was born in Missoula, Montana, on 20 January 1946. In his own words, he was there "just to be born" before the family moved — when he was only two months old — to Sandpoint, Idaho. His father, Donald,

worked for the Government's Department of Agriculture as a research scientist and was subject to frequent transfer, consigning the Lynch household to an itinerant lifestyle. After only two years in Sandpoint, where Lynch's brother John was born, the family moved again to Spokane, Washington, where another child, Martha, became the newest addition to the family. From there it was on to Durham, North Carolina, then to Boise, Idaho, and finally to Alexandria, Virginia. Lynch was only fourteen years old at that time.

One potential drawback to time-based structures, and to some extent any structure, is overreliance on them to the point that they seem to overshadow the content. Lynch's biography uses the time-based structure to open the biography but then soon jumps to other structures.

Context Based

Like time-based structures, context-based text structures grow out of the situation in which they are set. The specific structure varies according to that context and to what the writer wants to focus on: An essay

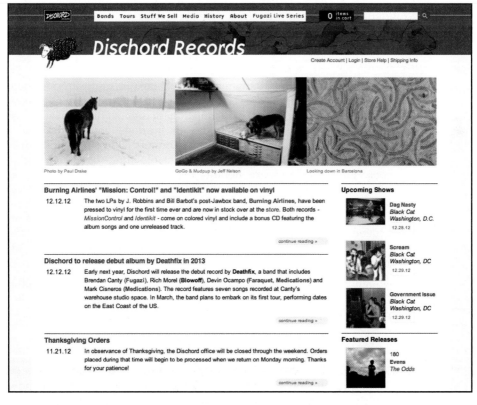

Dischord Records' website uses multiple structures to support different types of information seeking
Reprinted by permission of Dischord Records

about the United States, for example, could be structured by geographic region, by climate, by ethnicity, by dialect, or even by professional sports teams. The time-based structure discussed above is actually a type of context-based structure.

In some cases, texts offer multiple structures for users to select from based on their own needs. People visiting a record company's website might have different types of needs. Visitors to Dischord Records' site (see p. 83), for example, might be looking for items to purchase (supported by links in the top navigation bar), information about upcoming live shows (supported by the "Upcoming Shows" list in the right-hand column), or just news about the label and the bands on it (supported by the reverse-chronologically arranged list of news items in the bottom half of the page).

Weakness First

In situations where your audience seems to be aligned against you, particularly when your PACT chart identifies one or two key arguments against your point, consider dealing with those arguments first. Explain why those arguments are either incorrect or outweighed by other factors. Consider the opening of this article from audio production magazine *Tape Op*, in which Brad Williams tries to get readers engaged with what's often considered a dull topic, room acoustics:

> While hardly a glamorous concept, room acoustics represent a critical link in the recording or playback chain. While comprehensive room design is a complex cocktail of science, math and chance, certain obvious issues can be easily dealt with to improve your recordings — even in a home or project studio environment. One such problem is specular reflections, mirror-like reflections of sound that cause flutter echoes. Flutter echoes are hollow, metallic "bathroom" effects that honk at particular frequencies or discrete repeats. While absorption will control these issues by removing acoustic energy, you might be interested in diffusion instead — particularly if your space is already on the "dead" side. Diffusors come in many types, all designed with the objective of scattering reflected sound (relatively) equally in all directions.
>
> One popular style is the 2D Quadratic Residue diffusor (often called the BBC diffusor, after a paper published by the British Broadcasting Corporation).

Note how Williams acknowledges the relatively dull nature of the topic as well as its inherent complexity before pivoting to identifying both a specific problem and a specific solution. He does so quickly so that he can get to the main body of the article, which describes how to build this specific type of diffusor. He can move this quickly both because his argument is very efficient and compact and because his audience is composed of advanced amateur and professional recording engineers: They are already interested in improving audio quality. Williams has to convince them only that he has a specific, proven solution to a specific problem. Readers who recognize the description of flutter echo may want to solve it using the diffusors he describes.

In situations where readers are more actively opposed to a text's purpose, you might need to take much more time than Williams did to carefully describe the weakness, building up an argument that that weakness is either false or outweighed by other factors, often across many paragraphs or pages.

Strength First

You might take the opposite approach in situations where audiences are already likely to agree with you or when there are few serious opposing points or barriers to change. You can find extreme versions of this in advertising, where marketers often attempt to lead with such a strong argument that they hope viewers will forget about weak points. A political advertisement that trumpets the candidate's qualifications, for example, might either downplay weaknesses or simply ignore them. Similarly, celebratory texts such as awards ceremonies or obituaries will often focus primarily or exclusively on strengths.

Strength first can also work when you want to cue readers to remember or discover positive strong arguments that will attract them to your text, especially when there are not significant weaknesses. For example, Peter Reinhart's award-winning cookbook *The Bread Baker's Apprentice* opens with this narrative:

> On August 7, 1999, on a drizzly, chilly day typical to the region, thousands of pilgrims flooded a four-block area of southwest Portland, Oregon, in a park near Portland State University. They didn't come for religious reasons but to venerate with religious zeal their newly emerged passion for the world's most symbolically evocative foodstuff: bread. Not just bread, but good-as-it-gets bread, made by artisans of the Pacific Northwest using techniques discovered either accidentally or from the dissemination of arcane knowledge brought to this country only recently by European bakers through the Bread Bakers Guild of America, itself a throwback to days of yore. The Summer Loaf Festival, as it is called, is one of the first of what may soon be a national parade of tributes to the hottest food trend since, well, sliced bread. (p. 7)

Reinhart can assume that his audience is already ready to agree with him (they've purchased or borrowed his bread cookbook or at least are interested enough to be skimming it in a bookstore), so he opens by strengthening readers' interest (note the strong language: "venerate," "zeal," "evocative," and more). On the remaining introductory pages of the book, he describes the sensory experiences of smelling, touching, tasting, and seeing fresh artisan bread. He describes his own experiences as a teacher (lending to his credibility) and those of his students. He describes winning a major bread-baking competition. The cover of the book displays logos for several prominent awards given to the book. All of these are designed to take readers who are interested in the text and whip that interest into a frenzy.

You might have noted the opening sentence contains some less enthusiastic terms: the "drizzly, chilly day" in which the scene is set. Although this is not a strong point, it's raised and very quickly overcome in the subsequent sentences. Why open with this depressing imagery? Because it provides contrast to the strengths that immediately follow and because it isn't dwelled on (which would make the weakness of the scene more prominent).

In many cases, you'll mix structures for specific purposes like this. For example, you might start with a weakness that you then overcome with a strength and next bring up another weakness that you similarly deal with. This pro/con strategy would work well if you have a series of complex weaknesses that you need to deal with. You might choose this strategy because it allows you to dissect the complex situation. You can find it employed, often to devastating effect, in web discussion boards, where opponents will quote their adversary's full quote and insert their own comments, arguing point by point. Unfortunately, taking a stance that's too aggressive can also result in stronger disagreement — take care to deal honestly and generously with your adversaries.

Creating Transitions

In most cases, you want to make connections from one point to the next. Transitions provide several important things for readers: They alert readers that the topic is shifting. They also help readers see how point A connects to point B (and the overall place of both in the text). You can take cues from some of the structures we just discussed as suggestions for transitions. Linnea Snyder's 9/11 essay (p. 185), for example, uses "One is . . . while the other . . ." to connect two points. Brad Williams's article on acoustic treatment above moves from an overview to specifics with the phrase "One popular style. . . ."

A context-based structure can refer back to the context as the text moves from point to point. Hunter Thompson's *Fear and Loathing in Las Vegas* opens with "We were somewhere around Barstow on the edge of the desert when the drugs began to take hold" and moves forward in the landscape over the next several pages: "It was almost noon and we still had more than a hundred miles to go. They would be tough miles. . . . My attorney saw the hitchhiker long before I did. . . ."

A time-based structure can proceed in order over time. (Or the reverse: One of the most applauded features of the cult film *Memento* is the reverse-chronological order of the plot.) A differently structured text on teaching might just move through the class period in chronological order, using time-based terms to indicate movement into a new topic: "At the start of the class, students benefit from . . . During the class . . . At the close of class. . . ."

One of the most straightforward methods of making transitions is to simply state that you're making a transition. Many academic essays have introductions that explicitly state what the order is going to be. Here's the introduction to a short academic research paper about social networking programs:

> Do social networking programs like Twitter and Facebook help connect people to each other in communities or do they merely fragment and trivialize communication? To find out, I interviewed people who both love and loathe social networking apps. I also analyzed sample content from Twitter and Facebook as well as real-world conversations to compare the two. Finally, I researched how earlier communication technologies were received by users and critics. In the end, it appears that the reality is much more complex than simple positive and negative. Instead, social networking programs, like any communication technology, are what we make of them.

In the essay that follows this introduction, the transitions between the major sections can simply note that the text is now moving from A to B. In an essay that starts with the introduction above, the writer moves from the section analyzing the content of Twitter and Facebook posts compared to real-world conversation to the section on earlier communication technologies. To make the transition, he forges a connection between the two topics by pointing out a similarity between them that supports his argument:

> So if the content of Twitter and Facebook posts seems just as varied and rich as the content of real-world communication, why have these applications garnered such a bad rap compared to other technologies? It turns out a lot of communication technologies that we now think of as natural were originally both lauded and attacked. When the telephone was introduced, for example, wealthy people were aghast to find out that anyone — even someone from the lower classes — might be on the other end of the ringing line. (Marvin, 1988)

Making a meaningful connection like this helps the essay overall seem clearly reasoned and logical.

What about Introductions and Conclusions?

With very rare exceptions, you're best writing the main body of your text first and your introduction and conclusion last.

Why? Because writing is a messy process, full of unexpected turns, reversals, and detours. You want to be open to small or even large shifts in your direction or opinion, not tied down to reach a precise, predetermined conclusion. Even if your first draft manages to follow neatly along your outline, by the time you get to the end of your first draft you'll have a much richer, more detailed understanding of your argument. You'll be better equipped to write a powerful introduction and conclusion once you know exactly what it is you're introducing and concluding.

If you have time, you might want to wait a day or two after you've finished your first draft before working on your introduction or conclusion. Many writers find that putting a draft aside for a little while lets them see the draft with a fresher perspective.

Begin working on your introduction and conclusion by reading through your rough draft slowly. As you read, keep your audience in mind. Are you making arguments that connect with your readers' own opinions and inclinations? Are they going to be willing to make the change you want? Will they be making counterarguments?

When you're done, start to think about how you want to bring them into your text: How should your text start? Do you need to engage them with a short story or anecdote? Or do they just want the facts, no drama? Some of this will depend on the context they're in. A manager reading a formal proposal will probably be put off by a joke. Your best friend doesn't expect to get an e-mail from you that starts with a businesslike executive summary.

Starting with a Summary

A lot of academic writing begins with a straightforward overview of the text concluding with a thesis statement. Here's a rough draft of an introduction to an essay about file sharing and the music industry:

> In the last two decades, music listeners have embraced file sharing as the preferred method for obtaining a wide variety of music quickly, cheaply, and without the restrictions imposed by digital rights management. The music industry has responded with an army of lawyers and lobbyists who succeeded in writing laws that allowed them to sue normally law-abiding people for millions of dollars. In this paper, I will review the history of file sharing law, arguing that this hostile approach is an inappropriate, unsuccessful response to a changing technological landscape.

Like many essay introductions, this introduction begins broadly, setting up a conflict that the essay will attempt to solve or at least address.

Starting with a Story

Less academic essays often begin less formally and with a little more drama and creativity. This approach works best for audiences who are open to entertainment. Even in contexts where the audience is primarily seeking information, they might be more engaged by a short story that relates to the topic. In many cases, such introductions will be longer than a single paragraph because the story they tell needs room to develop. But in other cases, a carefully constructed, compact story contains a seed that the text then develops. Here's a version of a commencement speech that the late writer David Foster Wallace gave to the graduating class at Kenyon College:

> There are these two young fish swimming along, and they happen to meet an older fish swimming the other way, who nods at them and says, "Morning, boys, how's the water?" And the two young fish swim on for a bit, and then eventually one of them looks over at the other and goes, "What the hell is water?"

> If at this moment, you're worried that I plan to present myself here as the wise old fish explaining what water is to you younger fish, please don't be. I am not the wise old fish. The immediate point of the fish story is that the most obvious, ubiquitous, important realities are often the ones that are the hardest to see and talk about. Stated as an English sentence, of course, this is just a banal platitude—but the fact is that, in the day-to-day trenches of adult existence, banal platitudes can have life-or-death importance. That may sound like hyperbole, or abstract nonsense.

The opening story, a short fable here, makes a very simple point that Wallace builds on over the course of the speech. Interestingly, Wallace complicates what seems to be a simple point—young people aren't aware of what goes on around them—by turning the criticism on himself. Older people, he says, are as guilty of this problem as younger ones.

Fictional work often opens much more leisurely, setting tone or location rather than hammering home an explicit point. The four scenes from the short film "Mission Impossible" shown on page 90 offer an ambiguous opening. A person is sleeping on a couch while a TV plays in the background. Cut to an exterior shot of someone running frantically to the door of an apartment. The person from the first scene opens the door, groggy with sleep. The two talk quickly, laying out the dramatic situation that will drive the rest of the film.

Starting with a Dramatic Statement

One method for engaging readers involves grabbing their attention with a surprising statement, one that's dramatic, contradictory, or shocking. There are risks to this strategy given its lack of subtlety, but handled carefully a dramatic opening can pull readers in like a carnival barker luring people into a sideshow tent. Consider the foreword

● Four scenes from the short film "Mission Impossible"
Courtesy Zachary Durocher

to Studs Terkel's nonfiction book *Working*, which is composed of interviews with everyday people about their jobs and lives:

> This book, being about work, is, by its very nature, about violence — to the spirit as well as the body. It is about ulcers as well as accidents, about shouting matches as well as fistfights, about nervous breakdowns as well as kicking the dog around. It is, above all (or beneath all), about daily humiliations. To survive the day is a triumph enough for the walking wounded among the great many of us.

Terkel's opening statement shocks readers, who would not normally associate work with violence. The following sentences make a logical argument that work is, for many of us, often a form of violence. Work bends us to its demands, forces us to change who we are. So, as Terkel shows, work is a form of violence. After this dramatic opening, Terkel brings us the voices of those who work, lets them tell their stories, and shows us the lives of janitors, police officers, farmworkers.

Starting with an Abstract

In contexts where readers want information as quickly and efficiently as possible — for example, in scientific or business reports — effective introductions are very direct, almost blunt. Readers in these situations are often using the introduction to decide whether they'll take the time to read the rest of the text. Academic and research journal articles often start with a special form of introduction called an abstract, which readers use to decide whether to read the full text. Here's an example:

> Although college students today work and live in a remix culture, writing classes do not often give them the chance to practice remixing texts. There are many reasons for this, including old-fashioned ideas about what types of texts are valuable, what counts as creativity, and what it means to be a writer. But if we look at the world outside the classroom we can find numerous examples of remixed texts that are highly valued by different cultures. It's time to bring writing classrooms into the twenty first century by helping students learn ways of making remixed texts that will be valued both in and out of the classroom.

Abstracts usually start by staking a claim, noting a gap in current understanding of some phenomenon. The abstract then describes what the authors have done to address that gap. They often conclude by stating what action will be or needs to be taken in the future. Based on this information, readers decide whether the information in the article will be useful to them.

Ending with a Summary

Long, informative texts often end by summarizing the main points of the text and giving readers a direction. Texts that begin with an abstract can use this kind of conclusion, forming sort of a mirror image of the introduction. Here's the conclusion to the academic essay about remix culture that started with the abstract above:

> As I have showed above, being able to remix texts can be useful both in and out of the writing classroom. Common ideas about the value of "original" texts, about what counts as creativity, and what it means to be a writer have shifted. Although writing students are not often given the chance to practice these skills in the classroom, the situation needs to change in order to keep in step with changes that have already happened in the wider world.

The authors here explicitly refer back to earlier points, stating them again to help readers remember them. The short final paragraph gives readers (in this case, teachers of writing) a suggestion about what they should do in the future (and why it's important).

Ending by Suggesting New Beginnings

Even texts such as websites often provide conclusions. E-commerce sites like Amazon.com spend inordinate amounts of time and money researching the usability and user satisfaction of their interfaces. The order confirmation page does not simply tell users that their orders have been placed.

It also politely thanks them for placing the orders, offers them social media buttons so they can share news of their purchases with friends, and entices them to "Give Yourself a Little Something": a series of products that Amazon thinks you might want to buy. Only Amazon knows exactly how successful these efforts are at increasing customer satisfaction (and total purchases), but clearly the designers expect positive results.

Articles reporting scientific research also frequently end by proposing new research issues or questions. Science, like other fields, progresses by adding new knowledge to old. (As Isaac Newton said, "If I have seen farther it is by standing on the shoulders of giants.") A report on cellphone use and driving from the Centers for Disease Control and Prevention concludes with this paragraph:

> Many countries have made substantial improvements in reducing other risky driving behaviors, such as seat belt nonuse and alcohol-impaired driving, through a combination of legislation, sustained and highly visible enforcement, and ongoing public education campaigns to increase awareness of the risks and penalties associated with disobeying traffic laws. Countries could consider exploring the effectiveness of applying similar approaches to the problem of mobile device use while driving. Additionally, the effectiveness of emerging vehicle and mobile communication technologies (e.g., advanced crash warning and driver-monitoring technologies or applications that temporarily disable mobile devices while a vehicle is in motion) should be studied to assess their role in reducing crashes related to distracted driving.

Calls for additional research like this are a way for authors to begin forging a link from their work to that done in the future, either by themselves or others. Most research teams attempt to carve out areas of specialization, so they consciously try to link one research project to the next in this way.

Ending with a Quotation, Reflection, or Narrative

Texts that are used in contexts where readers are not driven as hard by information needs have more freedom to end in different ways. A profile of a person or a business, for example, might end with an overarching theme, point, or quotation that captures the nature of what's being described. Here's the final paragraph of a short profile of Mo Coppoletta's tattoo shop, The Family Business:

> Those who want customized work with an individual flair won't go wrong by making The Family Business their business. The artists aren't interested in what's emanating from other shops but focus on their own artistic principles. "Constant comparisons between shops can homogenize the work being produced and lessen the unique qualities of your own brand," says Coppoletta. "I look to my own interests and opinions in

order to build a singular voice for my business." It's that attitude toward tailor-made tattooing within a refined business setting that's making The Family Business become a brand name worldwide.

Fictional texts likewise often conclude by touching on overarching themes or emotions, not by stating them outright but by describing a scene. The conclusion to Téa Obreht's *The Tiger's Wife* returns to one of the main characters in a story told to her by her grandfather; the narrator has remained skeptical about the tiger, which her grandfather claims had numerous magical powers:

There is, however, and always has been, a place on Galina where the trees are thin, a wide space where the saplings have twisted away and light falls broken and dappled on the snow. There is a cave here, a large flat slab of stone where the sun is always cast. My grandfather's tiger lives there, in a glade where the winter does not go away. He is the hunter of stag and boar, a fighter of bears, a great source of confusion for the lynx, a rapt admirer of the colors of birds. He has forgotten the citadel, the nights of fire, his long and difficult journey to the mountain. Everything lies dead in his memory, except for the tiger's wife, for whom, on certain nights, he goes calling, making that tight note that falls and falls. The sound is lonely, and low, and no one hears it anymore.

The novel ends ambiguously, something that would not work for a functional document such as a proposal. But, for some readers interested in complex emotions, ambiguity is more interesting than cut-and-dried certainties. As with all writing, you need to take into account your readers and their context and purpose: Are they mature enough to handle a little ambiguity, or will they be happier with all the loose ends tied up?

Texts for Analysis

Read through the texts that follow as you try to determine what structure (or structures) each writer is employing. Does the writer explicitly mark the structure so that readers notice it, or is it subtle? Create a PACT chart for each text, attempting to identify what about the context, audience, and purpose led the writer to employ the structure that he or she did.

LEGAL DOCUMENT
Supreme Court of the United States, "Wal-Mart Stores, Inc. *v.* Dukes et al."

After the U.S. Supreme Court declined to allow a class-action lawsuit against Wal-Mart for allegedly discriminating against female employees, the *Christian Science Monitor* ran an editorial against the ruling, arguing that the limitations the Court placed on class-action lawsuits would make it nearly impossible to prove widespread corporate discrimination against women. On the following pages are an excerpt from the Supreme Court decision and the *Christian Science Monitor* editorial. How effective do you think each text is? Can you suggest an alternate structure for each? How did the genre for each (legal document and editorial) affect the structure?

The only corporate policy that the plaintiffs' evidence convincingly establishes is Wal-Mart's "policy" of *allowing discretion* by local supervisors over employment matters. On its face, of course, that is just the opposite of a uniform employment practice that would provide the commonality needed for a class action; it is a policy *against having* uniform employment practices. It is also a very common and presumptively reasonable way of doing business—one that we have said "should itself raise no inference of discriminatory conduct," *Watson* v. *Fort Worth Bank & Trust*, 487 U. S. 977, 990 (1988).

To be sure, we have recognized that, "in appropriate cases," giving discretion to lower-level supervisors can be the basis of Title VII liability under a disparate-impact theory—since "an employer's undisciplined system of subjective decision-making [can have] precisely the same effects as a system pervaded by impermissible intentional discrimination." *Id.*, at 990–991. But the recognition that this type of Title VII claim "can" exist does not lead to the conclusion that every employee in a company using a system of discretion has such a claim in common. To the contrary, left to their own devices most managers in any corporation—and surely most managers in a corporation that forbids sex discrimination—would select sex-neutral, performance-based criteria for hiring and promotion that produce no actionable disparity at all. Others may choose to reward various attributes that produce disparate impact—such as scores on general aptitude tests or educational achievements, see *Griggs* v. *Duke Power Co.*, 401 U. S. 424, 431–432 (1971). And still other managers may be guilty of intentional discrimination that produces a sex-based disparity. In such a company, demonstrating the invalidity of one manager's use of discretion will do nothing to demonstrate the invalidity of another's. A party seeking to certify a nationwide class will be unable to show that all the employees' Title VII claims will in fact depend on the answers to common questions.

Respondents have not identified a common mode of exercising discretion that pervades the entire company—aside from their reliance on Dr. Bielby's social frameworks analysis that we have rejected. In a company of Wal-Mart's size and geographical scope, it is quite unbelievable that all managers would exercise their discretion in a common way without some common direction. Respondents attempt to make that showing by means of statistical and anecdotal evidence, but their evidence falls well short.

The statistical evidence consists primarily of regression analyses performed by Dr. Richard Drogin, a statistician, and Dr. Marc Bendick, a labor economist. Drogin conducted his analysis region-by-region, comparing the number of women promoted into management positions with the percentage of women in the available pool of hourly workers. After considering regional and national data, Drogin concluded that "there are statistically significant disparities between men and women at Wal-Mart . . .[and] these disparities . . . can be explained only by gender discrimination." 603 F. 3d, at 604 (internal quotation marks omitted). Bendick compared work-force data from Wal-Mart and competitive retailers and concluded that Wal-Mart "promotes a lower percentage of women than its competitors." *Ibid.*

Even if they are taken at face value, these studies are insufficient to establish that respondents' theory can be proved on a classwide basis. In *Falcon*, we held that one named plaintiff's experience of discrimination was insufficient to infer that "discriminatory treatment is typical of [the employer's employment] practices." 457 U. S., at 158. A similar failure of inference arises here. As Judge Ikuta observed in her dissent, "[i]nformation about disparities at the regional and national level does not establish the existence of disparities at individual stores, let alone raise the inference that a company-wide policy of discrimination is implemented by discretionary decisions at the store and district level." 603 F. 3d, at 637. A regional pay disparity, for example, may be attributable to only a small set of Wal-Mart stores, and cannot by itself establish the uniform, store-by-store disparity upon which the plaintiffs' theory of commonality depends.

There is another, more fundamental, respect in which respondents' statistical proof fails. Even if it established (as it does not) a pay or promotion pattern that differs from the nationwide figures or the regional figures in *all* of Wal-Mart's 3,400 stores, that would still not demonstrate that commonality of issue exists. Some managers will claim that the availability of women, or qualified women, or interested women, in their stores' area does not mirror the national or regional statistics. And almost all of them will claim to have been applying some sex-neutral, performance-based criteria—whose nature and effects will differ from store to store. In the landmark case of ours which held that giving discretion to lower-level supervisors can be the basis of Title VII liability under a disparate-impact theory, the plurality opinion *conditioned* that holding on the corollary that merely proving that the discretionary system has produced a racial or sexual disparity *is not enough*. "[T]he plaintiff must begin by identifying the specific employment practice that is challenged." *Watson*, 487 U. S., at 994; accord, *Wards Cove Packing Co.* v. *Atonio*, 490 U. S. 642, 656 (1989) (approving that statement), superseded by statute on other grounds, 42 U. S. C. §2000e–2(k). That is all the more necessary when a class of plaintiffs is sought to be certified. Other than the bare existence of delegated discretion, respondents have identified no "specific employment practice"—much less one that ties all their 1.5 million claims together. Merely showing that Wal-Mart's policy of discretion has produced an overall sex-based disparity does not suffice.

EDITORIAL

Courtney E. Martin, "*Wal-Mart v. Dukes* Ruling Is Out of Sync with 21st Century Sex Discrimination"

Courtney E. Martin, an editor at feministing.com and senior correspondent at the *American Prospect,* presented an opposing viewpoint in response to the U.S. Supreme Court ruling in the *Wal-Mart v. Dukes* case. This editorial ran in the *Christian Science Monitor.*

In Wal-Mart v. Dukes, *the Supreme Court set a dangerous precedent when it ruled that the women in the class action suit could not prove a common culture of sex discrimination. But sexism is no longer written in official policy. It's engrained in culture.*

The Supreme Court's ruling in favor of "the world's biggest boss," as GritTV's Laura Flanders put it, in the *Wal-Mart v. Dukes* sex discrimination class action lawsuit this week is a major blow to working women across America. And perhaps even more important, it's a sign that some of the esteemed judges on our nation's highest court need a primer in how contemporary discrimination functions.

The Court decided 5–4 that up to 1.5 million former and current female employees couldn't file suit against Wal-Mart together as a class because there was scant evidence of institutionally sanctioned or organized discrimination by the company. But women make up over 65 percent of hourly employees at Wal-Mart, and only 34.5 percent of managers. In other words, Wal-Mart — like so many of America's biggest businesses — has a gender and leadership problem.

In his majority opinion, however, Justice Antonin Scalia argued that numbers like these, coupled with stories about the widespread exclusion of and humiliation of women, didn't constitute discrimination because, well, Wal-Mart has a non-discrimination policy.

Further, he wrote that Wal-Mart's policy of allowing discretion by local supervisors in employment practices — importantly, uncharacteristic of the corporation's overall micromanaging style — was "just the opposite of a uniform employment practice that would provide the commonality needed for a class action; it is a policy against having uniform employment practices."

A lesson in 21st century discrimination

Apparently Mr. Scalia needs a lesson in 21st century discrimination. This is a time in which discrimination of all kinds doesn't usually advertise itself on "white's only" water fountain signs and "woman wanted" ads for secretary positions in Sunday's neighborhood newspaper. It's a time when racism, sexism, and other forms of discrimination are entrenched in our culture — insidious, covert, often subtle. It's a time when the distribution of power — money, jobs, influence — is almost entirely dependent on informal relationships born of a still alarmingly segregated society.

It's not company rules that most brave working women have to challenge these days; it's informal and widespread exclusion. As Rinku Sen wrote in *ColorLines* magazine: "Certainly, there has been some blatantly sexist behavior among Wal-Mart managers . . . but mostly, Wal-Mart's system runs on silence."

At Wal-Mart, as with so many American companies, men speak the private language of promotion and negotiation, while women are left confused as to where the pipeline to power and new opportunities even starts. With women still taking on the majority of caretaking responsibilities, their second shift often prevents them from doing the kind of after-hours bonding necessary, were their male managers even willing to bring them into the "inner circle."

Culture is hard to legislate, but it's a real factor

Culture, of course, is harder to discuss, legislate, and change than policies, but that doesn't mean that our nation's highest court is off the hook. As Justice Ruth Bader Ginsburg pointed out in her dissenting opinion in this, the largest attempted class action suit ever: "Managers, like all humankind, may be prey to biases of which they are unaware. The risk of discrimination is heightened when those managers are predominantly of one sex, and are steeped in a corporate culture that perpetuates gender stereotypes."

It's not surprising that all three female judges on the Court, all of whom have most likely endured various forms of socially sanctioned discrimination in the past, ruled in favor of the Wal-Mart women. Ms. Ginsburg built a career, in part, prosecuting sex discrimination cases.

The most disturbing danger here is not that Scalia and the other four judges that sided with him seem to deny the continued existence of "good old boy" networks as forms of widespread discrimination that company policies can condone or mitigate. The most disturbing danger is that the Supreme Court has now created a precedent whereby plaintiffs, just to move past the pleading stage, must actually prove common harm according to evidentiary standards that are out of sync with the reality of how contemporary sexism most often functions in the workplace. Joanne Bamberger, a blogger at PunditMom and a lawyer, by training, calls this ruling "the most activist judicial move I've seen in a long time."

Sexism has gone "underground"

The irony, of course, is that the feminist movement has done such a good job fighting against institutional sexism, that it is now faced with an enemy that has — in a sense — gone underground. It's unlikely that male managers at Wal-Mart, even in conservative regions of the country, would feel entitled to advertise their preferences for promoting men, but they still feel just fine inviting the guys from work to Hooters for a managers' meeting — as real life evidence from the plaintiffs illustrated.

The women of Wal-Mart may not constitute a "class" in Scalia's antiquated vision, but they will continue on as a collective. This week's decision did not determine whether Wal-Mart has discriminated against individual women, so Joseph M. Sellers, a lawyer for the plaintiffs, told the *New York Times* that his clients are "determined to move forward" by filing individual claims with the Equal Employment Opportunity Commission. He plans on filing up to several thousand within the next couple of months.

Feminists are famous for arguing that the personal is political; in this case, the cultural is pivotal. It's a shame some of our nation's most esteemed judges were apparently not able to recognize that.

ABSTRACT
Edward Nęcka and Theresa Hlawacz, "Who Has an Artistic Temperament? Relationships between Creativity and Temperament among Artists and Bank Officers"

This abstract from a research article looks at the possible connections between creativity and personality.

In contrast to vast literature devoted to the relationships between creativity and personality, relatively few studies addressed the question of the creativity–temperament link. Temperament is conceptualized as the biologically rooted, mostly inborn, foundations for personality and other individual traits. Sixty artists and 60 bank officers participated in this study. Their psychometric creativity was measured with Urban and Jellen's (1986) Test for Creative Thinking–Drawing Production (TCT–DP) and an experimental task that required word categorization. Temperamental traits were measured with Strelau's Formal Characteristics of Behavior–Temperament Inventory (FCB–TI, 1997). It appeared that creativity was positively correlated with the temperamental trait of activity, and negatively with emotional reactivity, but only within the group of artists. Bank officers, who were generally less creative than artists, showed no relationships between creativity and temperament. These findings are interpreted in terms of the role of activity and emotional reactivity in development and expression of one's creative potential.

TWITTER FEED
Matt Stoffel

Matt Stoffel, an Internet and social media marketing manager, is an active Twitter user.

Reprinted by permission of Matt Stoffel. https://twitter.com/stoffelmatt/

BLOG
The Morning News

The Morning News, a web-based magazine, features essays, articles, art, culture, and humor.

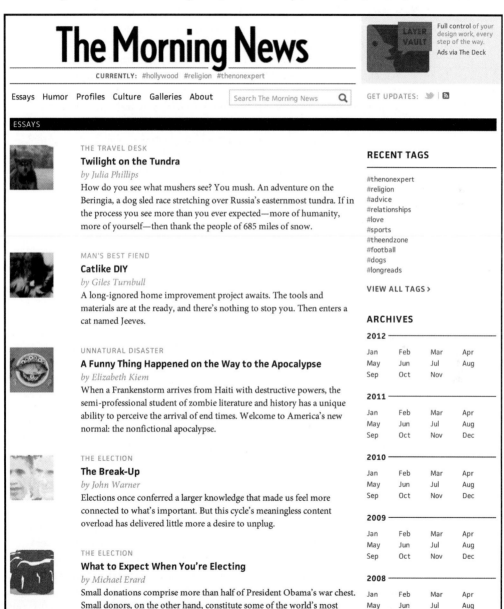

Exercises

1. Locate a short text (such as an editorial at a magazine or newspaper website) and describe how it is structured. Complete the PAC quadrants of a PACT chart. Then choose a completely different but appropriate structure for the author's purpose. Rewrite the text using the new structure.

2. Watch an episode of a television show on DVR or streaming video (you'll need to be able to pause and rewatch segments as you work). Using pen and paper, write a diagram of the show's structure. Come up with creative ways to represent patterns you notice in the show. For example, can you find sequences of generic events that seem to get repeated throughout the show? Is there a pattern to the way that events are set up? Are camera angles important? What about the soundtrack? Audience applause or laughter? Music? Annotate your diagram as necessary. Then compare your diagram with classmates' diagrams. What similarities and differences do you find between shows? Are there similarities within single genres (like sitcoms or dramas)?

3. Using pen and paper, diagram the structure across the comment thread from a web-based article on a moderately volatile topic (for example, government funding for alternative energy, problems of rising student loan debt, or even whether New York pizza is better than Chicago pizza). Analyze the structure both within and across comments. What patterns can you find? Do some structures seem to have predictable results (e.g., posts of type *x* are invariably followed by posts of type *y*)?

4. Find a TV commercial that you think works well, one that makes you want to purchase the product. (You can do a web search on "best commercials" to find some.) List the key elements in the commercial and then analyze the structure.

Scenario Connections

1. In Scenario 2, "Teamwork Problems," you're given a set of texts (syllabus material and e-mail messages) to draw on to respond to a problematic teammate. Review the scenario and select an overall structure for the text you'll create. Why is that structure most suitable? Are there weaknesses in that structure you'll need to be aware of as you write?

2. Asking people to change their behavior involves convincing them that their current actions pose some sort of problem. Scenario 9, "Educating Users about E-mail Scams," for example, calls on you to create educational materials for people at a senior center to help them avoid e-mail scams. Which of the introductions or starting points listed on pages 88-91 would work best? Describe the introduction or first thing viewers would see in your text — a PowerPoint slide and script of your opening comments, the main

image and text for a poster, the opening paragraph of a newsletter article, and so on. Also describe how that introduction will help convince your audience.

3. Scenario 13, "A Day in Your Online Life," asks you to gather data about your own use of a communication medium over a 24-hour period and then write a short analysis of that data. Although you haven't yet gathered the data, can you describe some structures that you might use for this type of analysis? Which structure (or structures) discussed on pages 78–86 do you think will work best, and why?

4. In Scenario 19, "Repurposing a Text" (p. 297), you'll take an existing text that deals with a very specialized or technical issue (such as an academic research paper) and repurpose it as an entertainment piece for a publication read by average, educated adults. Using terminology from this chapter, annotate one of the Background Texts from Scenario 19 to describe its structure. Select at least three elements of the structure you analyzed and write a brief explanation of why you think the author chose that structure.

Designing Visual Texts

All texts have visual design. Some, like traditional print novels, look very simple from a visual standpoint: page after page of paragraph after paragraph, broken only by occasional headings for new chapters. Other texts, like magazine advertisements or music videos, have very complicated, active visual designs. In this chapter, we'll start talking about — and working with — visual designs, thinking about how visual aspects help readers and users construct meanings. This chapter will give you some basic principles that you can draw on when you design texts of all types.

"Designing Texts? I Thought This Was a Book about Writing."

Why are we talking about "design" here? Because writing has shifted, expanding over the last several decades to include things besides letters on a page (or even on a computer screen). Written words are still important, but they now frequently take their place alongside images, video, and audio. In some cases, a text will be mostly words, with a few key images to illustrate points (figures in a formal report, for example). In other cases, texts may have very few (or even no) written words within them.

Consider the example on page 103, designed by Chris Talbot at Clarkson University for the campus radio station.

Like many radio station websites, the WTSC site is largely informative: tell users some news about the station, tell them what songs were recently played, and encourage them to listen to current and upcoming shows.

Could a simple, text-only site provide the same information? Sort of, but not really. How effective would this website be if we stripped out many of the visual design parts? See pages 104–05 for the results.

The look and feel of the whole site has shifted from relatively visually interesting — the colors, the graphics, the pictures — to visually dull. A lot of the basic information is still there, but along with a loss of visual interest, the text no longer supports one of the most frequent

● Website for WTSC, Clarkson University's campus radio station
Reprinted by permission of Chris Talbot

things done by readers on the web: skipping around the page. Skimming from topic to topic and clicking on links, for example, are now much more difficult because the headings and links no longer stand out visually. So in addition to generating interest, graphics and layout can structure information in ways that make it more usable for people.

In fact, graphics and layout are themselves types of information: The different color of the headings in the news section helps readers jump from one entry to the next. The clear spatial organization of different functional sections helps readers skip over the main news section if they're interested in finding links to things like the live audio stream or finding information about songs recently played on air.

WTSC The Source

91.1 FM Clarkson University

Your source for great music and entertainment since 1963!

Activities Fair, Wednesday, August 27th

Any Clarkson student interested in becoming part of the radio station as either a DJ or active member can come talk to our staff at the WTSC booth on Wednesday's activities fair in Cheel Arena. The fair is from 7-9pm and we'll be blasting out the good tunes so you can find us easily! After the activities fair there is a short information session immediately afterwards in the station. This will be as close to 9pm as we can get and the station is located next to the laundry room in the basement of the Hamlin-Powers complex, aka "the Pit." If you miss the activities fair and our meeting, you can still get involved by contacting Talbs at sm@radio.clarkson.edu

President Collins Interview, September 2nd at 8pm

The first of 8 (EIGHT) interviews with Clarkson University President Tony Collins in our own studio of WTSC. You can tune in to our station on Tuesday September 2nd at 8pm to listen in live! The interview will focus on the current progress of the new student center and be about 30 minutes long. If you have any questions that you want to be asked, send them to sm@radio.clarkson.edu. We look forward to having you listening in!

Radio.clarkson.edu Gets Facelift

There once was a time without automobiles, microwaves, and packaged ramen. There was a time without the Golden Knight, the internet, and "The Pill." All these things were the result of brilliant people making human tasks so much better. With this in

● Text-only version of WTSC website

mind, the managers and eboard members here at WTSC are now thinking: there once was a time when our website was so awful, so unhelpful, and so un-colorful. We now present to you our newly redesigned website—complete with colors! . . .

CURRENT ON-AIR SHOW

DJs Howie and the Wolfman

Show Name HW – Not A Clue

Listen Live: [HIGH] [LOW] [DIALUP]

Recently Played Songs View More

Artist Song

Scott Weiland But Not Tonight

Death Cab for Cutie Different Names for the Same Thing

Clap Your Hands Say Yeah Over and Over Again (Lost & Found)

Jurassic 5 Jurass Finish First

WTSC 91.1 FM – The Source Station ID

Currently 1:17 EST

Next show in 1 hour and 43 minutes

Today's Shows View All

Show Name Show Time (EST)

Mornings of a Funkagroovalistic Nature 10:00 AM-12:59 PM

Howie and the Wolfman 1:00 PM-2:59 PM

Beats 3:00 PM-4:59 PM

Funky Sac 5:00 PM-6:59 PM

Knight Time Black Out 7:00 PM-8:59 PM

● Numbers and arrows showing the likely path readers' eyes will take when looking for recently played songs
Reprinted by permission of Chris Talbot

Designers use methods such as these, often without even thinking consciously about them, to structure texts. You can use many of the same methods, whether you're working on a simple essay, a set of presentation slides, or a website.

Some Basic Design Principles

Although it's possible to design an effective document without knowing a lot of formal visual theory, knowing some basic design principles can jump-start your design learning. If you develop a toolbox of design strategies, you'll be less likely to fumble around when you're working on a text.

The next several sections will demonstrate what some of the following principles can help you do.

- Hierarchy
- Color
- Negative space
- Proximity
- Continuity
- Similarity
- Figure/ground
- Grids

Most of these principles come from gestalt theory, a way of describing how people make sense of visual information. All of these principles are rules of thumb, patterns that people *usually* follow when they're processing visual information. And you can't just apply them haphazardly, any more than you can build a house by simply nailing together every board on the job site. You have to think carefully about the changes you're trying to make with your writing, about your audiences and your contexts, and then draw on different design strategies to help you reach your goals.

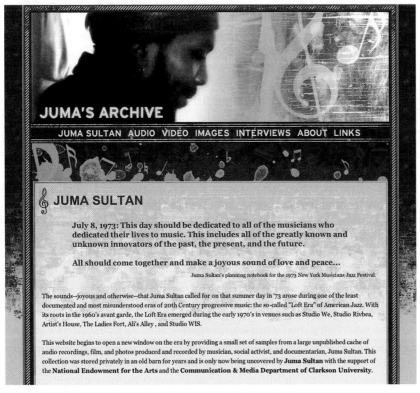

Jumasarchive.org screenshot reprinted by permission of Johndan Johnson-Eilola, P.h. D.

Reflect & Discuss

What parts of this image from the jazz music website Jumasarchive.org draw your eye to them? Can you guess some reasons that your eye is drawn to them? Pick an element on the page that doesn't attract your eye. What would you do to that element to make it stand out more?

Hierarchy

When we look at something, we don't give our immediate attention to everything at the same time (unless what we see completely overwhelms and confuses us). In most cases, we automatically sort what we see into levels of importance or hierarchy. In a well-designed text, the most important aspects, such as part and chapter headings in a book, are the most visually striking or highest in the hierarchy. Things that are a little less important, such as subheadings, are at lower levels in the hierarchy. These different levels should be pretty easy for viewers to sort out. In the manual for a power saw, warnings about the dangers of a rapidly spinning blade had better be much higher in the visual hierarchy than the reminder to send in a warranty card. Color also adds hierarchy. The original "Slipping" icon below is set in black. Changing the color makes the icon stand out from black and white text around it.

● Contrasting colors can make icons more powerful
Slipping by Louis Prado from The Noun Project

There are many ways to distinguish levels of hierarchy:

- **Size** (larger is higher)
- **Color tone** (brighter is higher)
- **Location** (toward top of page and toward left is higher)

The Adventure Planner website shown on page 109 illustrates how different principles guide readers' eyes, helping them decide what to pay attention to first. As this example demonstrates, the location of elements on the page along with their size and color affect how readers in Western print-based cultures process texts.

Color

Color can draw attention to key features in a text — you already know this if you've highlighted a textbook as you study. Contrasting, bright, or bold colors all call attention to elements on a page. Color can also be used to set mood. Darker colors are frequently perceived as more formal, lighter colors as less formal (literally "lighter"), and bright primary colors as playful or childlike, as demonstrated in the website for Kids .gov shown on the facing page.

Text in the main heading/banner is much larger and bolder than anything else on the page.

Text in navigation bar is smaller than main title and set against a noncontrasting background to subordinate it.

At a second level in the hierarchy are the images just under the banner. These images act as buttons to link to subsections of the site.

The banner is also located at the top of the page, which is where Western print readers are trained to look.

Similarly, in Western print-based cultures, things farther down the page are usually less important.

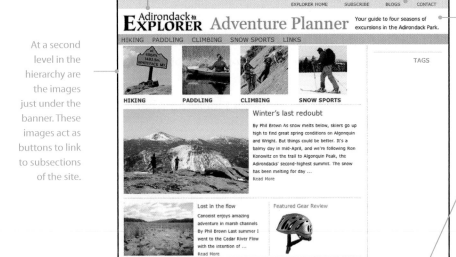

● Use of multiple techniques establishes hierarchy among design elements
Reprinted by permission of Adirondack Explorer

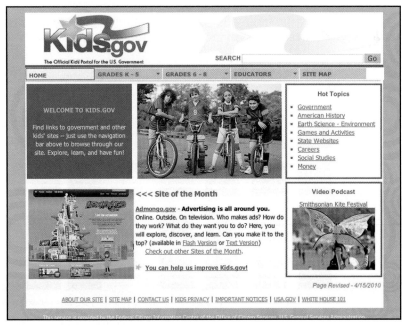

● Bright primary colors suggest playfulness

Negative Space: The Gaps between Objects

One crucial concept of gestalt theory is the importance of the space *between* objects: negative space or white space. Negative space is the "background" of an image, which is often white but might be any color (the white space of a Stop sign is colored bright red). You may not think about this unused space very much because it seems so neutral and bland — it's literally in the background — but negative space is what separates design elements from each other, providing structure and often hierarchy.

Proximity: Birds of a Feather Flock Together

Most people assume objects that are grouped together are somehow related. This human tendency makes proximity — the spatial relationships among groups of objects — an important design consideration. Your readers will likely categorize things cognitively based on the visual groupings.

In the examples below, the set of sixteen blocks on the left is usually seen as one large collection of blocks, while the same sixteen blocks in the example on the right are normally perceived as four separate areas, each composed of four blocks. Objects separated by small gaps are understood to be in groups (the basis of a gestalt theory called *continuity*, which is covered on page 111).

Proximity can be used to structure collections of information in your designs. By grouping related items, you help readers more effectively process information by allowing them to focus on specific chunks — those in grouped proximity — at any point.

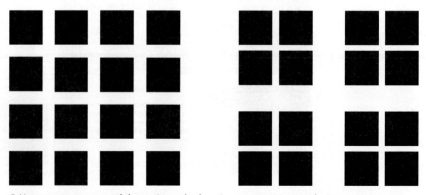

How squares are spaced determines whether viewers see one set with sixteen squares or four sets with four squares each

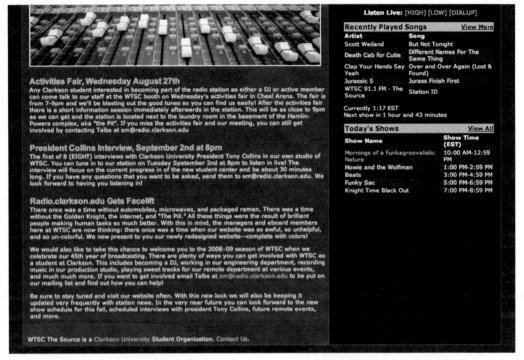

● Related types of information (weblog posts, recent songs, and show times) are grouped near each other
Reprinted by permission of Chris Talbot

At the WTSC website, stories are located near each other (in the left column) and specific "event" information (songs, shows) is grouped together on the right.

Continuity: How the Eye Continues across Gaps

Our eyes continually scan images, reacting to what we're seeing, moving from one individual element to the next. The arrangement of the individual elements can influence how our eyes move. Once our eyes are moving in a certain direction, they may keep going in that direction, leaping gaps to go from one object to the next, providing continuity. (Gestalt theorists actually call this term "continuance," but "continuity" is probably a more familiar term.)

Readers in Western cultures tend to skim in a large Z-shaped pattern, from top left to bottom right. Lines can reinforce that movement, further guiding readers to move in the direction they were headed already. In the example at the top of page 112, the arrow tends

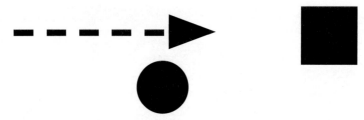

● The linear arrow provides continuity, directing the eye toward the more distant square rather than the closer circle

to direct the eye all the way across the page to the square; most readers would notice the circle last.

Even minor things like shaded rows on a table can help keep readers' eyes moving in the correct direction. For example, if the table at the top of page 113 didn't have shaded rows, readers would be likely to read down columns (due to close proximity) rather than across rows.

● Crosswalk markings often use continuity, with a series of bold, white rectangles that pedestrians and motorists interpret as a line

Today's Shows	View All
Show Name	**Show Time (EST)**
Mornings of a Funkagroovalistic Nature	10:00 AM-12:59 PM
Howie and the Wolfman	1:00 PM-2:59 PM
Beats	3:00 PM-4:59 PM
Funky Sac	5:00 PM-6:59 PM
Knight Time Black Out	7:00 PM-8:59 PM

Reprinted by permission of Chris Talbot

Similarity: How Objects Are Grouped

The eye also tends to group similar objects, even when they're separated by some space. Most people would describe the figure below as groups of circles and squares; a few might take the next step and identify a diagonal line of circles against a background of squares. But few would describe the figure simply as four columns or four rows or sixteen objects.

In the absence of other strong influences, similarity will even cause viewers to cognitively group objects across fairly large spaces. When you look at the image of various buttons on page 114 you will probably start trying to sort the buttons into categories (even before you realize it): by size, by color, by material. Images that don't support gestalt processing tend to seem a little confusing. And images that seem to

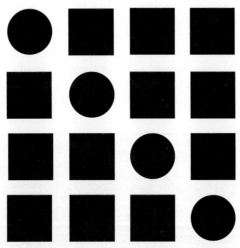

● Similarity of circles creates a diagonal line against a field of squares

Reflect & Discuss

Assume someone described this image as a diagonal line of circles set against a field of squares. Besides similarity, what other gestalt principles are they relying on to come up with that?

● Similarity might cause you to sort these buttons into visual categories by color, size, or material
Eleonora Kolomiyets/Shutterstock

support multiple, conflicting ways of being read by using gestalt principles seem pointless and random.

You might not have given it much thought, but even something as simple as a consistent format for things like headings helps readers process visual information. The consistent bold, yellow headings in the main body column of the WTSC website help readers both identify the titles of articles and let them skip from one article to the next with-

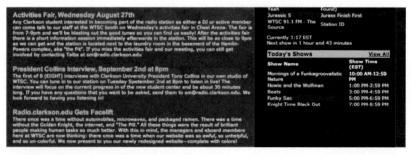

● Headings distinguished from body text by color
Reprinted by permission of Chris Talbot

Similar formatting in headings indicates similar level of importance.

NEGATIVE space separates design elements.

Close proximity of introductory sentence to bulleted list suggests they are connected.

NARRATIVE

ABSTRACT: THE JUMA SULTAN ARCHIVE

The Project's Importance to the Humanities

Of all the genres of American Jazz, probably the least documented is the period that has become known sometimes as the "black avant garde" or "Loft Era" of Jazz. This period encompasses the late 1960s through the 1970s. This project helps to provide a new window on the era by preserving and making accessible an unpublished cache of audio recordings, film, and photos owned by former musician and musician-labor-organizer Juma Sultan.

Principal Activities and Expected Results

1. **Preserve a collection** of unpublished, live, analog recordings of major American jazz artists of what is commonly referred to as the "black avant garde" or "loft era" jazz, recorded in the 1960's and 70's by musician, social activist, and documentarian, Juma Sultan. Preservation will be done by transferring the analog data to digital formats. Currently, the original analog recordings are still in their original tape boxes and film canisters stored primarily in cardboard boxes. (See photos in the Appendix 1.)

2. **Document each recording** by researching and identifying where possible the players, dates, and venues.

3. **Enable access** to these recordings and their historical documentation for musicians, jazz researchers, and, where allowable by copyright, the general public through a dedicated website which is hosted by the Eastman Kodak Center for Excellence in Communication (EKCEC) in association with the Department of Communication and Media in Clarkson University's School of Arts & Sciences.

This site has been developed with funds from a $10,000.00 grant by the National Endowment for the Arts: "The Aboriginal Music Society Project: The Lost Tapes of Juma Sultan, NEA/Clarkson University contract no. 06-3100-7226. The working title of the website is "Juma's Archive" (www.jumasarchive.org - **See Appendix 2 for website example**).

The website now contains:
- 30 digitized audio recordings (30 second clips)
- 13 digitized video versions of original 16mm film (30 second clips)
- 14 digitized photographs (with watermarks)
- An oral history of the era based on interviews with Juma Sultan
- A collection of links to external websites related to the musicians and the loft jazz era

NOTE: Because most, if not all, of the recordings recovered so far are bound by copyright in some form or another, the website only provides 30 second samples of these recordings. However, the full recordings are/will be available to researchers and musicians who wish to travel to Clarkson University to listen to – but not copy – any recording in the digital archive.

4. **Continue to develop a video documentary** about the archive. A 25-minute version will soon become available for viewing on the website. With further funding we hope to travel to interview other key participants in the era, such as, Sonny Simmons, Rashied Ali, Dave Burrell, Grachan Moncur III, Sam Rivers, Pharoah Sanders, Archie Shepp, and George Wein for a projected 50 to 55 minute documentary.

● Design principles at work in a business document

out having to read everything on the page — the titles are like stepping stones that readers can jump to. If the formatting varied from one heading to the next, readers wouldn't know what direction to head in.

In most cases, multiple gestalt principles are used at the same time to provide visual and logical structure in a text. Even a standard business document such as the grant proposal below includes elements of proximity and similarity to help readers understand the content as a whole.

Figure/Ground: How Objects Stand Out

When we focus on an object on a page or a screen, other aspects of what we see fade into the background. The part that we focus on is called the *figure,* and the part that fades away is the *ground*. When

Reflect & Discuss

How have gestalt principles been used in the design of this book? What aspects of the size and location of the text help you understand how the portions relate to one another?

you're looking at something like black ink on white paper, separating the figure from the ground seems pretty simple (even automatic). In most cases, there's more ground than figure — isolating the figure object against a lot of contrasting background is a good way to call attention to the figure.

But in more complicated situations, figuring out what part is figure and what's ground can be more difficult. For example, you may see the image below as four black blocks or as a white cross on a black background. Or you might move back and forth between the two, not really able to figure out what part is figure and what is ground.

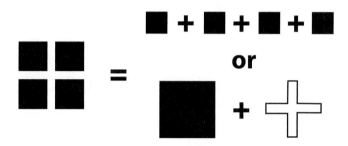

In fact, some designers intentionally cause this slight tension between figure and ground relationships, even switching back and forth in ways that create suspense.

When you look at the figure of a person in profile on the left, you most likely initially read the black part of the image as the foreground: a man facing to the right. But you may then notice another way of reading the image: A man, upside down, facing left, with white as the foreground and black as the background.

Because many texts use dark figures on light backgrounds, switching that pattern can give even a small element of a page some impact. The WTSC page makes headings stand out by using bright yellow text (see p. 114) or white text (next page) on a black background in the main section of the page.

Grids: Structuring Pages

There are numerous ways to structure or "lay out" text and graphics on a page or screen, but to simplify things let's cover one common method: the implied grid. In the grid system, you create a set of vertical and horizontal lines on a blank page and use these lines to guide the placement and alignment of content on the page. When the design is complete, the grid lines themselves are removed. Because the content falls on the (implied) lines, viewers see the page as being aligned to a grid even though the lines are not present.

Rodin Anton/Shutterstock

CURRENT ON-AIR SHOW

● White letters on a black ground increase visual interest
Reprinted by permission of Chris Talbot

In grid layouts, the content does not necessarily limit itself to occupying single cells. As the magazine page on page 118 illustrates, some elements can span more than one cell. This practice actually makes the layout more interesting to viewers and serves to "pull together" the page. Another way to increase visual interest is to break the grid. The magazine page, in fact, deviates from an even grid vertically and horizontally. As with many design strategies, adhering completely to a very rigid system can seem dull — the grid is just a starting point.

The number of horizontal and vertical lines used in a grid system can vary from one layout to the next. The simplest grid, of course, would be a single block spanning the height and width of a page. Slightly more complex would be single vertical and horizontal lines cutting a page into quarters. In practice, the simplest grid usually splits the page into thirds — this allows some variation and visual interest. But grids of four or five lines are not uncommon. In layouts with a lot of individual items such as a product catalog, even more lines might be used.

Grid systems are useful because, among other things, they offer a way to maintain a consistent look across multiple pages, they speed up the process of laying out multiple pages, and they split columns of text into readable widths. Columns of text that are too wide tend to cause eye strain as readers scan words across the page. Grids are extremely important in texts that have small type sizes and relatively wide pages or screens, such as newspapers and websites. The WTSC site (p. 103) and the Adventure Planner site (p. 109) both use modified grid systems.

As mentioned above, there are many other ways to structure pages: classic book cover designs are often centered horizontally on the page. The Absolut ad shown on page 127 adopts this simple (and safe) format. The Adbusters ad on page 127 uses a more free-form, open approach.

● In the magazine page on the left, photos, text, and other elements are placed on a grid like the one shown on the right
"Races and Places" magazine page from Runner's World, March 2013, p. 113. Reprinted by permission.

Letters as Visual Design: Typography

Although you undoubtedly have dozens or even hundreds of fonts (or more) on your computer, you may not have realized there's a professional discipline, hundreds of years old, devoted to the creation, use, and study of fonts or type: typography. Twenty or thirty years ago, most people wrote without thinking much about typography. Most typewriters and early computers offered only one font. Even those that allowed average users to use multiple fonts often supported only two or three. But as with graphic design in general, the computer changed all that with the introduction of programs and operating systems that allowed users to choose among dozens or hundreds of fonts on the fly — even using multiple fonts within a single word.

Unfortunately, what the computer *didn't* give users was knowledge of visual design principles. Early documents produced with "desktop publishing" programs often looked like ransom notes, sporting huge numbers of fonts in ways that unintentionally weakened the overall

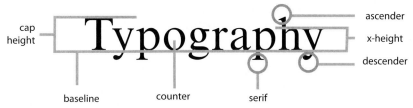

● Typographers define specialized terms for different parts of letters to make it easier to compare one font to another. Some of these terms are used on the facing page.

goal of the text. Just because you *can* use 40 fonts in your résumé doesn't mean you *should*.

Most users today have settled into a dull but relatively safe routine of using a small number of common fonts for most of their documents — Times New Roman and Helvetica, for example. These fonts can be used badly (and they often are), but it's hard to go way off track with them. But even those fonts can often be used more effectively than you might suspect. And learning some typography basics will also help you branch out in ways that will make your documents more successful.

Paying Attention: Type as Transparency

One of the difficulties of paying attention to typography (as with most types of communication) is that our first instinct is to value transparency. Type, we think, should not have a message of its own but only transport the "real" message of a text. If users are distracted by the typeface a text is set in, they're not paying attention to what the text is really saying.

While it's true that we don't want readers to *consciously* notice the typefaces we choose, we do want type to communicate with them. Good typography often communicates important messages in subtle ways. We notice this most often when something just seems a little *off*, but we can't put our finger on the reason. The letters on the page may be slightly squished together, making them a little more difficult to read. Or the length of lines of text on a page may be too long, causing our eyes to skitter to lines above or below the one we're trying to read — we can recover, maybe without even noticing it, but the strain slowly adds up. Eventually, without knowing quite why, we put the text aside because we no longer feel like reading it. So good use of type may not be immediately obvious to readers, but it's there.

Second, written texts can't take place without typefaces — they *are* part of the message. Even choosing between two very commonly used typefaces — Arial and Times New Roman on a website, for example — sends the message, "This is fairly standard." The message that "we're conventional" is itself a message. There's no such thing as pure objectivity: Every text comes *from* a viewpoint. Using typography well requires you to understand the ways in which type contributes to the message.

Font? Typeface? A Note about Terminology

In general, most people will know what you're talking about whether you use the term "font" or "typeface." But to people that study type the two terms have important differences. Fonts are specific versions of a typeface. Most popular typefaces like Helvetica have many specific fonts of that typeface, produced by different companies and with slight variations from one to the next. It's not something you probably need to worry about too much, but it's useful to know the two terms aren't exactly identical.

Typefaces: Serif, Sans Serif, and Novelty

Although there are many ways to categorize type, one simple method splits typefaces into two categories: those with serifs (see the figure below) and those without. In general, typefaces with serifs tend to look more classic or conservative, while those without serifs (called sans serif) tend to look more modern. A third category, often called novelty, includes typefaces with a wide range of characteristics, often so distinctive that the font itself seems to speak as loudly as the words themselves.

Lorem ipsum dolor sit amet, consectetuer adipiscing elit. Nunc odio arcu, venenatis et, placerat a, sollicitudin non, lectus. Phasellus quam nunc, euismod et, euismod in, viverra pulvinar, dolor. In mauris arcu, convallis nec, fringilla nec, pretium vitae, est. Maecenas fermentum.

This is text set in a sans serif font, Gill Sans 10 point.

Lorem ipsum dolor sit amet, consectetuer adipiscing elit. Nunc odio arcu, venenatis et, placerat a, sollicitudin non, lectus. Phasellus quam nunc, euismod et, euismod in, viverra pulvinar, dolor. In mauris arcu, convallis nec, fringilla nec, pretium vitae, est. Maecenas fermentum.

This is text set in a serif font, New Baskerville 10 point.

Lorem ipsum dolor sit amet, consectetuer adipiscing elit. Nunc odio arcu, venenatis et, placerat a, sollicitudin non, lectus. Phasellus quam nunc, euismod et.

This is text set in a decorative font that is primarily sans serif but includes some serifs (such as on the number 1). OCRA 10 point.

● From left to right, a sans serif typeface, a serif typeface, and a novelty typeface that includes elements of both

Typography

Myriad Pro

Lorem ipsum dolor sit amet, consectetuer adipiscing elit. Aliquam sollicitudin suscipit purus. Cras quis justo. Aliquam euismod elit placerat sem lacinia bibendum. Class aptent taciti sociosqu ad litora torquent per conubia nostra, per inceptos himenaeos. Lorem ipsum dolor sit amet, consectetuer adipiscing elit. Praesent congue justo et massa. Integer molestie.

Typography

Helvetica

Lorem ipsum dolor sit amet, consectetuer adipiscing elit. Aliquam sollicitudin suscipit purus. Cras quis justo. Aliquam euismod elit placerat sem lacinia bibendum. Class aptent taciti sociosqu ad litora torquent per conubia nostra, per inceptos himenaeos. Lorem ipsum dolor sit amet, consectetuer adipiscing elit. Praesent congue justo et massa. Integer molestie.

Typography

Lucida Sans

Lorem ipsum dolor sit amet, consectetuer adipiscing elit. Aliquam sollicitudin suscipit purus. Cras quis justo. Aliquam euismod elit placerat sem lacinia bibendum. Class aptent taciti sociosqu ad litora torquent per conubia nostra, per inceptos himenaeos. Lorem ipsum dolor sit amet, consectetuer adipiscing elit. Praesent congue justo et massa. Integer molestie.

o o o

Lowercase "o" in Myriad Pro,
Helvetica, and Lucida Sans

● Variations across sans serif typefaces

Matching Type to Audience, Context, and Purpose

The three typefaces above all look somewhat similar. They are all sans serif faces. But if you look at them closely, you'll begin to see subtle but important differences. Most striking is the differing amounts of space taken up by each. The short Lucida Sans text example takes up several more lines than the even shorter Myriad Pro example. There are several reasons for this difference, but in general it has to do with Lucida Sans being a more "open" face. As the lowercase letter "o" from each typeface shows, Myriad Pro's "o" is much smaller than Lucida Sans's "o".

These differences are there for a reason: Lucida Sans was designed specifically to be highly readable in lower-resolution contexts (faxes and computer screens) where the openness of the font allows easier reading. In other words, Myriad Pro and Helvetica were designed for the high-resolution world of print while Lucida Sans was designed for the relatively lower resolution world of computer screens.

These differences also have other effects: Lucida Sans has a less formal feel to it, what you might call "playful" if you were the kind of person who described typefaces with imaginative terms. All faces have "feelings" to them, even if you don't normally think much about fonts. If Lucida Sans is playful, Helvetica is often considered modernist (in the sense of precision machinery), while a font like Comic Sans oscillates between being thought as playful (by many, many inexperienced

To be or not to be — that is the question:

Whether 'tis nobler in the mind to suffer

The slings and arrows of outra

Or to take arms against a sea

And, by opposing, end them. To

No more — and by a sleep to s

The heartache and the thousa

That flesh is heir to — 'tis a c

Devoutly to be wished. To die,

To sleep, perchance to dream.

For in that sleep of death wha

When we have shuffled off th

Must give us pause.

14 JUNE 2014

SEAN HOLLISTER
255 WINSTONE STREET, APARTMENT 8
LAFAYETTE, INDIANA 49203

DEAR MR. HOLLISTER:

WE ARE WRITING TODAY TO REQUEST IMMEDIATE PAYMENT OF YOUR ACCOUNT AT LUCID RECORDS. YOUR ACCOUNT IS CURRENTLY 47 DAYS OVERDUE IN THE AMOUNT OF $274.38. WE HAVE ASSESSED A $10 LATE CHARGE TO YOUR ACCOUNT, MAKING THE TOTAL DUE $284.38.

WE ARE ONLY ABLE TO EXTEND CREDIT TO CUSTOMERS FOR SHORT-TERM PURPOSES. AS THE TERMS OF YOUR CREDIT AGREEMENT STATED, YOUR ACCOUNT MUST BE PAID IN FULL BY THE FIRST OF EACH MONTH.

IF YOU WOULD LIKE TO DISCUSS THIS MATTER, PLEASE CONTACT ME AT THE PHONE NUMBER BELOW.

SINCERELY,

JULISSA MARTINEZ
LUCID RECORDS
27 MAIN STREET
WEST LAFAYETTE, INDIANA 49201
(800)555-1234

● A novelty font is a poor choice for a business letter; Comic Sans is a poor choice for Hamlet's soliloquy

designers) and being considered inappropriate for most uses (by many, many experienced designers).

Unless you're being intentionally clumsy, Comic Sans is probably a poor choice for serious texts. And a "novelty" font such as the one shown above probably hurts the overall purpose of a business letter attempting to collect on an overdue account.

Choosing a Typeface and a Font

In most cases, readers shouldn't notice typography. When they do notice, readers aren't paying attention to the message. Business letters, like scripts for moody dramas, research papers, or autobiographies, normally don't

Department of
Communication & Media

EDWARD ARMSTRONG
U N I V E R S I T Y

April 3, 2014

Mary S. Lopez
673 South Street
Grass Lake, MI 49240

Dear Ms. Lopez,

I'm delighted to inform you that you have been selected as the 2015
Raymond C. Jones Communication Scholar for 2015. The scholarship,
founded in memory of alumnus Raymond C. James (BS 1984), recognizes junior students who show exceptional promise in the field of communication. The award includes a full tuition stipend as well as a $1,000
grant to cover travel expenses to a communication-related professional
conference of your choosing.

The selection committee noted the remarkable quality of the portfolio
you submitted as part of your application packet, in particular the interactive media texts you completed during your internship this year.

The award will be announced during our program's annual awards banquet at 8 p.m. on Friday, May 9. We would be honored if you would join
us at the banquet to accept the award in person. Please let me know by
May 1 if you'll be able to attend.

Sincerely,

Dr. Francine Welty

Dr. Francine Welty
Chair, Communication Awards Selection Committee
Professor of English
Edward Armstrong University
Potsdam, NY 13699
voice: 315-555-5154
e-mail: fwelty@edwardarmstrong.edu

● A business letter using relatively simple, neutral type

Reflect & Discuss

In 2011, researchers at Indiana University and Princeton found that fonts that are slightly difficult to read (including Comic Sans) actually improved learning in some experiments. The researchers suggest that the improved effort required might increase performance. Why might making something harder to read also make that reading more memorable? What are the challenges to using this tactic?

want to call attention to the font being used. Although there are many strategies used to structure the business letter on page 123, the type is handled very simply: Times New Roman (a typeface so commonly used that it draws little attention to itself) in roman (regular) and bold fonts.

Of course, distinctive fonts are not necessarily a bad strategy. Viewers often have strong expectations about what different type means. Used wisely, distinctive fonts can strengthen a message. Compare the two versions of the U.S. Constitution on page 125. The first, set in Comic Sans, is probably more legible than the second. But the second, written in script by hand, signals that the text is an important historical document. (Even today, hand lettering signals attention to detail — wedding invitations are still sometimes written in calligraphy and addressed carefully by hand.) For many viewers in the United States, the large three-word introductory phrase identifies both the document and its historical context immediately. The context can also affect how readers perceive the meaning: If the audience is in a U.S. citizenship class and understanding the content is of paramount importance, Comic Sans might be more successful than script. But better would be a more readable font such as Palatino or Gill Sans because the unevenness of Comic Sans tends to cause reading difficulties.

Deciding What Media You Can Handle

As part of your thinking about design, you'll want to consider carefully whether you have the expertise (or can gain the expertise) to create a text in the medium you've chosen. Creating complex visual designs or multimedia texts on a computer seems extraordinarily easy — especially if you've seen the process only in software commercials. It's rarely that easy.

In addition to the artistic talent required to design a good (let alone great) animation or interactive website, the technical skill required can be daunting. That should not dissuade you from trying, but test the waters before diving in. For example, if you decide that your community service project for a local senior citizens' drop-in center would best be served by 30-second TV commercials run on a community cable channel, start by creating a 5-second commercial. See what things, if any, trip you up. Will you be able to resolve the problems? Can you afford to hire outside help, even just someone to train you? You'll want to address those questions before you commit to a project you can't adequately support.

If you're working with relatively complex media, you may be able to locate simplified applications that provide "training wheels" to get you started. For example, if you want to create video but don't have experience with shooting and editing that medium, don't start with a high-end camera and a complicated application like Adobe Premiere or Final Cut Pro. Instead, you might opt for using an iPhone and an app such as Cinefy (as shown on page 126), which offers very easy-to-use tools for structuring and editing video.

We the People of the United States, in Order to form a more perfect Union, establish Justice, insure domestic Tranquility, provide for the common defense, promote the general Welfare, and secure the Blessings of Liberty to ourselves and our Posterity, do ordain and establish this Constitution for the United States of America.

Article. I. - The Legislative Branch

Section 1 - The Legislature

All legislature Powers herein granted shall be vested in a Congress of the United States, which shall consist of a Senate and House of Representatives.

Section 2 - The House

The House of Representatives shall be composed of Members chosen every second Year by the People of the several States, and the Electors in each State shall have the Qualifications requisite for Electors of the most numerous Branch of the State Legislature.

No Person shall be a Representative who shall not have attained to the Age of twenty five Years, and been seven Years a Citizen of the United States, and who shall not, when elected, be an Inhabitant of that State in which he shall be chosen.

● Which of the two texts is more effective given the document's context, purpose, and audience?

The National Archives, 8601 Adelphi Road, College Park, MD 20740-6001

● In the iphone app Cinefy, a user has access to separate timelines for editing video, audio, and special effects. A Publish button allows the user to upload the finished video to the web.

Designing a Text: An Example

Designing texts brings another set of complicating but empowering aspects to writing. If you understand both words and images, you'll have a larger toolbox of strategies to bring to any writing problem. That doesn't mean you pull out all the stops for every project — that will often just lead to overly designed, self-indulgent texts that don't fit well with your audiences, purposes, and contexts.

Instead, designing a text should be a process of slowly working through your PACT framework, using material in each quadrant to inform decisions about the others as you go. The analyses you do might suggest that the context and audience are so well known and rigid you have no real choice but to use a specific type of text. Job application letters, for example, don't normally include novelty fonts, bright colors, or other features that seem like visual design. Instead, they seem perfectly neutral. (In fact, that's part of their design strength: They say, "I'm businesslike, professional, and reasonable. Trust me.") The brief PACT diagram below was created for a job application letter — the purpose, audience, and context all make it clear that a simple, conservative business letter is the best fit.

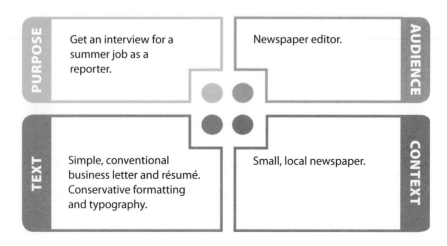

PURPOSE	AUDIENCE
Get an interview for a summer job as a reporter.	Newspaper editor.
TEXT	**CONTEXT**
Simple, conventional business letter and résumé. Conservative formatting and typography.	Small, local newspaper.

Let's look at an example of a more creative design process. In her writing class, Chan and her classmates have been looking at the role of advertising in our cultures — how it structures meaning, how it encourages viewers to think (and then act) in certain ways. Beer ads, for example, tend to portray enjoyable situations in which beer is one primary component: parties, watching big football games with friends, having a good time in the bar after a hard-fought pickup football game. Perfume ads (another easy target) make an intangible, invisible product a subtle but crucial component in romance and elegance. Fast-food ads show gatherings of friends or family bonding over a bag of french fries, bread, meat products, and soft drinks.

● "Follow the flock": an Adbusters parody ad taking design elements from ads being satirized
Courtesy of Adbusters Media Foundation

As Chan and her classmates have been discussing, advertisements for products both play off of and reinforce desires, sometimes linking new desires (for a particular commercial product) to deeper, more common desires (success, belongingness, happiness).

For this assignment, Chan has been asked to work on a variation of the assignment in Scenario 5, "Creating a Parody Ad." Her class has looked at parody ads from places like Adbusters and Yes Men, things that *look* like conventional advertisements but with a message that opposes the traditional messages usually contained in ads: *Don't buy this product*.

To get started, Chan looks at a series of ads in magazines. As she does this, she takes notes about the messages in the ads and how they are constructed, thinking about how each ad might be reversed: Who is the audience this ad intends to reach? How can we flip the intention of this ad into a situation the audience will find amusing? Maybe amusement isn't the intention we want. What if we want to shock them?

● An ad from the popular Absolut vodka campaign
© Caro/Alamy

After viewing some Adbusters spoof ads based on the popular Absolut vodka campaign, Chan decides to create an additional Absolut spoof ad. Chan has mixed feelings about alcohol consumption. Like many college students (and other adults), she thinks drinking seems like one ingredient of a fun evening out with friends. But she's also seen the side effects of overconsumption; she even knew several people who were killed in drunken driving accidents. So while she's not interested in creating an ad that demonizes moderate, responsible social drinking, she mulls over the idea of an ad that creates a message about the problems of drinking and driving, using the Absolut Vodka style to get her message across.

Chan starts sketching out some notes (below), beginning with a list of big or broad changes she wants to make in her audience.

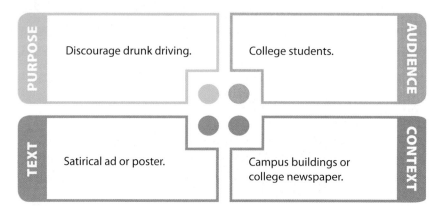

This is pretty broad, so she starts to break down that very brief but complicated term "satirical." Chan wants to create a text that is a satire. She needs to come up with concrete ways to do that. She looks back over the Absolut ads to see whether she can figure out more about how they work. She leaves aside her overall goals for now and looks more at the immediate, concrete objects in the ads — the design techniques being used to actually create the text. The ad campaign generally includes two techniques:

- Some object or arrangement of objects that form the outline of the iconic Absolut bottle
- A large caption that reads "Absolut" and then a noun that plays with or makes a pun about the picture

None of these are the *satire*, though, the grim humor that turns the ad from a pro-vodka image to an anti-drunk-driving image. Satire works by setting a context (and expectations) to lure viewers or readers in and then shifting the context to make the meaning more powerful. Obviously, she needs to add in some sort of image related to drunk driving — the most obvious option would be an accident scene.

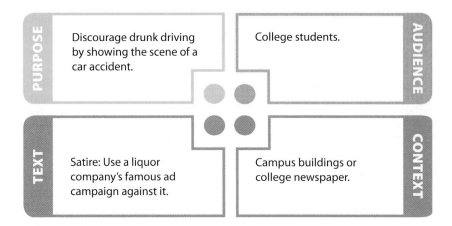

She feels like she's getting somewhere. Now she knows she can start working back and forth within the framework to fill in gaps and come up with more ideas. She sees another cell she can fill in: Where might a bottle outline show up in a drunken driving accident scene? On the road next to a wrecked car, maybe next to the chalked victim outline on the asphalt that's commonly seen in movies and on TV. Wait, here's an idea: Have the chalk body outline be the Absolut bottle. The caption for the image comes pretty quickly after that. She now has a framework she can use to help her start working on drafting the ad.

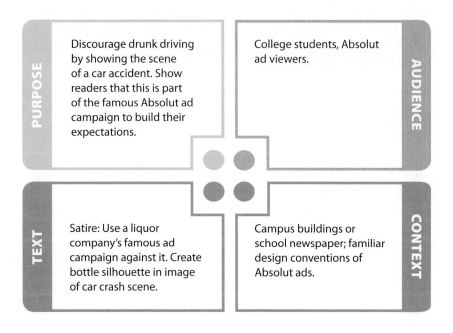

Top: © David R. Frazier Photolibrary, Inc./Alamy; Middle: © Viktor Koppan/
epa/Corbis; Bottom: © ZUMA Press, Inc./Alamy

Creative work like this is rarely linear. And there's still a lot of work to be done; Chan just has the concept at this point. She moves back and forth between image searches on the web and her planning table, saving some images to disk, noting their URLs so she can let her teacher know where she got source material (and in case she needs to secure copyright permission to use the images as part of an actual public ad campaign rather than just a class assignment). She prints some out and sketches on them, trying to find the bottle shape that's her goal. She rejects many because they are so gruesome she can't imagine working with them for any length of time. She looks for a while at images of automobile test crashes, but they seem too colorful and bright; they're also disconnected from the whole negative connotation angle she's after. She decides she wants something darker, with more threatening connotations, like old crime scene photos.

Eventually she locates a photo of an accident scene (see bottom left), showing first responders helping a victim.

She has all her main components — slogan, image, basic message — so she starts sketching the ad out on paper. She knows from looking at the other Absolut ads (both real and satire) that they have a vertically centered orientation with the main image focal point near the top and the slogan near the bottom.

Her crime scene image is fairly complicated, with several police cars and officers. She knows this is going to cause some figure/ground issues (see pp. 115–16) because of the complexity of the image, so she starts by cutting out some of the extra things (see p. 131).

As she works with the image, she tries to envision where the Absolut bottle outline should go. She notices that the undercarriage of the

● Chan's cropped photo

● Black-and-white version with Chan's slogan and placeholder text

car already has strong vertical lines. Those might be useful because the bottle itself is mainly composed of vertical lines. The image is also still pretty busy, so to get readers to focus on the car she carefully selects the outlines of the car, then inverts the selection so that the background is selected instead. This allows her to work with matte tools in her image-editing program to decrease the contrast in the background. She hopes this will overcome the tendency for readers' eyes to follow the lines of the road (out of the image); the reduced contrast seems to help. She converts the image to monochrome, black and white, which seems to help set up a hierarchy (p. 108), with the overturned car more prominent. The loss of bright colors also seems to make the image starker, more violent (p. 108).

The conversion to black and white also helps the complexity of the background: viewers would initially sort all of the people into multiple groups based on the color of their clothes (firefighters, EMTs, police officers) according to the principle of similarity (pp. 113–15). In black and white the people tend to just look like one group, making the image simpler and more powerful.

She begins by putting the slogan onto the cropped image, tweaking the font until it's similar to what she's seen in the ads, a very bold sans serif (p. 120). A little research online tells her that the main font is Futura Extra Bold Condensed. She doesn't have that font on her

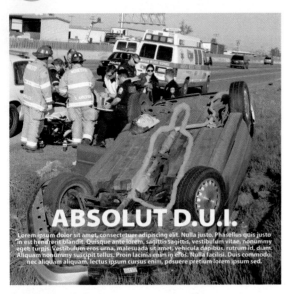

● Chan's first draft

computer so she selects something similar and tells herself she'll check a campus computer; the replacement would be pretty quick. She inserts some placeholder text, at a very small size, under the slogan. This is where the chatty or sarcastic body text shows up in the Absolut ads. She's not worried about that content right now since she's just working on the layout. But she needs a block of *something* there. The text is small enough that continuity (see pp. 111–12) will make it look just like a block of text, even if the words don't make any sense at this point.

Chan remembers the missing component: the chalk-outlined bottle. She sketches that onto the car's undercarriage using a soft brush and a graphics tablet. The line of the bottle strengthens the continuity of the layout (p. 111). Perfect (at least for a first draft). After she e-mails the attachment to her instructor for feedback, she wonders whether she could reverse the image so that the people were on the right and the car on the left. This would help bring the reader into the image better but would also require her to fix the letters on the firefighters' jackets and on the ambulance and police car. She could do it but it will be time consuming. She'll experiment with that in the next draft to see if it's worth the effort.

Putting It All Together

This chapter has covered a wide range of techniques for applying graphic design principles to texts you create. These principles can help not only with texts you might think of as being "designed" (posters, web pages, advertisements) but also with more traditional texts (essays, reports, letters).

In most cases, creating a text starts with the familiar aspects of purpose, audience, context, and text. Fill in what you know first in a PACT chart: That will help you determine what type of text will be most successful.

After you've done some thinking about your text and worked with the PACT chart, take some time to look at what other people have done.

Good design must take into account your audience's expectations. Although sometimes you can defy expectations and succeed, it's a risky gamble; be sure the surprise you cause in your audience is a positive one.

To take a common example, standard academic essays typically have very conservative designs. Good ones are usually designed very carefully, with attention paid to font choice, headings, and negative space to help people easily read them, highlighting key information through design choices (headings to denote new sections, italics to emphasize a word or indicate a book title, indenting to set off a long quotation). But it's rare to see a standard academic essay that includes flashy graphics, wild type, or lots of color, even if the essay uses those aspects in a very solid design. Good design must take into account the purpose, audience, and context.

After you've explored your purpose, audience, and context and examined some effective examples, you'll need to decide what type of process you're going to follow. As with other aspects of writing, some people work best by sketching designs out to get a rough layout and then going back to create the necessary text. Other people want to create all of their text first and then apply design techniques to that material. Like Chan in the example on pages 127–32, most people are somewhere in the middle, creating some text and then working on the design, adding to and revising their text as they continue to work on the design.

The specifics of the project will also influence your work process: The website for a campus radio station lends itself to starting from the graphic design side (choosing a color scheme, creating graphics), while a personal response essay might begin by generating the text and looking hard at design only near the end.

As you work, ask yourself how your readers are going to interpret your document in terms of design:

- Is the most important element on the page or screen visually prominent?
- Are the hierarchical relationships among elements of the text made clear? Do the most important elements stand out while the less important ones stay back?
- Will readers' or viewers' eyes move along the page or screen in a way that leads them through important information?
- Does the layout generally meet your audience's expectations?

Consider all of the techniques and principles discussed in this chapter as a toolbox that can help you address these questions.

Texts for Analysis

Unless you're a graphic artist or designer, you probably don't think a lot about design — you just use it, without being aware of it, to understand what you're seeing. Ironically, good design is often invisible or automatic: It just works. As you look at the texts below, refer to the discussion of design principles on pages 106–18. Which principles seem to be at work here? Which of them seem to be most important in understanding why and how each text works?

- Hierarchy
- Color
- Negative space
- Proximity
- Continuity
- Similarity
- Figure/Ground
- Grids

PHOTOGRAPH
"Sunset in a Winter Forest"

Leonid Ikan/Shutterstock

"Live Blues, February 23, 2011"

This poster advertises a blues guitarist and singer performing at a local bar.

Brien O'Keefe

POSTER
RIAA, "Internet Safety Checklist"

This poster was distributed by the Recording Industry Association of America. RIAA's primary work involves preventing people from illegally downloading or copying music and helping impose penalties on those who do. Music Rules! is an RIAA campaign to protect intellectual property (music and movies) from piracy.

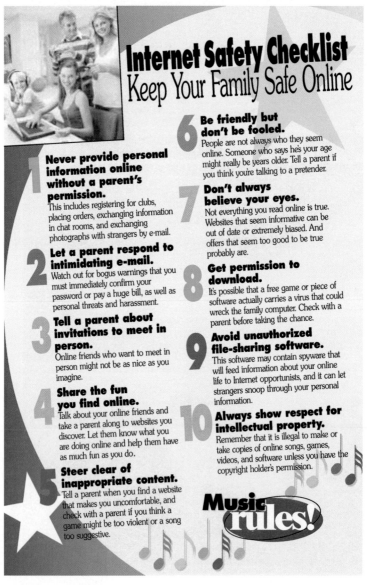

Music Rules! Internet Safety Checklist. Reprinted by permission of the Pause Parent Play Project.

POSTER
Pause Parent Play, "Parents Thwart Flesh-Eating Cyborgs"

This poster from Pause Parent Play's website encourages parents to work with their children on appropriate media use.

David & Goliath Creative Agency

Exercises

1. Analyze an artistic painting in terms of the design principles discussed in this chapter. Print the image out at reduced size so you have room to write in the margins. Annotate the image to show how the principles are being used. Try to find at least four principles being used. You can locate images in printed collections or at websites such as Artcyclopedia (www.artcyclopedia.com).

2. Analyze a flyer for a campus event or group. Locate a flyer or poster for a campus event (if you're taking the poster from a public bulletin board, be sure to take one only for an event that has already passed). Based on what you know about the campus organization, the event, and the text itself, create a brief PACT chart. Analyze how well the text works according to the graphic design guidelines covered in this chapter. Are there revisions you would suggest to make the flyer more effective?

3. Design a 2-inch button for a social cause. Given the limitations of a 2-inch button, your message will need to be both very strong and very simple. You can develop a logo, a short bit of text, and/or graphics to construct your message.

4. Take an academic paper that you've written and redesign the layout for a new genre. You'll need to be creative with your PACT chart as you do your redesign: Can you still achieve your original purpose, or do you need to rethink that? Some translations will be more difficult: Going from a five-page essay to a bulletin board will require some gymnastics. You might find yourself leaning more on parody and irony, making entertainment your purpose. (This exercise is similar to the more in-depth version in Scenario 19, "Repurposing a Text, on page 297.")

    You'll want to also analyze the target genre: What design features do texts in that genre draw on heavily? What are the conventions?

    Possible types of texts include these:

   - Graphic novel (use example from Comic Life or other software)

   - Flyer

   - Billboard by the side of a highway

   - Magazine article

   - Radio audiomagazine

   - CD or DVD box

   - Political campaign poster

   - Movie trailer

    For longer, more complex formats such as a magazine or graphic novel, your instructor might give you permission to design only a few pages of a projected much-longer work.

5. Take a typography field trip. Go off campus and locate three noteworthy examples of typography in the wild. The examples can be either good or bad, but they should be interesting. Remember that fonts are neither good nor bad in a vacuum; consider their contexts, purposes, and audiences. Take

photos of each example and write a brief (600-word) analysis that includes the images and explains how the typography in each relates (or fails to relate) to its apparent context, purpose, and audience.

Scenario Connections

1. Scenario 3, "Arguing for a Handwritten Letter? Or E-mail?" involves analyzing the pros and cons of handwritten letters and e-mail messages. You can read some of the arguments in favor of or against each in the Background Texts for the scenario. As you'll note, the personal and aesthetically pleasing nature of handwriting is often discussed by those in favor of letters. With a web image search, locate an example of handwriting that you would like to have if you were writing a letter to a specific relative such as a grandparent or grandchild. Then locate a font that seems appropriate to that same relative. Why did you make the choices you made? If you had to pick either the style of handwriting or the font you found, which one would you pick? Why?

2. Scenario 5, "Creating a Parody Ad," is similar to the assignment Chan worked on in the example on pages 127–32. Choose a real advertisement that you might want to create a parody of for this scenario. Using terms from this chapter, write a short description of the distinctive aspects of the ad that you'll want to draw from to create your parody. What design principles does the ad rely on? What style of typography does it use? How do readers' eyes move through the text? How does the design create hierarchy among the various elements? Are there any aspects of the ad that don't work well?

3. Scenario 15, "Designing an Organization's Graphic Identity," asks you to design coherent, consistent guidelines for "graphic identity" for a campus organization. After reviewing the scenario (including the Background Texts), pick a campus organization to work for. Select from one to three colors to use in the graphic identity and describe why those colors match the organization's purpose and audience. Design at least one graphic element (logo or logotype) that will be included as part of the group's identity. (Note: If you plan to actually provide the organization with the graphic identity materials, you should contact it first for permission and also involve the group in the design process. If you're just using the materials in your class, you do not need the organization's permission, but it might not hurt to ask.)

4. Scenario 14, "Designing Cover Art for Digital Music (p. 292)," gives you some raw materials that you'll work with to create a mockup for a new record label's website. For the sake of the assignment, assume you have access to any font you like. Choose one font for headings and one for body text. Use terminology from the typography section of this chapter (starting on page 118) and describe why those fonts are effective choices given your audience and purpose. Identify one font that you think would *not* work well for the site's purpose and audience.

Managing Writing Projects

If you want your writing to change things, you have to manage it effectively. At its simplest, managing a writing project involves answering these two questions:

1. What needs to happen?
2. How do I make all those things happen?

As with most writing tasks, the answers to these questions can be very straightforward or very complicated. Consider a simple example: You drive to your friend Carolyn's apartment to pick her up on the way to a movie. From the parking lot outside her apartment, you send her a text message: "i'm here". Carolyn quickly replies, "b right dn." In 30 seconds, she opens the passenger-side door of your car.

In this situation, the answers to the two questions seem pretty simple:

1. What needs to happen? *Carolyn needs to come down to the parking lot and get into the car.*
2. How do I make all those things happen? *I'll text Carolyn and tell her I'm here.*

Although you might not have thought about it, the simplicity of those answers relies on a lot of other things already being in place: that Carolyn has her phone with her and turned on, that she isn't still mad after you made fun of the (goofy) shirt she was wearing yesterday, that she's actually *in* the apartment and isn't on the other side of town waiting for you at the movie theater because she thought you'd agreed to meet at the theater, that she knows what your car looks like. Any of these things being out of place would require more complicated plans and responses.

Still, the situation is familiar enough and simple enough that little planning or management is required. But once you start to engage with larger, more complicated problems, you'll find it useful to think about writing as a project that needs some management.

Thinking about writing as project management can not only make your writing more effective, it can keep your project from crashing to a halt in a pile of missed deadlines and missing information.

Reflect & Discuss

What strategies have you used for managing large projects? These could be writing projects, the process of selecting and applying to a college, running an event, or just choosing and buying holiday gifts for family and friends. What strategies have been successful? What ones haven't worked well for you? Are there things you know you should be doing but currently don't? Why?

Tasks: Identifying What Work Needs to Be Done

Although a lot of people just wade into a project, for complex work you probably want to plan a little. The first step is in identifying what work needs to be done so you can start figuring out how long it will take, what resources you might need, and other issues that can make or break your project.

Breaking a Large Project into Smaller Tasks

If even a very common writing situation with a very simple purpose involves a lot of things, how do you deal with writing situations that are complicated at the start? Consider another example: writing a 10-page research paper that analyzes how arguments about global warming are constructed, which is due in two weeks for your environmental science class. At first glance, this writing situation also has a very simple task.

What needs to happen? You can use the description your instructor used as part of the assignment description:

> Write a 10-page paper analyzing how articles from three different popular magazines describe research on global warming.

This sounds pretty straightforward, but if you think about the second question, things start to get more complicated.

How do I make that happen?

> Sit down the night before the paper is due and start typing frantically. Crash and burn in a flamboyant cloud of caffeine and cursing at approximately 5:30 a.m. and beg the instructor for an extension.

And you wouldn't be the first person to answer the question that way. You might be more effective, though, if you looked back at question one and broke down your answer into its concrete parts—the things you need to do:

- write a 10-page paper
- analyzing how
- articles from three different popular magazines
- describe research on global warming

This process of breaking down large projects into smaller tasks is an important aspect of project management: A project that seemed so large you couldn't get your arms around it can be broken into chunks small enough for you to lift.

Putting Tasks in a Sequence

But choosing how to break down that project requires careful thought: You can't just break off any chunk and start working on it: Some portions rely on other parts. You don't spend a lot of time carefully proofreading a rough draft that will be substantially changed in two days. And you can't analyze an article that you haven't located yet.

So you might start by looking at the quick list of tasks we came up with and think about how to order them: What needs to happen in what sequence?

1. Locate three articles about global warming.
2. Skim through each article to get a sense of what's in it.
3. Begin working on a PACT chart for the paper.
4. Decide on a method or framework for analyzing how research on global warming is described based on material in the PACT chart.
5. Write a paper describing this analysis while referring to (and possibly revising) the PACT chart.

Remember here (and throughout your writing processes) that most writing is not a simple linear activity. Even though we can list out steps in order, we may find that we occasionally step backward to an earlier step. For example, when we're writing the paper we might realize that there's a gap in our analysis or some other problem that requires us to find more arguments or do some additional analysis. Maybe on a more careful reading, we realize one of the articles doesn't seem appropriate. That's fine — our linear ordered list is just a method for ordering our work, but it's not something we are completely bound to.

Determining the Scope and Duration of Tasks

Each of these tasks should probably be broken down a little more until the resulting pieces are of manageable sizes. What's a manageable size? That depends on you and on the task. If you've analyzed dozens and dozens of arguments about global warming, you probably don't need to break that task down much more. However, if this is the first assignment in a class on environmental writing and you don't have a lot of experience with analyzing texts, you might want to make this step more detailed. At this point, it's also useful to start thinking about the scope of the tasks (how much time they take) and constraints ("milestones," such as a draft being due in class on a certain date).

1. Review assignment and textbook chapter (1 hr)
2. Browse web to locate three articles (1 hr)
3. Read articles (2 hrs)
4. Develop PACT chart (1 hr)
5. Outline key points to analyze using PACT chart (1 hr)
6. Outline paper w/PACT (0.5 hrs)
7. Write draft 1 of paper (5 hrs, **due Monday, 11/3**)
8. Check draft against assignment requirements and PACT chart (0.5 hrs)

9. Peer-review draft in class (1 hr)
10. Revise based on comments (3 hrs)
11. Proofread (0.5 hrs)
12. Turn in final draft at class (**due Monday, 11/10**)

As you map out your project, don't forget to consider information you already have on hand — notes from class, readings, your PACT chart, or other materials that might help. If, for example, your class analyzed a magazine article last week, look back to your notes to see what process everyone followed and how long it took. If there's a text-book in your class that covers the process, review it as well. And while it should go without saying, read through the actual assignment care-fully and review the assignment again while you work: You'd be sur-prised how often students work hard to complete an assignment only to find out they missed key requirements or did something the wrong way because they didn't read the assignment sheet carefully or review it again before turning the project in.

Timelines: Identifying *When* Work Needs to Be Done

Woody Allen once said that time was nature's way of keeping every-thing from happening at once. A project timeline serves a similar func-tion: It spreads your individual tasks out so that you can deal with them one at a time. Timelines also make sure that you meet deadlines (such as the two draft deadlines in the list above). Timelines can help you coordinate work on this project with all the other work you're doing: your other class work, meetings, meals, job, and everything else on your schedule. By coordinating these things, you (try to) make sure you have time to get everything done.

As with the list of tasks you've generated, you should remember that the timeline is a *tool* to help structure your work. It's easy to spend the majority of your time obsessing about the layout of your timeline or the font you're using in your list of tasks, to the point that you're engag-ing only in "meta" work — work *about* work — and never actually com-pleting your real work.

Organizing Tasks into a Timeline

Timelines organize tasks. You won't be surprised to find out that timelines can be very simple (Draft 1 due Wed; Final revision due Monday) or very complicated (see the next section on Gantt charts). Timelines for large team projects can become amazingly complex because the timeline needs to organize the work of multiple people, some of whom cannot start tasks until other people have finished earlier tasks.

GANTT CHARTS Usually, the more complex the lists of tasks the more complex the timeline. A Gantt chart is one type of complex timeline that can be used to allocate resources (rooms, equipment, or even people) and for multiperson projects. Although very large, complex projects may require specialized project management software such as OmniPlan or Microsoft Project, any spreadsheet program such as those in Google Drive or Zoho can be used to create Gantt charts. The structure of the chart highlights, for example, where overdue work on the part of one team member slows down another team member.

You can create a Gantt chart such as the one below by listing your main tasks in order down the left column and the dates in the top row. Then fill in the cells to indicate when you will work on each specific task. You can color-code the cells if you like (such as yellow

		M	Tu	W	Th	F	Sa	Su	M	Tu	W	Th	F	Sa	Su	M	Tu	W	Th	F
		10	10	10	10	10	10	10	10	10	10	10	10	10	10	10	10	10	10	10
		13	14	15	16	17	18	19	20	21	22	23	24	25	26	27	28	29	30	31
Research																				
	Run Survey				S+R	S+R	S+R	S+R	S+R											
	Interview Center Director	R																		
	Analyze Survey Results								S+R											
	Compare to Other Schools						J+K	J+K												
Drafting																				
	Construct Survey	J+K	J+K																	
	Create Stylesheet			J																
	Methods Section				J+K	J+K			J+K	J+K				J	J					
	Survey Results									S+R	S+R									
	Recommendations											J	J			S	S			
	Figures											K	K			K	K			
	Full Draft																	J+R		
Reviewing																				
	Methods						S	S				R	R	R						
	Results																			
	Recommendations													K	K					
	Figures													S	S					
	Full Draft																		S+K	
	Copyedit/Proof Final																			ALL
	Staff:	J:	Jennifer																	
		K:	Kyle																	
		R:	Rebecca																	
		S:	Sean																	

● A Gantt chart for a team research project. Tasks are listed in the left column and dates in the top rows. The initials in individual cells indicate which team members will work on each task at each stage of the project.

Tips for Working on Gantt Charts

- *Identify set "milestone" dates and fill those activities in first.* If your first draft is due in class on Tuesday, November 11, fill that in. You'll have to work around due dates and other milestones because they're already set.

- *Identify dependencies — tasks that can't take place until some earlier task has been completed.* For example, if you need to create an outline before you create the first draft, be sure that your Gantt chart reflects that. Dependencies are often a major issue for team projects because you don't want one person sitting around waiting because another person hasn't finished a necessary part of the project. You can't proofread the draft if your teammate is still revising it.

- *Build in some cushioning by over-estimating the time required for tasks where possible.*

For larger, more complex projects, you might even specifically schedule in a week's cushion at the end so you have some leeway if the project gets behind schedule. Better to have it and not need it than need it and not have it.

- *Keep your Gantt chart current.* If you miss a deadline, go through and figure out where you're going to make up that time. Will it come from your slack time or cushion? Or do you have to speed up other tasks?

- *For very complex projects (especially team projects), consider taking the time to learn a dedicated project management program such as OmniPlan or Microsoft Project.* These programs feature things like resource management, automatic recalculations of all tasks when the time for one task changes, dependency checking, and more.

for work that you have to do on campus and green for work you can do at home).

CALENDARS For our environmental science research paper, we'll stay with a simpler approach; we'll enter things into the same calendar that holds our other scheduling information. This will help coordinate work on the assignment with everything else to make sure there aren't huge conflicts.

Calendar programs like Google Calendar allow you to set up multiple calendars such as one for classes, one for social events, and one for your intramural sports team. You can decide to have all calendars show up on the same screen or selectively hide calendars to make one easy to scan. This capability lets you set up dedicated calendars for specific projects or classes, showing or hiding calendar views as necessary to help you track complex projects or many smaller ones. The example at the top of page 146 shows a Google Calendar set up for the environmental science paper assignment. You can add shared calendars into the mix so that teammates can choose to show their teammates' calendars to find possible meeting times.

● A Google Calendar set up for a specific project. Scheduling in time to finish each task two days before it's due will give you "slack" time in case you fall behind schedule.

Focusing on Action and Duration

As you write out tasks, remember to think in terms of *action*: What will you be doing and for how long? So rather than simply writing "Draft 1 due" (which is a fairly lifeless and uninformative statement), you'd write, "Write draft 1 (4 hours)." This might seem like a small thing, but thinking in terms of activity and timespan helps you break down larger projects into workable chunks.

Figuring out exactly how much time to dedicate to different writing tasks is very difficult because it varies from one writer to another. Some people spend a very large amount of time on earlier stages such as brainstorming and outlining, but then write a solid, first, full draft; other writers spend less time in the early stages, preferring to write a very loose first draft that they'll revise many times. Overestimate how much time you need and take notes on your timeline showing how much time you actually spent on each task. You can then use those notes to help you make more accurate schedules for future projects.

The table on the left shows examples of vague action statements and better ones. As you can see from the "Better" column,

Vague	Better
Research »	• Locate articles in library's online database (1 hr) (**due January 17 in class**)
	• Review articles for key trends (2 hrs)
Draft 1 due »	• Organize notes into outline (1 hr)
	• Convert outline to draft (5 hrs)
	• Revise rough draft for peer crit (1 hr) (**due January 26 in class**)
Finish paper »	• Review comments (0.5 hrs)
	• Revise final based on comments (3 hrs)
	• Proofread final draft (0.5 hrs)
	• Turn in final draft in class (**due February 2 in class**)

● Vague action statements and better instructions

more detail is usually a good idea. And notice that the items include not only actions ("Proofread final draft") and durations ("0.5 hrs") but also deadlines ("due January 26 in class").

Managing Information

You may be the kind of person who is meticulous about organization: color-coded highlighting system for marking up your textbooks; neatly typed labels on file folders; and web-based, automated backup program for your computer. Or you might be closer to the other extreme: tattered sheets of paper with scrawled notes sticking out of your textbooks, stacks of unorganized papers towering precariously on your desk, and backups — what's a backup?

Even if you're an obsessively organized person, managing information during a writing project can require something a little different than your normal system. If you're the nonplanner type, picking even a couple of the strategies below would be a good start.

Tips for Managing Virtual Information

- **Set up a notes folder.** Create a directory or folder on your hard drive to hold all materials related to this specific writing project. Name it something informative — not "Paper 1" but "ENGL 102 - History of Punk Rock Research Paper."

- **Create additional subfolders as necessary.** If you're creating a lot of files (for example, by clipping web pages to disk), create subdirectories to keep your main project folder from getting swamped. The example on page 149 shows folders, subfolders, and file names for a writing class.

- **Create a folder in your mail app if you're doing much work on the project in e-mail.**

- **Use a backup system.** There are two types of people: those who have lost files due to a drive crash and those who will in the future. Your backup system can be as simple as burning a CD-R of your project directory every week, but a more robust system is better.

Automated systems like web-based CrashPlan or Apple's Time Machine back up files automatically, taking the least reliable part of a backup system — the user — out of the equation.

- **Give your files informative names.** Naming files well is probably more important than naming folders well. You might get away with names like "draft 1.docx" for very short projects, but larger research projects call for better names. And if you're submitting papers to peers or your instructor online, including your initials or name in the file name will be helpful. You might even go as far as including dates. "ENGL 102 Enviro Proposal 1.28.12 JJ-E d1.docx" is better than "proposal.docx."

- **Keep multiple drafts of projects.** Don't simply overwrite your old draft with a new draft. Instead, put successive draft numbers in the file name, starting a new major draft by saving

(continued)

Tips for Managing Virtual Information
(continued)

your work to a new file with the new number in the file name. The older drafts are another form of insurance against detours (that idea you had at 3 a.m. for reordering your main points might have been a bad direction to take) or corrupted files.

- *Keep "scrap" folders on your hard drive and don't throw things away until you're sure you'll never need them again.* Save course materials, at least until the end of the semester after grades are completed. If you're not working

with video or other large files, hard drive space probably isn't an issue.

- *Use web-based services like Google Drive or Dropbox so that you can get at project materials from any computer that has web access —* whether you're at the library, the computer lab, a friend's apartment, or your parents' house during a short break.

- *Think carefully before deleting old projects.* If you're going to be applying for a job that focuses on content creation or design, you might be expected to provide a portfolio that showcases your best work.

Tips for Managing Print Information

- *Make stacks of related materials.* You can bring structure to masses of paper by stacking them in a neat corner on your desk, on a bookshelf, or on the floor.

- *Designate certain areas of your workspace for different types of information:* materials waiting to be read (journal articles or books) stacked in one area, materials already reviewed that will be actively used during drafting in another area, and materials that didn't prove to be useful stacked in yet another. Exactly where you put each stack is up to you, but in general the materials that you'll use the most should be closer to you. Things used less frequently can be farther away or even in storage.

- *Put loose papers into folders based on the project:* drafts that you've printed and marked up for revision, photocopies of articles or other things. Write the project name on the front of the folder and/or the tab. If you find that you want to keep materials from many projects for a long time, invest in a small filing cabinet with hangers for folders.

- *Use color-coded sticky notes to tag different types of information or color-coded folders for different projects:* green notes for arguments in

favor of a position but red or yellow notes for those opposing it, for example.

- *Make marginal notes on raw material indicating how you think you can use it.* Cross-reference things (both digital and print). For example, if one paper criticizes another one, make notes on both so you'll remember the connection.

- *Consider using print notebooks.* Although print notebooks are slowly declining in use in favor of laptops, tablets, and smartphones, notebooks may provide an easier-to-use interface for free-form communication: You can draw and write text in the same space in ways that are difficult to do with smartphones or computers. This is largely a personal preference, but one worth thinking about.

- *Avoid throwing papers away until the project is finished and graded.* Sometimes, an article you copied or a note you jotted down at the start of a project might seem useless partway into your work, only to reemerge as a key element later on. While you can't keep everything forever, you can set up a folder or box marked "Hold" to gather these maybe-useful-maybe-not materials until the project is truly completed.

```
Name
▼ 📁 2015 SPRING COURSES
   ▶ 📁 CALC105
   ▶ 📁 CS101
   ▼ 📁 ENGL101
      ▼ 📁 Chapter 1 – Understanding
      ▼ 📁 Chapter 2 – Approaching Situations
            📄 Exercise 2 notes – commercials.docx
         ▶ 📁 S2 – Voting
            📄 Text analyses – credit cards.docx
      ▶ 📁 Chapter 3 – First Drafts
      ▶ 📁 Chapter 4 – Structuring
      ▼ 📁 Chapter 7 – Research
         ▼ 📁 environmental research paper F13
            ▼ 📁 assignment handouts
                  📄 arguing w/data copy.pdf
                  📄 grading guidelines copy.pdf
                  📄 paper formatting guidelines.pdf
            ▶ 📁 brainstorming
               📄 climate change paper.ooutline
            ▶ 📁 climate change skeptics
            ▼ 📁 drafts
                  📄 climate change research d1.1.doc
                  📄 climate change research d2.0.doc
               ▶ 📁 peer review notes
               📄 environmental paper outline d1 copy.oo3
               📄 environmental paper outline d2.0.oo3
               📄 environmental paper outline d2.1.oo3
         ▼ 📁 maps
```

● Files with informative names, organized into folders and subfolders

Don't obsess about organization. Writing projects often develop rhythms, a slow shift from order to chaos, back and forth. Contrary to what you might think, a little (or even a lot of) chaos can be useful. First, if you spend all your time making sure you're perfectly organized, you won't have time to actually write or design. Second, chaos can help you see things in new ways. Seeing two apparently unrelated articles next to each other might spark a new connection in your mind or show you a different side of an argument. At the same time, don't use "productive" chaos as an excuse to just let everything fall apart. Periodically take time to go through the pile of papers on your desk (and floor) and put them back in order or devote some time to organizing the files on your hard drive and backing them up.

Text for Analysis

BLOG POST

Gina Trapani, "Geek to Live: Organizing 'My Documents'"

Gina Trapani is the founder and editor of Lifehacker, the popular site that offers "tips, tricks, and downloads for getting things done and living life better." Here she offers her tips for organizing the "My Documents" folder on your computer. As you read, consider the questions she poses at the end of the post: "What does your 'My Documents' look like? Why does it (or doesn't it) work for you?" Do the methods she suggests seem like sensible practice or overkill?

Last week we discussed how to organize your paperwork with a filing cabinet, some manila folders, and a label maker. Today we're going to tackle that virtual yellow folder on your computer called "My Documents."

If your current file organization system works for you, congratulations. But if you frequently find yourself letting files clutter your computer's desktop, or if you spend time arranging files in a deep, complicated hierarchy of fine-grained folders, it's time for a revamp. Remember, with simplicity comes effortlessness. A few simple but flexible buckets can get your bits and bytes under control so you can spend less time moving files around and more time getting work done.

There are a million and one ways to arrange files and folders on disk. Some might argue that spending a moment even thinking about it in the age of desktop search is unnecessary. That may be true, but some semblance of order will clear your desktop and your mind and make you "ready for anything." Over the years I've come up with a six folder structure for "My Documents" which I create on every computer I use without fail. This scheme accommodates every file I might come across, keeps my desktop clear, smoothly fits in with an automated backup system, and also makes command line file wrangling a breeze.

This is just one way that won't work for everyone, but there may be something here to help you get your digital documents under control. In alphabetical order, my six main folders are called: **bak**, **docs**, **docs-archive**, **junkdrawer**, **multimedia**, and **scripts**. Here's a quick rundown of what each does and what it might contain.

1. **bak:** I spend a lot of time at the command line, so I always opt for shortened file names. In this case, bak is short for backup—but it isn't what you think. Your data backups will reside on external disks, but the bak folder holds application-specific exported backup data. For instance, your bak folder might contain your Firefox and Thunderbird MozBackup files (you backup before you install new extensions, right?), your Quicken file backup, your Address Book exported CSV, or a dump of your weblog's database.

2. **docs:** Docs is the big kahuna of all the six folders. It's the place where all the working files for your currently in-progress tasks, projects, and clients go. Docs changes often and frequently, and should be purged often. I have many sub folders in docs, like "finance," "clients," and "creative-writing." The "clients"

folder has sub folders too, like "lifehacker" and "kinja." That gets us 3 sub folders in, and that's usually as deep as I'm willing to go.

3. **docs-archive:** Your docs file should be purged of no longer "working" files frequently. "Closed" files — on a completed project, for a former employer, for past tax years — should go into your docs-archive. This archive exists just for reference and search, but the separate folder keeps all that extra stuff from cluttering up docs, which is basically your working task dashboard. The files in docs-archive don't change much if ever, and so you can back them up on a different (less frequent) schedule as a result.

4. **junkdrawer:** The junkdrawer (or temp, or tmp) is a temporary holding pen for files you're messing around with but don't need to save long-term. Firefox and Thunderbird should both save to junkdrawer by default for downloads and mail attachments. When I'm cropping and sharpening photos to upload, checking out a video, or just testing out a script or program, into junkdrawer the files go. Files I decide I want to keep graduate from junkdrawer into docs; otherwise, the automated hard drive janitor I wrote about awhile back comes sweeping through and deletes anything older than 2 weeks from junkdrawer while I sleep.

5. **multimedia:** Here's where your music, video, and photos folders go. In terms of managing your media within this folder, I'm generally content to let iTunes and Picasa take care of things. Of course your preference may vary, but the benefit of having all those space-hogging sound, video, and image files under one multimedia umbrella parent folder is backup. Chances are your multimedia backup scheme will be different than your documents backup because of the lesser change frequency and the gigabytage required. Drop 'em all here in the multimedia folder and you're good to go. Keep in mind that sharing your media with a home web server works nicely with an overarching multimedia folder, too.

6. **scripts:** The scripts folder is where any executable script or shortcut lives. Here I keep my previously-mentioned weight logger and janitor scripts, any batch scripts, and Windows shortcuts for quick launching programs.

A word about Windows' default home directory

As I said, I'm a big fan of short and to the point file paths. Windows' default user documents directory is something like:

> C:\Documents and Settings\Gina\My Documents\

To which I say, "For the love of all that is good and holy, why, Microsoft, why?"

I can appreciate human-readable folder names, but I do lots of command line work and scripting, and I don't ever want to have to remember to enclose my home directory path in quotes or remember the slashes to escape spaces. So to make things easier, I always change the "My Documents" directory to c:\home\gina\. This consistently lowercase path sans spaces is much easier to type, remember, and much more scriptable.

To change your documents directory in Windows, right-click on the "My Documents" icon. Under Properties, hit the Move button.

Choose the new location. Windows will politely ask if you'd like to move all your documents from the old location to the new one. Go ahead and do that if you need to.

Beyond the big 6

If you've read this far, then I'm going to let you in on a little secret: these aren't the only folders that live in my home directory. Being a programmer and web developer, if the workstation I'm on is a development machine, I also frequently work within a "code" folder and a "webserver" folder (the root of my Apache installation). Also, many Windows applications take it upon themselves to create folders in "My Documents." Sometimes I leave 'em, other times I'll explicitly set where stuff gets saved—like my Trillian IM logs or Thunderbird mail archives location (docs and docs-archive, respectively).

But enough about me. There must be strong feelings out there about filing versus piling and what the best folder structure is. So, lifehackers, show us your filing mojo. What does your "My Documents" look like? Why does it (or doesn't it) work for you?

Exercises

1. Analyze the organization of files on your hard drive. What are the main directories you use? How is information organized in those directories? Do you have a system for organizing your information? If so, how did you come up with it? If not, does the lack of structure ever lead to problems? What do you see as the strongest and weakest points of your organization scheme? Write a short (750- to 1,000-word) summary and analysis of your findings.

Compare your own analysis with other students' in class. What similarities do you see? What differences? Can you find techniques that you'd like to apply to your own organizing practices?

2. Interview a professor about how he or she organizes an office to support writing (even faculty in a discipline such as visual or performing arts spend a great deal of time writing). During the interview, ask for a description of how information is physically organized in the office—are books, journals, and other printed texts organized? What principle guides the organization? What materials are on the desk? Why? Ask the professor to walk you through a relatively common writing project that he or she recently completed (of anything—a journal article, a committee report, a novel, and so on). What kinds of materials were used? Where did he or she place the materials? Did the materials move from place to place over the course of the project? Write a short (750- to 1,000-word) summary and analysis of your findings.

Alternately (or in addition, for a larger exercise), ask the professor to describe how the hard drive on his or her office computer is organized using questions from exercise 1. Are there separate folders or directories for each class or major project? What method is used for naming them?

3. Go to a large photo-sharing site such as Flickr or Picasa and search on the term "workspace." Locate examples of the following:
   - messiest workspace
   - neatest workspace
   - most creative workspace
   - largest workspace
   - smallest workspace

   Imagine yourself in each of them while working on a project, working with different resources such as books, printouts, and drafts. What aspects of each would be useful or productive to you? What aspects would hinder your work? Finally, which of these workspaces resembles your own? Write a 1,000-word narrative or short story in the first person ("I") in which you describe what it would be like to work in one of the spaces you found.

4. Start a backup system of some type (web-based; separate hard drive; or periodic, scheduled copies to another medium). Write a short (500-word) informal report on the system, including a description and how much cost and effort is involved. Do you think you'll be able to continue using it, or is it too much hassle? (If you already have a backup system, you can use that for your description.)

Scenario Connections

1. For Scenario 6, "Writing a Profile for a Magazine" (p. 280), you'll be interviewing a person to write a profile about them. After reviewing the scenario and the material in this chapter about breaking down tasks (starting on p. 141), create a list of tasks you'll need to accomplish. You should break down larger tasks until they are at an actionable level such as "Call Mona Grey to see whether I can interview her" and "Write first draft of interview questions." Sort your tasks into chronological order and assign a rough estimate of how many minutes or hours each will take. If you're working with a peer-review team, ask it to look at the tasks and times to give you feedback on whether they seem reasonable.

2. In Scenario 14, "Designing Cover Art for Digital Music" (p. 292), you'll create three different cover art options for a fictional band as well as a presentation about your designs. Large, complex projects like this one require careful scheduling. Create a list of tasks and a Gantt chart for your project. Don't forget to include time to learn any technologies you're not familiar with, time for research and designing, and time for getting feedback on both your designs and the presentation for revisions.

3. Scenario 15, "Designing an Organization's Graphic Identity," involves creating multiple components (a logo, several types of sample texts, and a brief graphic identity manual). Create a broken-down task list and then put the tasks into a calendar that will help you finish the project on time.

4. Scenario 20, "Revising a Campus File-Sharing Policy," asks you to conduct research on the legal issues surrounding file sharing and then to revise your campus's policy (or the policy provided in the Background Texts for the scenario). Using the tips on pages 147–48, develop a plan for how you will manage virtual and print information for this project. What system will you use to name and keep track of your files? Where will you store the print information you need to work with? What methods of organization have you used successfully in the past? Write a short description of your plan.

Getting Information and Writing from Research

In some cases, you'll be able to write simply from things you already know or things you can find out with minimal effort — a text message to a friend asking for notes in a class you missed, an essay about a story you've read, a cover letter for the résumé you're submitting for a job. But in other cases, you won't know enough to write an effective text. You might need to do research to write an informed opinion, make an effective argument, or design a compelling ad campaign. Research informs many types of writing, from traditional academic papers that argue for a particular point of view by quoting sources, to political ads honed through feedback from focus groups and surveys.

Writing from research uses many of the things you know how to do already: understanding your context and understanding how your writing can lead to change in that context, knowing how to work effectively in teams, writing effective sentences and paragraphs, and more. This chapter covers the aspects of writing that are specific to working with sources:

1. Identifying what information you need
2. Developing a research plan
3. Doing secondary research
4. Doing primary research
5. Taking notes
6. Connecting your research to your writing

For writing projects, your research activities will usually start before any concrete writing tasks, but they may overlap with the early stages of writing. For example, for a long essay that contrasts three opposing philosophical views you might begin researching and writing about one of those views before starting research on the others. Or, after an initial round of research, you might start writing and then realize you need to find more information to argue a specific key point. This is why it's crucial to build extra time into your research and writing activities, as discussed in Chapter 6 on page 145, to leave slack time for unforeseen work.

It's useful to see research as a conversation, as engagement with other voices. When you write from research, you are commenting on the ideas of others, linking ideas from various sources, and contributing to an ongoing dialogue among people over time. Researchers play ideas off one another, adding their own thinking and research to a community of like-minded people. The texts you write are a contribution to the community's conversation, an attempt to change how the members of a community think or act.

Identifying Information You Need

Texts written from research can be driven by a **purpose** (doing research to choose a course of action), by their **audience** (doing research about or in relation to a person or group of people), by their **context** (doing research in response to a specific request or need), or by other **texts** (responding to or writing about other texts).

As you saw in Chapter 2, identifying your purpose, audience, context, and text are recursive, fluid processes that can start with any of the four aspects, moving among all four until you've developed enough of a framework to begin writing — or, in this case, doing the research that will inform the writing. Asking questions about each aspect can help you identify the information you need to gather in your research.

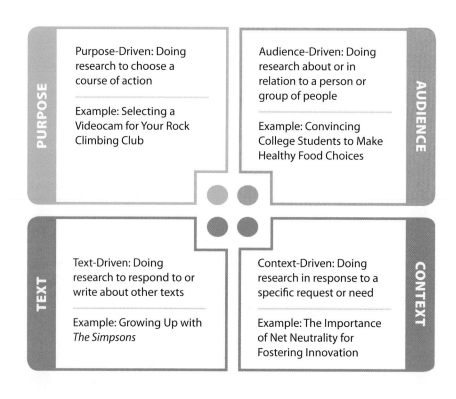

PURPOSE

Purpose-Driven: Doing research to choose a course of action

Example: Selecting a Videocam for Your Rock Climbing Club

AUDIENCE

Audience-Driven: Doing research about or in relation to a person or group of people

Example: Convincing College Students to Make Healthy Food Choices

TEXT

Text-Driven: Doing research to respond to or write about other texts

Example: Growing Up with *The Simpsons*

CONTEXT

Context-Driven: Doing research in response to a specific request or need

Example: The Importance of Net Neutrality for Fostering Innovation

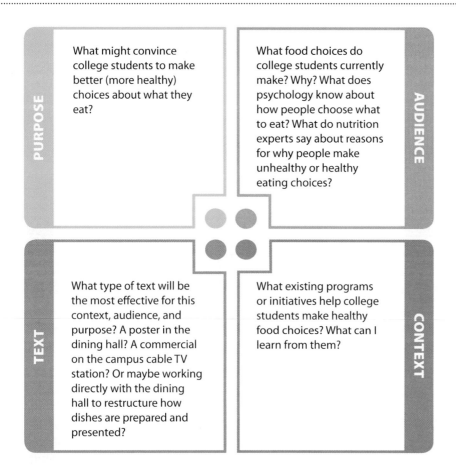

PURPOSE
What might convince college students to make better (more healthy) choices about what they eat?

AUDIENCE
What food choices do college students currently make? Why? What does psychology know about how people choose what to eat? What do nutrition experts say about reasons for why people make unhealthy or healthy eating choices?

TEXT
What type of text will be the most effective for this context, audience, and purpose? A poster in the dining hall? A commercial on the campus cable TV station? Or maybe working directly with the dining hall to restructure how dishes are prepared and presented?

CONTEXT
What existing programs or initiatives help college students make healthy food choices? What can I learn from them?

(If you need help coming up with questions, consult the PACT chart in Chapter 2 on pages 42–43 for ideas.)

Here's a quick example. Someone trying to convince college students to make better choices about foods they eat might decide to do research about underlying causes and potential solutions, as shown by the developing PACT chart above. The audience column suggests that some background reading in psychology and nutrition might be useful in coming up with strategies.

Likewise, writing a text about the importance of "net neutrality" (preventing powerful companies from controlling Internet access and speed by prioritizing some types of traffic over others) will involve asking questions about context (see the PACT chart on p. 158). In answering those questions, your work might spill over into other categories as you realize you need to do some additional research to find out whether you even need to create a text at all.

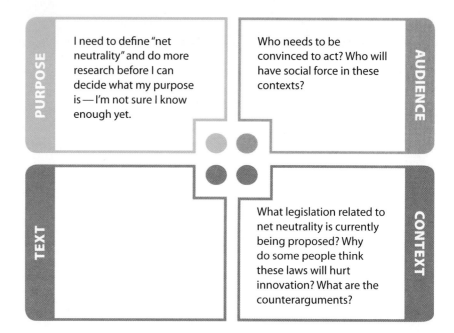

PURPOSE

I need to define "net neutrality" and do more research before I can decide what my purpose is — I'm not sure I know enough yet.

AUDIENCE

Who needs to be convinced to act? Who will have social force in these contexts?

TEXT

CONTEXT

What legislation related to net neutrality is currently being proposed? Why do some people think these laws will hurt innovation? What are the counterarguments?

Developing a Research Plan

As you begin identifying what information you need for your writing, think about how you're going to actually *get* that information (both the where and the how). Also think about the quality of the information you need. What information will best meet your readers' needs and your purpose? What evidence will convince them to make the change you're suggesting? For example, if your goal is to convince students that file-sharing programs clog the campus network, statistical data on network usage that identifies the cause of bottlenecks will likely be more convincing than quotations based on isolated, personal observations by students. Using your PACT notes to develop a research plan will help you make decisions about what kind of research to do and how to prioritize your research activities.

Decide What Kind of Research To Do: Primary or Secondary

Research can be broken into two main categories: primary and secondary. Primary research usually involves going directly to a source: interviewing someone about his or her work, for example, or conducting a survey to find out a group's attitudes. Secondary research involves reading *about* something: reading a journal article that summarizes primary research such as survey findings, for example.

Neither type of research is necessarily better than the other; they just differ in how close you get to the source of information.

Primary Research	Secondary Research
• Interviews	• Wikipedia
• Usability tests	• Web searches
• Surveys	• Specialized search engine or database searches
• Product tests	
• Observations of things or events	• Abstracts
• Measurements of things or events (at one time or over time)	• Books or journal articles
	• Documentaries or other video
• Direct comparisons among things	

In most cases, you'll want to start with some secondary research: If the information already exists, don't repeat the primary research unless you have good reason. It's better to use (and cite) that information and then build on it. If you were writing a research paper about poverty in the United States, for example, you probably wouldn't have the time, expertise, or sources to actually conduct census surveys and interviews (primary research activities); instead, you would probably want to access U.S. Census data about levels of poverty in a government web database (a secondary research activity). But if you wanted to include some information on income levels of students at your own university, you might want to conduct an anonymous survey of students at your school (a primary research activity).

Primary research usually requires more work. In this example, in addition to the work of doing the survey, you would probably also need to check whether the survey needs to be approved by your school's dean of students office or the institutional review board, which has to review and approve research on campus that involves human subjects. But you might find that the dean of students office already has this data and is willing to share it, turning your primary research plan into a simpler secondary research activity.

Primary and secondary research influence each other because a good primary researcher always does secondary research to see what's already been done (and what those doing it think about), while secondary researchers reflect on, critique, and synthesize the results of primary research to suggest additional primary research. In fact, most academic articles that deal with primary research include a significant section (called something like "Literature Review") in which the primary researchers discuss what secondary research has already been done. In writing projects, you'll also often do some mix of primary and secondary research, but the proportions of each will depend on your specific projects.

List and Prioritize Your Research Activities

Once you've used your PACT chart to think about what information you need and what types of research you should do, begin listing and prioritizing your research activities. Begin by listing out what information you need and where you think you can find it. Then sort the list based on the importance of the information: What issues are most crucial to convincing your audience? What are least crucial? Below is a partial list of issues arising from the food choices example discussed earlier. You'll see that the list includes both primary sources (talking to students and dining hall staff) and secondary sources (reading journal articles).

What Do I Need?		Where Can I Find It?
The psychology of food choice/ what makes us decide what to eat?	»	Psychology journals
Restrictions on school dining hall about what can be served, time constraints, etc.	»	Talk to a dining hall cook or search online for interviews or news articles
Surveys on how college students choose what to eat	»	Nutrition journals (online at library portal); ask some college students

Next, list the specific research actions you need to take. Be sure to write your actions out as concrete steps rather than general topics. With each action, write an estimate of how much time the task will take. For example, for your hypothetical research on file sharing,

Get info about file-sharing use on campus

is so general that it would be difficult to estimate how long this task might take. But something like

Contact IT department for bandwidth usage reports
Distribute survey on file-sharing use for students

provides enough information that you can estimate how long the tasks might take.

Then, for each action list any dependencies — things that must be completed before that task can be started. "Distribute survey," for example, would require you to have already created the survey.

Instructor's Manual

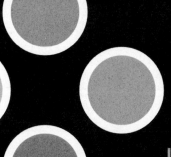

Changing Writing

A Guide with Scenarios

Johndan Johnson-Eilola

INSTRUCTOR'S MANUAL FOR

Changing Writing

A Guide with Scenarios

Johndan Johnson-Eilola
Clarkson University

BEDFORD/ST. MARTIN'S

Boston • New York

Contents

Introduction

This brief guide to teaching with *Changing Writing: A Guide with Scenarios* consists of several resources to help with your course planning, teaching, and assessment.

- **Three sample syllabi** illustrate different ways to combine the readings, scenarios, and exercises in *Changing Writing* for 15-week courses that meet two or three times a week. Each of these courses suggests a different emphasis: One culminates in the publication of a class online magazine; another emphasizes research. You can customize the syllabi and assignments by using the other resources in this manual.

- **Suggestions for teaching the scenarios** offer ideas for adapting the scenarios in the integrated media for *Changing Writing* to create different types of assignments, as well as ideas for creating related activities to suit your course goals.

- **The index of scenarios and exercises** lists all of the book's exercises, scenario connections, and scenarios according to the types of writing or course topics they involve. For example, if you wish to find assignments to support your teaching of argument, assignments that involve multimodal composition, or assignments that lend themselves to collaborative writing, this index can help you.

- **A sample rubric** suggests criteria for evaluating student work, including audio, video, and web projects.

- **A list of LaunchPad Solo contents** at the end of this manual suggests additional tutorials and activities that are available to students along with the scenarios.

Sample Syllabus 1

This syllabus for a 15-week course that meets three times a week includes seven scenarios, a research paper, collaborative writing, and peer review. It culminates in the publication of a class online magazine.

Week 1

HOUR 1

Discuss: Class introductions, syllabus overview

For next class: Read the introduction, How Writing Is Changing, pages 3–7; bring an example of a text type you use daily to the next class.

HOUR 2

Discuss: Introduction and text types

For next class: Read Chapter 1, Building a Framework for Reading and Writing, pages 8–14 (up to "Applying the Framework as a Reader").

HOUR 3

Discuss: Chapter 1, pages 8–14

For next class: Read Chapter 1, pages 15–30 (rest of chapter); do Chapter 1, Exercise 1 (PACT analysis of a letter to the editor).

Week 2

HOUR 1

Due: Chapter 1, Exercise 1

Discuss: Chapter 1, pages 15–30 (rest of chapter); Scenario 11, "A Story from Your Digital Life"

Activity: Chapter 1, Reflect & Discuss, page 17 (analyzing graffiti), OR Chapter 1, Texts for Analysis, page 28 (cigarette ad)

For next class: Read Chapter 2, Approaching Writing Situations, pages 31–47.

HOUR 2

Discuss: Chapter 2, pages 31–47

For next class: Scenario 11, "A Story from Your Digital Life"

HOUR 3

Due: Scenario 11, "A Story from Your Digital Life"

Discuss: Chapter 2, Texts for Analysis, page 44 (credit card ad)

Activity: Chapter 2, Reflect & Discuss, page 32 (household disagreement)

For next class: Chapter 2, Exercise 1 (essay analyzing TV ads)

Week 3

HOUR 1

Due: Essay for Chapter 2, Exercise 1

Discuss: Scenario 1, "Advocating Voter Registration on Campus"

Activity: Guest lecture from writing center director or visit to writing center

For next class: Chapter 2, Scenario Connection 1 (creating a PACT chart for Scenario 1)

HOUR 2

Due: PACT chart for Scenario 1

Discuss: Peer review of PACT chart

For next class: Draft for Scenario 1

HOUR 3

Due: Draft for Scenario 1

Discuss: Peer review of drafts

For next class: Revise draft; read Chapter 3, Starting to Write, pages 48–56 (up to "Ideas and How to Have Them").

Week 4

HOUR 1

Due: Revised draft for Scenario 1

Discuss: Chapter 3, pages 48–56

For next class: Read Chapter 3, Starting to Write, pages 56–63 (up to "Moving from Ideas to a Draft").

HOUR 2

Discuss: Chapter 3, pages 56–63

Activity: Chapter 3, Reflect & Discuss, page 56 (strategies for generating ideas)

For next class: Read Chapter 3, pages 64–74 (rest of chapter); do Chapter 3, Exercises 1 and 2 — create a single short essay combining responses to both exercises.

HOUR 3

Due: Annotated photo and essays for Chapter 3, Exercises 1 and 2

Discuss: Chapter 3, pages 64–74; Scenario 5, "Creating a Parody Ad" (collaborative project)

Activity: Group discussion of scenario ideas

For next class: Draft for Scenario 5

Week 5

HOUR 1

Due: Draft for Scenario 5

Discuss: Full-class critiques of drafts

For next class: Begin revising draft for Scenario 5; read Chapter 4, Structuring Your Texts, pages 75–87 (up to "What about Introductions and Conclusions?").

HOUR 2

Discuss: Chapter 4, pages 75–87

Activity: Chapter 4, Exercise 4 (view TV commercial in class and analyze in small teams)

For next class: Read Chapter 4, pages 88–101 (rest of chapter); do Chapter 4, Exercise 3 (analyzing posted comments on the web); finish revising draft for Scenario 5.

HOUR 3

Due: Final draft for Scenario 5; Chapter 4, Exercise 3

Discuss: Chapter 4, pages 88–101; Scenario 19, "Repurposing a Text"

For next class: Choose your original text and new publication for Scenario 19; read Chapter 5, Designing Visual Texts, pages 102–18 (up to "Letters as Visual Design: Typography").

Week 6

HOUR 1

Due: Text and publication selected for Scenario 19

Discuss: Chapter 5, pages 102–18

Activity: Chapter 5, Reflect & Discuss, page 113 (gestalt principles)

For next class: Draft for Scenario 19; read Chapter 5, pages 118–39 (rest of chapter).

HOUR 2

Due: Draft for Scenario 19

Discuss: Chapter 5, pages 118–39; peer review of drafts for Scenario 19; Scenario 7, "Podcasting Campus Life for Prospective Students" (brainstorm in small groups)

For next class: Revise draft for Scenario 19; do Chapter 5, Exercise 3 (social cause button).

HOUR 3

Due: Button design for Chapter 5, Exercise 3; final draft for Scenario 19

Discuss: Group discussion of Exercise 3

Activity: Chapter 5, Texts for Analysis, page 134 (winter sunset photo)

For next class: Read Chapter 6, Managing Writing Projects, pages 140–54; draft podcast script for Scenario 7; start recommended activity from Chapter 6, Text for Analysis (organizing "My Documents" folder).

Week 7: Mid-Semester Break

Week 8

HOUR 1

Due: Podcast script for Scenario 7

Discuss: Full-class critiques of scripts

For next class: Read Chapter 7, "Getting Information and Writing from Research," pages 155–71 (up to "Being an Ethical Researcher").

HOUR 2

Discuss: Chapter 7, pages 155–71

For next class: Chapter 7, Exercise 1 (arguing against an article — this will be the basis for your research paper); read Chapter 7, pages 171–99 (rest of chapter).

HOUR 3

Activity: Library tour with research librarian (*Note:* Consider scheduling the library tour in a separate class period if there's time.)

Discuss: Chapter 7, pages 171–99

For next class: Report on results of Chapter 6, Text for Analysis (organizing "My Documents" folder); rough cut of podcast for Scenario 7.

Week 9

HOUR 1

Due: Rough cut of podcast for Scenario 7; report on results of Chapter 6, Text for Analysis (organizing "My Documents" folder).

Discuss: Full-class critiques of podcasts

For next class: Read Chapter 7, Text for Analysis (sample research paper); begin revising podcasts; find five professional sources for research paper and write an annotated bibliography.

HOUR 2

Due: Annotated bibliography including five scholarly sources for research paper

Discuss: Chapter 7, Text for Analysis (sample research paper)

For next class: Continue revising podcasts.

HOUR 3

Due: Final podcast for Scenario 7

Discuss: Play podcasts in class.

For next class: Research paper outline

Week 10

HOUR 1

Due: Research paper outline

Discuss: Peer review of research paper outlines; MLA format for research papers and works cited

For next class: Read Chapter 9, Revising Your Texts, pages 225–45; begin drafting research paper; bring to next class a section of one original text you're using for your research paper and a paraphrase you wrote.

HOUR 2

Discuss: Chapter 9; paraphrase assignment

Activity: Discuss tools for managing information (notes, bibliographic information).

For next class: Do Chapter 9, Exercise 3 (meet with a writing center tutor about draft of research paper).

HOUR 3

Due: First draft of research paper (*Note:* If you prefer to allow more revision time, make this draft due in Hour 2.)

Discuss: Responses to Chapter 9, Exercise 3; peer review of research paper drafts

Activity: Sign up for teacher conferences (10-minute blocks next week).

Week 11

Individual conferences by appointment. Revised draft is due by noon the day before your conference.

For next class: Finish research paper; read Chapter 8, Writing with Other People, pages 200–11 (up to "How to Give Feedback").

Week 12

HOUR 1

Due: Research paper

Discuss: Chapter 8, pages 200–11

Activity: Chapter 8, Reflect & Discuss, page 200 (your best collaborative experience) and page 207 (PACT chart)

For next class: Read Scenario 10, "Writing a Restaurant Review"; find an example of a restaurant review and bring it to next class.

HOUR 2

Discuss: Scenario 10, "Writing a Restaurant Review" (to be done in groups and include photos)

Activity: Assign teams for restaurant review; meet to brainstorm ideas for restaurant; schedule restaurant visit.

Activity: Full-class discussion of restaurant reviews; complete PACT charts.

For next class: Read Chapter 8, pages 211–24 (rest of chapter).

HOUR 3

Discuss: Chapter 8, pages 211–24

Activity: Discuss style sheets in Microsoft Word (use for restaurant review). (*Note:* If not using Microsoft Word, discuss style sheets in another application or the creation of style guides in general.)

Activity: Chapter 8, Exercise 1 (characteristics of good and bad team members)

Week 13

HOUR 1

Discuss: Scenario 6, "Writing a Profile for a Magazine"

Activity: Full-class review of a sample profile (the Background Text in Scenario 9 or another example)

HOUR 2

Due: Draft of restaurant review for Scenario 10

Activity: Full-class critique of restaurant reviews (*Note:* Consider inviting a local journalist to discuss restaurant reviews.)

For next class: Revise restaurant review; read Chapter 10, Publishing Your Texts, pages 246–60.

HOUR 3

Due: Final draft of restaurant review for Scenario 10

Discuss: Chapter 10; creating a class online magazine in WordPress (www.wordpress.org)

Activity: Review possible templates; vote on one for online magazine.

For next class: Conduct interview for Scenario 6.

Week 14

HOUR 1

Due: Bring notes from interview for Scenario 6.

Discuss: Interviews

For next class: Draft profile for Scenario 6.

HOUR 2

Due: Draft of profile for Scenario 6

Activity: Peer review of drafts

For next class: Revise profile; do Chapter 10, Exercise 2 (using media technology tutorials).

HOUR 3

Due: Final draft of profile for Scenario 6; Chapter 10, Exercise 2

Discuss: Chapter 10, Exercise 2

Activity: Using restaurant review teams, edit all restaurant reviews and magazine profiles for the class online magazine (edit for style, length, layout, and location of pictures).

For next class: Finish any editing not completed in class.

Week 15

HOUR 1

Due: Final layouts of reviews and profiles

Activity: Post restaurant reviews and profiles to class magazine site. Leave posts in draft mode for editing and proofreading. Assign teams to sets of articles.

Activity: In teams, review and proofread assigned set of articles.

Discuss: Visit from campus marketing staff member to discuss press releases

HOUR 2

Due: Final magazine articles

Activity: Publish magazine articles; write press release as a full class and submit to campus marketing office.

HOUR 3

Activity: Course summary and evaluations. If necessary, revise press release after feedback from campus marketing office.

Sample Syllabus 2

This syllabus for a 15-week course that meets three times a week focuses on research-based writing and omits Chapter 5 (Designing Visual Texts) and Chapter 10 (Publishing Your Texts). This syllabus includes four scenarios, two research-based papers (one short, one longer), and a series of short informal student presentations on writing tools. In the presentations, a group of two or three students will demonstrate technologies ranging from outlining features in Microsoft Word to surveying features in Google Drive to creating timelines in Excel. (You can preview Chapter 7 for some starting points if you like.)

Week 1

HOUR 1

Discuss: Class introductions, syllabus overview

For next class: Read the introduction, How Writing Is Changing, pages 3–7; bring an example of a text type you use daily to class.

HOUR 2

Due: Introduction and text types

Discuss: Chapter 1, Texts for Analysis

For next class: Read Chapter 1, Building a Framework for Reading and Writing, pages 8–14 (up to "Applying the Framework as a Reader"); do Chapter 1, Exercise 1 (PACT analysis of a letter to the editor).

HOUR 3

Due: Chapter 1, Exercise 1

Discuss: Chapter 1, pages 8–14; short overview of oral presentations on writing tools

Activity: Create presentation teams; begin thinking about what tools to present (selections due week 4).

For next class: Read Chapter 1, pages 15–30 (rest of chapter); do Chapter 1, Exercise 4 (e-mail inbox).

Week 2

HOUR 1

Due: Chapter 1, Exercise 4

Activity: In small teams, share Chapter 1, Exercise 4 responses.

Discuss: Chapter 1, pages 15–30 (rest of chapter); Chapter 1, Reflect & Discuss, page 10 ("Provençal Pizza" excerpt)

For next class: Read Chapter 2, Approaching Writing Situations, pages 31–47; do Chapter 2, Exercise 3 (letter to former self).

HOUR 2

Due: Chapter 2, Exercise 3

Discuss: Overview of software for creating posters (instructor's choice)

Activity: View three TV commercials in class and discuss responses to questions in Chapter 2, Exercise 1 (discuss only; omit essay).

For next class: Create PACT chart for Scenario 8, "Drafting a Poster about Online Privacy."

HOUR 3

Due: PACT chart for Scenario 8

Discuss: Talk about PACT charts for sample posters (instructor selected).

Activity: In small teams, compare PACT charts for Scenario 8.

For next class: Poster for Scenario 8

Week 3

HOUR 1

Due: Poster for Scenario 8

Discuss: Intro/tutorial on brainstorming and outlining software (instructor selected)

For next class: Read Chapter 3, Starting to Write, pages 48–63 (up to "Moving from Ideas to a Draft"); do Chapter 3, Exercise 5 (generating ideas and outlining an editorial) — use one or more applications demonstrated today.

HOUR 2

Due: Chapter 3, Exercise 5

Discuss: Chapter 3, pages 48–63; Research Paper 1 assignment overview; style guide (instructor's choice)

Activity: Small-group discussion of Chapter 3, Exercise 5 responses

For next class: Read Chapter 3, pages 64–74 (rest of chapter); do Chapter 3, Exercise 1 (analyze your own writing space).

HOUR 3

Due: Annotated photo and essay for Chapter 3, Exercise 1

Discuss: Identifying reliable, scholarly sources (see Chapter 7, "Tips for Avoiding Bias in Research" and Reflect & Discuss, page 172)

Activity: Library tour or visit from library staff

For next class: Read Chapter 7, Getting Information and Writing from Research, pages 155–73 (up to "Working with Sources"); Chapter 7, Exercise 1 (letter to the editor).

Week 4

HOUR 1

Due: Three ideas for Research Paper 1; Chapter 7, Exercise 1

Activity: In small groups, exchange Chapter 7, Exercise 1 responses. Read your partner's letter to the editor and discuss whether you agree or disagree and why.

Discuss: Research as a communal practice (instructor shares a scholarly article he or she wrote or read in grad school, discusses connections to previous work); review bibliographic style guide (instructor's choice).

For next class: Read Chapter 7, pages 173–99 (rest of chapter); create annotated bibliography including at least three scholarly sources; form teams for writing tool presentation.

HOUR 2

Due: Annotated bibliography (three scholarly sources); your team's choices for writing tool presentation

Discuss: Chapter 7, Text for Analysis, page 184 (sample research paper); how to track sources

Activity: Explore word-processor features (instructor's choice; likely options include style sheets, commenting features, track changes, running header/footer, autotext); sign up for writing tool presentation dates.

For next class: Chapter 7, pages 173–99 (rest of chapter); create annotated bibliography including at least six scholarly sources; bring texts to class as well.

HOUR 3

Due: Annotated bibliography including at least six scholarly sources; bring texts to class as well.

Discuss: Overview of structure in research papers; choosing when to summarize and when to quote

Activity: In pairs, select one of the texts that you've gathered for the bibliography (one per team) and analyze its structure using concepts from the textbook.

For next class: Read Chapter 4, Structuring Your Texts, pages 75–101; bring research notes to next class; draft outline for Research Paper 1.

Week 5

HOUR 1

Due: Research notes and outline for Research Paper 1

Activity: Small-team reviews of outlines

Discuss: Research plans and timelines; compare research notes in small groups and discuss strategies.

For next class: Work on full draft of Research Paper 1 (due Hour 3).

HOUR 2

Discuss: Team 1 Writing Tool Presentation

Activity: Work on Research Paper 1 for remainder of hour.

For next class: Draft 1 of Research Paper 1

HOUR 3

Due: Draft 1 of Research Paper 1

Discuss: Short overview of peer-review guidelines

Activity: Peer review of research paper draft

For next class: Write a summary of your revision plans based on peer reviews; revise Research Paper 1.

Week 6

HOUR 1

Due: Draft 2 of Research Paper 1 with summary of revision plans

Activity: Sign up for Research Paper 1 meetings with instructor.

HOUR 2

No class: Individual meetings with instructor to discuss Research Paper 1. Bring your research notes and something to take notes with (pen and paper or laptop).

For next class: Revise Research Paper 1.

HOUR 3

Due: Final draft of Research Paper 1

Discuss: Team 2 Writing Tool Presentation

For next class: Three ideas for Research Paper 2; read Chapter 6, Managing Writing Projects, pages 140–54.

Week 7: Mid-Semester Break

Week 8

HOUR 1

Due: Three ideas for Research Paper 2

Discuss: Chapter 6, pages 140–54

Activity: Create timelines (choice of software up to instructor); start working on a timeline for Research Paper 2 using known dates from syllabus.

For next class: Chapter 6, Exercise 1 (analyzing file organization)

HOUR 2

Due: Chapter 6, Exercise 1

Discuss: Outlining software

Activity: In small teams, break this large project into at least 10 smaller tasks: buying a new car after you graduate and take your first job. Where do group members disagree about steps? Why? (*Note:* You could also make this an assignment to be completed before class.)

HOUR 3

Discuss: Style and voice in scholarly sources; copyediting and proofreading

Activity: Edit a sample text for clarity, strong voice, grammar, and punctuation; share results with small group. How do your editing and proofreading decisions differ? Why? (Use the sample text your instructor provides or Chapter 8, Text for Analysis, page 216.)

Activity: Share results for Chapter 6, Exercise 1. Do you notice any similarities? Differences? Strategies you might adopt?

For next class: Timeline for Research Paper 2; Chapter 6, Exercise 2 (interviewing a faculty member about file organization)

Week 9

HOUR 1

Due: Timeline for Research Paper 2; Chapter 6, Exercise 2

Activity: In small groups, share results of Chapter 6, Exercises 1 and 2 (both students and faculty). Are there differences between faculty and students? Are all faculty alike?

Discuss: Each team reports back three key findings to class.

For next class: Annotated bibliography for Research Paper 2 (at least five sources)

HOUR 2

Due: Annotated bibliography for Research Paper 2 (at least five sources)

Discuss: Team 3 Writing Tool Presentation

Activity: Small-group review of bibliographies; Chapter 6, Exercise 3 (images of workspaces)

For next class: Read Chapter 9, Revising Your Texts, pages 225–45; begin drafting Research Paper 2.

HOUR 3

Discuss: Chapter 9, pages 225–45

Activity: In small groups, provide feedback (summary and marginal) to the writer of the Chapter 9 Text for Analysis. Exchange feedback with another team. Read the feedback you were provided. How does it make you feel? Will it help during revising? Is it detailed and concrete or vague and hesitant? What might you tell the reviewer to do differently in his or her review?

For next class: Annotated bibliography for Research Paper 2 (at least 10 sources)

Week 10

HOUR 1

Due: Annotated bibliography for Research Paper 2 (at least 10 sources)

Discuss: Review strategies for providing feedback.

Activity: Small-group reviews of bibliographies

For next class: Chapter 9, Exercise 5 (your strengths and weaknesses)

HOUR 2

Due: Chapter 9, Exercise 5

Discuss: Team 4 Writing Tool Presentation

Activity: Small-group discussion of Chapter 9, Exercise 5 responses

For next class: Outline for Research Paper 2

HOUR 3

Due: Outline for Research Paper 2

Discuss: Scenario 9, "Educating Users about E-mail Scams"

Activity: In small groups, work through the scenario in class; create a 500-word article for a newsletter.

Week 11
HOUR 1
Activity: Finish Scenario 9 in class.

For next class: Begin drafting Research Paper 2

HOUR 2
Due: Scenario 9

Discuss: Team 5 Writing Tool Presentation

For next class: Draft 1 of Research Paper 2

HOUR 3
Due: Draft 1 of Research Paper 2

Discuss: Weblog software overview for final project (instructor's choice: WordPress, blogger; could opt for print magazine)

Activity: Sign up for authoring privileges, create one post, insert one graphic.

For next class: Draft 2 of Research Paper 2

Week 12
HOUR 1
No class: individual meetings with instructor for Research Paper 2

For next class: Revision plan for Research Paper 2

HOUR 2:
Discuss: Team 6 Writing Tool Presentation

Activity: Work on revising Research Paper 2 in class.

For next class: Final draft of Research Paper 2

HOUR 3
Due: Final draft of Research Paper 2

Discuss: Scenario 19, "Repurposing a Text" (use as the basis to revise either Research Paper 1 or 2 for mass audience)

For next class: Read Scenario 20, "Revising a Campus File-Sharing Policy."

Week 13
HOUR 1
Discuss: Scenario 20, "Revising a Campus File-Sharing Policy"

Activity: Break into teams for Scenario 20; begin work in class.

For next class: Timeline for Scenario 20

HOUR 2

Due: Timeline for Scenario 20

Discuss: Team 7 Writing Tool Presentation

For next class: Scenario 20 short memo; revision plans for a repurposed paper for Scenario 19

HOUR 3

Due: Scenario 20 short memo; revision plans for a repurposed paper for Scenario 19

Activity: Full-class review of Scenario 20 short memos

For next class: Draft 1 of file-sharing policy for Scenario 20

Week 14

HOUR 1

Due: Draft 1 of file-sharing policy for Scenario 20

Activity: Full-class review of policies for Scenario 20

For next class: Final draft of Scenario 20 policy and memo

HOUR 2

Due: Final draft of Scenario 20 policy and memo

Discuss: Team 8 Writing Tool Presentation

Activity: Short tutorial on image editing and cropping for web publication

For next class: Draft 1 of repurposed paper for Scenario 19

HOUR 3

Due: Draft 1 of repurposed paper for Scenario 19

Discuss: Web publishing platform (Instructor's choice: WordPress, Blogger, etc.; could substitute a traditional print magazine if desired)

Activity: Small-group review of repurposed papers

For next class: Images for repurposed paper

Week 15

HOUR 1

Due: Images for repurposed paper (copyright cleared)

Activity: Small-group discussion of images and repurposed paper; assignment of table of contents page and articles to student teams for editing, proofreading, and posting to website

For next class: Final draft of repurposed paper for Scenario 19

HOUR 2

Due: Final draft of repurposed paper for Scenario 19

Activity: Finish editing, proofreading, and posting articles to website.

HOUR 3

Discuss: Course summary

Activity: Course evaluations

Finals Week

Course website completed.

Sample Syllabus 3

This syllabus assumes a 15-week course with two class periods per week. It includes four scenarios and culminates with a research paper.

Week 1

HOUR 1

Discuss: Introductions; syllabus overview

Activity: In small groups, talk about where you write (how it looks, what's around you, what your routines are, etc.).

For next class: Read introduction, How Writing Is Changing, pages 3–7; bring a piece of writing you like to next class (fiction, nonfiction, song lyrics, etc.) along with a PACT chart you've completed for that text.

HOUR 2

Due: PACT chart for a piece of writing you like

Discuss: Sampling of texts you brought in (instructor starts); what counts as a "text"?

Activity: In small teams, pick one text and discuss how it could be translated to a new medium (poem becomes short story, play becomes news broadcast, etc.). What would be gained? What lost? How would the PACT chart change?

For next class: Read Chapter 1, Building a Framework for Reading and Writing, pages 8–30; read Chapter 1, Texts for Analysis, page 21 (Twitter instant-messaging etiquette).

Week 2

HOUR 1

Due: Chapter 1, Texts for Analysis (Twitter instant-messaging etiquette)

Discuss: Chapter 1, pages 8–30

Activity: In small groups, create a list of etiquette tips for another technology (be sure to create a PACT chart to guide your work).

For next class: Read Chapter 2, Approaching Writing Situations, pages 31–47; read Scenario 2, "Teamwork Problems."

HOUR 2

Discuss: Chapter 2 and Text for Analysis, page 44 (credit card ad)

Activity: Visit to writing center or in-class visit from staff; assign teams and start work on Scenario 2.

For next class: Scenario 2

Week 3

HOUR 1

Due: Scenario 2

Activity: Teams present their Scenario 2 responses (rest of class takes instructor role and responds to each).

For next class: Read Chapter 3, Starting to Write, pages 48–56 (up to "Ideas and How to Have Them"); do Chapter 3, Exercise 1 (analyzing your writing space).

HOUR 2

Due: Chapter 3, Exercise 1

Discuss: Writing tools demonstration (instructor's choice)

Activity: In small groups, share Chapter 3, Exercise 1; discuss what you like and dislike about your space.

For next class: Read rest of Chapter 3, pages 56–74; read Scenario 9, "Educating Users about E-mail Scams."

Week 4

HOUR 1

Discuss: Invention strategies; Scenario 9 (limit scenario to 1,000-word article)

Activity: Small groups brainstorm ideas for Scenario 9 article (but final article will be individually written).

For next class: Scenario 9

HOUR 2

Due: Scenario 9

Activity: Small groups share Scenario 9 responses; each group selects one to read to rest of class.

For next class: Read Chapter 4, Structuring Your Texts, pages 75–101.

Week 5

HOUR 1

Discuss: Chapter 4

Activity: Full class diagrams the structure of a short text (Chapter 4 Texts for Analysis or instructor's choice).

For next class: Chapter 4, Exercise 3 (diagramming a comment thread)

HOUR 2

Due: Chapter 4, Exercise 3

Discuss: Alternate structures (return to activity from previous class)

Activity: Outlining software tutorial (in word processor or separate app)

For next class: Chapter 5, Designing Visual Texts, pages 102–18 (up to "Letters as Visual Design: Typography"); find examples of three different design principles from the chapter for next class.

Week 6

HOUR 1

Due: Examples of three different design principles

Discuss: Chapter 5, pages 102–18

Activity: Small groups share design principle examples and then share most interesting with rest of class.

For next class: Chapter 5, Exercise 1 (analyze an artistic painting); read Scenario 5, "Creating a Parody Ad," and choose topic for your ad.

HOUR 2

Due: Chapter 5, Exercise 1; topic for Scenario 5

Activity: Small-group discussions of Chapter 5, Exercise 1

Activity: Full class designs a visual text (instructor's choice — possibly a poster recruiting students to this class); basic tutorial on image-editing software (instructor's choice); tips on using stock image sites

For next class: Read Chapter 5, pages 118–39 (rest of chapter), and Chapter 6, Managing Writing Projects, pages 140–54

Week 7: Mid-Semester Break

Week 8

HOUR 1

Discuss: Chapters 5 and 6; research paper project

For next class: Chapter 6, Exercise 1 (analyzing file organization); Scenario 5 ideas (PACT diagrams and sketches for three possible ads)

HOUR 2

Due: Scenario 5 ideas (PACT diagrams and sketches for three possible ads)

Activity: In small groups, review Scenario 5 ideas.

For next class: Read Chapter 7, Getting Information and Writing from Research, pages 155–80 (up to "Using Sources"); list initial ideas for research paper.

Week 9

HOUR 1

Due: Scenario 5 ad; initial ideas for research paper

Discuss: Chapter 7, pages 155–80; style guides (overview different disciplines and then focus on style guide being used in this class)

Activity: Small-group review of Scenario 5 drafts

For next class: Read Chapter 7, pages 180–99 (rest of chapter); timeline for research paper; begin revising ad for Scenario 5 (due Week 10, Hour 2).

HOUR 2

Due: Timeline for research paper

Discuss: Refining a research paper topic; how to hunt for sources

Activity: Library tour

For next class: Research paper topic and three annotated sources

Week 10

HOUR 1

Due: Research paper topic and three annotated sources

Discuss: Paraphrasing and quoting; why quotations and references are important (research/scholarship as an ongoing conversation in a discipline)

Activity: Paraphrasing and quoting exercise (give students text excerpts and ask them to paraphrase or quote from each using appropriate style guide rules)

For next class: Read Chapter 7, Text for Analysis, page 184 (sample research paper); do Chapter 7, Exercise 4 (use the notes you've made for the research paper so far).

HOUR 2

Due: Final version of ad for Scenario 5; Chapter 7, Exercise 4

Discuss: Chapter 7, Text for Analysis (sample research paper)

Activity: In small groups, discuss Chapter 7, Exercise 4.

For next class: Ten annotated sources for research paper

Week 11
HOUR 1

Due: Ten annotated sources for research paper

Discuss: Review of Chapter 4

For next class: Review your timeline for the research paper and make any necessary changes; use the Track Changes feature in Microsoft Word to highlight what you've changed. Write a brief list of issues you're having with this project.

HOUR 2

Due: Updated timeline and list of issues

Discuss: Moving from notes to outlines

Activity: Outline tutorial (in word processor or separate app).

For next class: Research paper outline

Week 12
HOUR 1

Due: Research paper outline

Discuss: Moving from outlines to drafts

Activity: Sign up for individual conferences.

For next class: Chapter 9, Revising Your Texts, pages 225–45

HOUR 2

No class: individual meetings with instructor

For next class: Research paper, draft 1

Week 13
HOUR 1

Due: Research paper, draft 1

Discuss: Revision plans

Activity: Small-group review of drafts

For next class: Chapter 8, Writing with Other People, pages 200–24; Scenario 10, "Writing a Restaurant Review"

HOUR 2

Discuss: Chapter 8, pages 200–24

Activity: Chapter 8, Exercise 1 (in small groups)

For next class: Research paper, draft 2; begin work on Scenario 10.

Week 14
HOUR 1
Due: Research paper, draft 2

Activity: Small-group review of research paper drafts; sign up for research paper draft conferences.

For next class: Bring notes from your small-group review to individual conference with instructor.

HOUR 2
No class: individual conferences on research paper drafts

Week 15
HOUR 1
Due: Scenario 10 draft

Activity: Full-class review of Scenario 10 draft

For next class: Revise Scenario 10 draft.

HOUR 2
Due: Final draft for Scenario 10

Discuss: Course summary; last-minute reminders and Q &A about research papers

Activity: Course evaluations

For next class: Research paper, final draft

Finals Week
Due: Research paper, final draft

Suggestions for Teaching the Scenarios

The scenarios in *Changing Writing* are designed to be flexible and adaptable. This section offers suggestions for adapting each of the scenarios and creating related activities to suit different types of assignments and course goals.

Scenario 1, Advocating Voter Registration on Campus

- Push the assignment toward one type of text to focus on different pedagogical goals: posters for work on visual design, editorials for textual skills, or formal presentations for work on oral presentation.

- To work on less formal (but still important) texts, consider asking students to construct a strategy and several samples for a social media platform (Twitter, Facebook, etc.).

- If you have time, include a required draft along with in-class feedback.

- Launch the assignment with primary research: Have the class brainstorm ways in which to gather concrete data (surveys of students, focus groups on existing voter registration materials, brief interviews with individual students, etc.). Assign a group to each research topic and give them one week to design and run their research projects. Groups report back to the class with results.

- If your class is near an election cycle (national or local), ask students to create their texts for publication. Consider asking a local voter registration worker or a balanced group of politicians to visit your class to discuss voting and citizenship. (Check with your campus administration regarding political activity on campus: Nonpartisan or balanced discussions are generally allowed, but biased coverage — inviting candidates of only one party — may not be.)

- Use this scenario's context, audience, and purpose as an opportunity for a short research paper on voter registration among college students. Ask students to find sources that will help them analyze the current situation, including what factors encourage or discourage students from registering to vote. The final section of the paper should argue for one or more specific strategies to employ on your campus for increasing student voter registration.

Scenario 3, Arguing for a Handwritten Letter? Or E-mail?

25

Scenario 2, Teamwork Problems

- Allow students to switch the scenario context from classroom to workplace. This shift might provide nontraditional students with an opportunity to connect their academic and corporate/organizational lives.

- Ask students to consider a situation in which they've let someone down. Ask them to create a PACT chart that describes how they responded — or should have responded — to the situation. How can they apply what they've learned from that experience in their plan for responding to this scenario?

- Assign a short (1,000-word) personal narrative to students in which they write about a problem they faced in a team context (academic or otherwise), how they felt about it, how they dealt with it, and how that experience affected them afterward.

- Put students into small groups and have them frame a response to the situation collaboratively.

- After they complete the assignment, ask students to take the position of the problematic team member. How might that team member respond to the text the students created? If the problematic team member wants to own up to the difficulties he created, how could he propose making the situation right? What response would convince both his teammates and his instructor?

- Ask the students to address their text to Jake rather than the instructor.

- Have students do research on teamwork before creating their texts. How do experts recommend dealing with problematic team members? What strategies might resolve the situation? Assuming there's still time left in the scenario before the project is completed, could students use this research to develop a PACT chart to address the situation without taking the issue to the instructor? (*Note:* This option could also function as a stand-alone assignment in the form of a short academic research paper.)

Scenario 3, Arguing for a Handwritten Letter? Or E-mail?

- Have students pick a relatively long e-mail they recently sent or received and translate it into one or more tweets. Let them write a short essay summarizing their thought processes during that work: How did the 140-character limit change their communication strategies? How did they choose what elements from the original e-mail to keep out or leave in? Did their grammar or spelling change? How effective would the message be in the new medium?

- Focus the scenario by asking students to take a position rather than arguing for both sides.

- Ask students to do online research on earlier forms of communication and write a short essay describing how one of those forms might have encouraged different habits (time and materials involved, reproducibility, dissemination, reading, etc.). You could focus the assignment by pointing students toward one specific technology (e.g., oral storytelling, hand-lettered book manuscripts, telegraph, stone tablets, papyrus scrolls) or leave the technology choice to the students.

- Challenge students to find the earliest complaint about a communication technology and its effect on people.

- Explore the visual rhetoric of handwriting by having students discuss examples of handwriting (an image search for "handwriting" on the web will offer a wide variety). Ignoring the textual content of the message, ask them to brainstorm adjectives for each example: Playful? Precise? Extravagant? Childish? Ceremonial?

- Assign a journal entry in which students write about what they like and dislike about their own handwriting. (If students' journals are online, consider having them complete this journal by hand, possibly scanning the results to post to their online journal.)

- Conduct an academic-style debate in class with each side supporting either handwritten letters or e-mail. Ask each team to select a spokesperson for the debate and then give each team 20 minutes to brainstorm supporting points; tell them to also identify counterarguments that they'll need to defend against. Debate the topic during the remainder of class (allow 5 minutes for post-debate analysis of weak and strong points).

Scenario 4, Making Invisible Things Visible: Mapping Data

- This scenario is relatively complex, so consider requiring multiple drafts with review and comments by you or students.

- You might focus the assignment by specifying some parameters, from picking a singular geographical region (e.g., the town your school resides in or each student's hometown) to providing an actual social issue (the location of public parks compared to socioeconomic factors). An initial phase of such a project might ask students to propose and then vote for what area to focus on.

- Assign a short personal narrative or journal entry in which students talk about differences in two geographical areas near where they grew up: economic, social, architectural, or otherwise. Ask them to describe how they felt as they were in each area and why.

- A shorter assignment could simply ask students to use the Questions to Keep in Mind to write a short paper that analyzes a specific map (one that they locate or that you provide).

- After a tour of library resources (onsite and web), assign students to write a short annotated bibliography on using maps for social change: three sources with complete bibliographic information (tell them what style guide to use) and a 100-word annotation for the article. If students need starting points, provide them with search terms such as "postmodern geography," "community mapping," or "mapping social change." You could also point them toward journals such as *Economic Geography, Political Geography, Urban Geography, International Migration Review* or ask them to locate the geography journals section in your campus library or library website.

- Ask students to find a political speech that makes claims about a specific region that the students test by actually mapping data.

Scenario 5, Creating a Parody Ad

- Create a more ambitious assignment by asking students to create 15- or 30-second TV or radio ads. (You might consider putting students into teams for this option.) If your campus has a student-run TV or radio station, see whether staff are willing to help your students produce the ads (and/or potentially run them).

- Create a shorter scenario in which students complete PACT charts and rough sketches but do not complete the polished final version of their ads.

- Ask students to research copyright law and write a short report — citing specific, appropriate sources — that describes whether (and why) these parody ads are legal or illegal (or somewhere in between). For example, is Adbusters legal in its use of Ronald McDonald's likeness?

- Include peer review where each student (or group if you're using that option) presents a rough draft of his or her ad for feedback.

- Choose some current campus initiative (e.g., recycling, wellness, community service) and invite someone involved to speak to the class about the initiative (why it's important, challenges faced, etc.). Have students use the initiative as the topic for their ads.

- Ask students to find parody ads online (have them search on "spoof ad" or "parody ad" if they need direction) and then complete PACT charts analyzing how each works. Discuss their findings in class: Are there common strategies?

Scenario 6, Writing a Profile for a Magazine

- Limit the assignment by asking students to interview each other for the magazine profile.
- Ask students to copy the text from a profile they find into a file and then annotate or analyze the rhetorical moves the writer makes in their attempt to construct an interesting profile. Have students look at both the high and surface levels, both the overall picture (a brilliant but flawed genius; a troubled artist; a humble, hardworking parent) and the details (a gleam in the eye, old but meticulously kept shoes, a firm handshake).
- Focus the assignment by selecting a single site for interviews: For example, ask a local senior center to coordinate interview subjects for your students. Have the students create general ground rules about length of articles, use of images, and other basics, then let them interview subjects and write short articles. For a briefer version, allow students to gather simple oral histories in the subjects' own words (rather than using the interview as a source for a profile).
- Create a class publication that includes the interviews (website, weblog, print magazine). You could also include other scenario material such as restaurant reviews from Scenario 10.
- To allow work in design, ask students to format their interview as if it were to appear in a magazine, complete with headings, multiple columns, pull quotes, images, and running headers and footers. After the interview, start the design discussion by looking at sample profiles in magazines, analyzing how they are structured.
- Allow the whole class to interview one visitor (a campus official, a local celebrity, an alumnus). Have each student write a profile based on the notes each takes during the interview. Share and discuss the profiles in class or in small groups: What different aspects did each decide to focus on? What aspects seemed to appear in many profiles? What features seemed to characterize the strongest profiles?

Scenario 7, Podcasting Campus Life for Prospective Students

- Shorten the assignment by asking students to do background research and create the written script (but not record the actual podcast).
- If your students have access to video equipment and editing software, ask them to create v-casts (video podcasts). These might include straight narration but also tours of campus locations.
- Put students into small development teams and have them create more ambitious (higher quality or more complex) texts.

- To generate ideas and raw material for podcasts, asks students to write first-person narratives about their single favorite location on campus. Have them describe what it's like for them to be in the spot (focusing on sensory data) and reflect on why they appreciate the experience.

- Invite someone from campus recruiting or marketing to talk to your class about current strategies, constraints, and audience research. Ask whether they'll provide feedback on the student podcasts or consider actually publishing the podcasts on your school's website.

- Switch the medium: Instead of a podcast, ask students to create a Flickr album, graphic novel, or 15-second radio promo.

Scenario 8, Drafting a Poster about Online Privacy

- Explore more design options by asking students to create three design sketches and get feedback during a class critique before choosing one to develop into a final draft.

- Ask students to create real or mocked-up web pages rather than posters.

- Have students analyze the rhetorical moves being made in actual cyberstalking incidents (a published account that you provide or one that they find in online press).

- Ask student to write a brief (500-word) essay defending a specific age at which people should have unlimited and unmonitored access to the Internet.

- Ask students to consider their own selves at the age described in this scenario. What arguments — logic, horror story, reputation, personal safety — might have convinced them to be careful about online privacy? What arguments might not have convinced them?

- Change the audience from students to parents. Ask students to talk or write about how their strategies would differ because of this change. (This would also be a useful follow-up discussion topic if students completed the original assignment: How would their strategies differ if they created posters for parents rather than students? Would a poster still be the best medium? How might their PACT charts change?)

- For a shorter assignment, have students do online research about cyberstalking or other online danger ad campaigns. Ask students to collect several examples and then create hypothetical PACT charts that explain the strategies employed in the ads. Also (or instead) assign a very short research paper about online privacy: What types of threats to youth are currently out there? How likely, statistically, are teens to experience invasions of their privacy for each type? What are the recommendations for recognizing and avoiding these threats?

Scenario 9, Educating Users about E-mail Scams

- Ask students to read PayPal's advice about avoiding scams before they work on their PACT charts.

- Focus the assignment on one specific medium. This can allow you to make the assignment simpler (e.g., by sticking with a short textual article for a newsletter) or more complex (by assigning 30-second video PSAs or posters). Narrowing the assignment to one medium can also allow you the ability to provide hands-on tutorials for that specific medium.

- Ask students to do research on fraud or scams targeted at senior citizens. Are there common strategies employed? Are there general strategies that seniors can use to avoid being tricked?

- Allow students to select a single example of an e-mail scam (or assign one specific example to all students). Have them complete a PACT chart for the scam and then write a 1,000-word essay that analyzes how that e-mail scam attempts to trick its audience.

- Partner with a local senior center to create materials that will actually be used at the center. Invite a staff member from the center to visit your class to discuss strategies. Organize a field trip to the center so that your students can talk to people about how they evaluate the trustworthiness of e-mail.

Scenario 10, Writing a Restaurant Review

- Limit the geographical scope of the assignment by having students review on-campus dining facilities.

- Have students reflect on the topic by writing a 1,000-word personal narrative about their favorite restaurant experience. Include sensory details, conversations, other participants (with the student or at other tables), descriptions of staff, and more. What made this visit special?

- Compare reviews by having students all visit and review the same restaurant. In class discussion, explore the reasons for differences among the reviewers. How objective do students think restaurant reviews are? Is it possible that some reviews varied due to random circumstances or personal tastes?

- Ask students to write a short, textual analysis of two reviews of a specific restaurant — one from a professional publication and one from a crowdsourced venue such as TripAdvisor or Yelp. How does the writing style of each differ? What are the goals of each venue and review? What are the pros and cons of each from the perspective of someone considering a visit to the restaurant?

- After the students complete their reviews, ask them to take the position of restaurant staff. Ask them to complete a PACT chart from the staff member's perspective.

- Ask students to imagine that they are staff members of the restaurant, writing a response that will be published along with the review. What strategies might they employ? What tone should the response take? Remind students that the audience for the response is not the reviewer but the readers who have just finished reading the review, which may have been positive, negative, or mixed.

- Transform this into a collaborative project: put students into small groups and have them visit a restaurant together. (For this option you may want to create a short list of restaurants to review, including on-campus options, and let students pick which team to join. This might help students avoid restaurants they're not inclined to visit due to restrictions based on diet, budget, or travel options.)

- Ask students to research this question and report back to class: When does a negative restaurant review stray into slander or libel? Have them cite specific cases or laws (including definitions of the terms).

- Expand the assignment by requiring students to create a two-minute segment designed to air on a local television or radio news or morning talk show.

Scenario 11, A Story from Your Digital Life

- Give students practice at working with new media by asking students to create two-minute videos that include personal narration and screenshots recreating their experiences.

- Help students learn primary research skills by having them interview one another in pairs or small groups to write individual or collaborative essays on their media experiences.

- Pivot the assignment by asking students to write about a nontechnical language learning experience. Ask them to reflect on a time when they found out something about language in general: a rhetorical move they made or observed, an amusing or a revelatory anecdote they experienced, or a linguistic roadblock they ran into.

- Ask students to learn to use the basics of a new communication technology (e.g., video or audio editing, weblog authoring, presentation app), keeping a diary so that they can write a short essay about their experiences.

Scenario 12, Analyzing Your Media Diet

- Give students public speaking experience by asking them to create and deliver five-minute presentations, including samples of the media they experienced.

- Focus on primary statistical research by having your class agree on a common framework for the diaries (categories, format, etc.) so that the diaries can be pooled and analyzed for trends (or lack thereof).

- After the assignment is completed, ask students to write (or just discuss) how they might have changed their methods to get better data: What parts of completing the logs were difficult? Are there gaps in the data? How representative or scientific do they think their data is?

- Switch the focus of the diary to a different type of communication: face-to-face personal interactions with other people, communication from teachers to class, reading textbooks for a class, use of consumer technologies.

- Ask students to locate three research-based articles on one specific medium they encountered (e.g., locate research on how teens use text messaging). Use this activity as a bibliographic exercise by requiring students to report their results in writing using a specific style guide's format and/or writing a summary of each article.

Scenario 13, A Day in Your Online Life

- An alternative version of this assignment could ask students to track all of their online communications, not just a single medium. This might offer more discussion about how each technology affords different types of communication.

- Ask students to summarize, in a short research paper, generational differences in adoption and ways of using a specific communication technology. Or, as a shorter assignment, ask students to locate, read, and summarize for the class a research-based article on differing uses of a specific technology — the differences could be due to age but also gender, economic status, geographic location, or something else. Ask the class to attempt to poke holes in the research, offering other explanations for the differences.

- Consider asking students to complete PACT charts for some of the communications they are analyzing. In their analyses, they can discuss any trends or other interesting features they note across the PACT charts.

- To focus more on visual rhetoric, you could ask students to chart the data in multiple ways (e.g., bar chart versus scatter plot), discussing which type of graphic seems to work best for the purposes of their analyses.

- Provide more focus (and opportunity for discussion) by requiring students to focus on one communication technology that they all use (the web, a word processor, etc.). Discuss similarities and differences among students in small-group or full-class discussions.

- Consider doing this assignment along with your students, especially if you choose the above option to focus on a single communication technology. Discuss with them any differences between your data and theirs (if any) and whether they seem due to generational, occupational, or other reasons.

Scenario 14, Designing Cover Art for Digital Music

- As a starting point to this assignment, ask students to write a short personal essay or journal entry in which they describe why they like a specific album, CD, or iTunes cover. What are the visual features that evoke strong feelings? What aspects of those feelings are based in nonvisual things such as memories that relate to listening to that music? Do they like the cover because of its design or in spite of its design?

- Although the scenario only requires creating a PowerPoint presentation, you could give students the opportunity to get some oral presentations skills by having them deliver the talk to the class. The class can then provide feedback on the design options presented.

- You might focus the assignment by giving students a specific genre of music to cover rather than leaving the choice up them. This would allow deeper discussion of design conventions within that specific genre.

- Convert this to a real-world project by having students work with actual musicians and bands. (This option would work particularly well if your school has a music or performing arts department.)

- Put a spin on the assignment by asking students to take a cover in one genre to translate into another genre. Or take a cover from one historical era and rework it to fit within a different era. Or both: For example, allow them to take a 1970s Led Zeppelin album cover and redesign it in the mode of a 1950s-era Blue Note 1500-series bebop cover. Doing so would also open up opportunities to more discussion about how genres are created and modified within communities.

Scenario 15, Designing an Organization's Graphic Identity

- For a shorter version of this assignment, have students reverse-engineer a graphic identity manual. Give them a range of texts from an organization and ask them to describe what rules guide the graphic identity revealed in the texts. What determines type, color, logo or logotype use, or other features that are consistent across the group of texts? Lead a short guided class discussion based on a single group of texts from an organization or allow students to form small teams.

- Assign an analysis paper in which students identify categories in logo or logotype design for a specific category of organization (soft drink brand, political group, grocery store, auto company, etc.). Locate at least 10 examples of logo or logotype and sort them into categories. What are the visual features that mark each category? What are the rhetorical reasons behind those visual features (e.g., some automotive logos connote history and tradition while others point to innovation using specific visual strategies).

- As a short take-home assignment with follow-up class discussion, ask students to pick an organization that has a large web presence. Complete a generic PACT chart for the organization and bring it to class for discussion: Who are the audiences and contexts for that organization's work? What overall purpose does the organization have? How does the graphic identity of the organization work to support these things?

- Ask someone from your campus marketing office (or other relevant office) to talk about how your campus achieves a coherent graphic identity across its texts. If the marketing group has an official (or unofficial) set of graphic identity guidelines, ask your representative whether he or she can share them as part of class discussion.

- As a journal assignment or short personal essay, ask students to write about a commercial product that they have a relatively strong allegiance to (one that's associated with a visual identity element such as a logo, brand color, or even font). Can they see any connection between the visual aspect of the visual identity element and their feeling about the product itself? For example, Coke undoubtedly hopes its freehand script logotype corresponds to consumer's experiences: playful, bright, casual, and easygoing. (The same logo in a typewriter-inspired font like Courier would be a mismatch.)

- Allow students to switch the context: Rather than develop a graphic identity for an organization, ask them to develop one for themselves. Require them to complete the PACT chart to set a specific context. Are they going on the job market after graduation? Are they forming a startup company or opening a freelance consultancy? Are they in a band? Perhaps just looking to create a distinctive identity for the texts they write (e.g., letters, Twitter, or Facebook homepage)?

Scenario 16, Designing a Website for Doglake Records

- This is a fairly complex project, so it might work well as a team or even full-class assignment.

- This scenario might also work well as a simple class discussion: Develop a PACT chart as a full class. Ask students to sketch (with pen and paper or in a layout program) some very quick designs over the course of 20 minutes in class or before class. Then share the ideas in small teams or a full class. Vote on the most promising sketches.

- For a shorter assignment, assign students only a single page for the website (you can choose the page or allow students to pick one of the four described in the scenario).

- Start the project with some primary research. Ask students to write a short research paper in which they analyze the websites for five record labels in the same general genre as Doglake Records. What are the similarities across the five sites? What are the differences? Which seems the most likely to be successful? Consider both visual and textual elements of the sites.

- Ask students to select the website for a record label they aren't familiar with and to then create a PACT chart for that label.

- Start a discussion about genre by putting students into teams to analyze sites for specific genres of music. Each team will pick one type (punk, pop, classic country, etc.) and find five labels in that genre. Ask them to describe (in a short written or oral report) what similarities they found across the five sites and what differences they found. The students should look at all visual aspects of the main page: structures, colors, type, tone, content, graphics, and more.

Scenario 17, Designing a Newsletter for the Zeeland Farmers' Market

- If the season's right, ask students to visit a local farmers' market. Take notes about the customers and vendors: How do people portray themselves? How do they dress and act? What do they say? How are the booths configured, both the contents of single booths and the relationship among booths? Have students use their notes as primary resources as they complete a PACT chart for their Zeeland Farmers' Market newsletter.

- Allow students to form functional teams to complete the assignment. Teams will assign members to these roles: manager, copyeditor, photo editor, layout artist. If your class has completed Chapter 6, Managing Writing Projects, have them complete a Gantt chart to organize their work.

- Create a briefer version of this assignment by having students locate an existing farmers' market newsletter online that needs significant revision. Ask them to use the content of the existing newsletter to create a new version. (*Note:* Avoid publishing the new versions, both for reasons of copyright and ethics. Farmers' markets are chronically understaffed and underfunded, so public critique would reflect badly on your class. You might consider requiring your students to select only out-of-state markets to lessen the chance of exposure.)

- Have students research the locovore movement, which encourages people to eat food that is produced locally. Have them use reliable objective sources to write a short article for the newsletter (using that research) that encourages people to shop at their local farmers' market.

- Focus on textual revision by giving students one or more of the longer texts included in the assignment. Have them copy the text into a word processor and edit the story to improve it. You could also provide a target word count that will require decreasing the length of the story by 25 percent or more. Ask them to write a short explanation of the decisions they made during editing.

Scenario 18, Creating a Facebook Page for an Organization

- If students already belong to organizations that have a Facebook presence, allow them to redesign those organizations' pages.

- For a much shorter assignment, ask students to read the Background Text. Then have them pick an existing business with a Facebook Timeline. Write a short report or give a short presentation that analyzes the business's timeline given the advice in the background reading. (You might also use this as a launching activity for a variation of the scenario that asks students to redesign an existing Facebook Timeline.)

- As a supplement to the assignment, ask students how a business's Facebook goals differ from a person's. Are there elements in the PACT chart for each that are very different? Would some use different terms for the same thing (e.g., "sale" for business versus "like" for an individual)?

- Assign a journal entry in which students reflect on how and why they use Facebook. For those who do not use the site, ask them to reflect on why. Or if they used to use the site but have now stopped, describe what motivated that decision.

- For an assignment on genre, ask students to pick an organization that has a Facebook Timeline as well as other social media or web presence (website, Pinterest or Tumblr page, Twitter account, etc.). Have them create PACT charts for two of the texts. Use the PACT charts to discuss how and why each text differs.

- Create a Facebook presence for your class and have the class create content for a timeline over the course of the semester. Initially students could submit potential content to you for decisions about what to run; later you could put individuals or teams in charge of creating the timeline.

Scenario 19, Repurposing a Text

- Allow comparisons across student work by assigning all students the same source text. (Choose something specialized but not too complex for students to follow.) After they've completed the assignment, put them into small teams to share the results. Ask them to talk about how each version differed. What did each decide to focus on? What did each omit? Were there similar strategies?

- Scale back the complexity of the original text by specifying a simpler target audience for the repurposed text: Give them a government report on nutritional needs for children and ask them to translate that into an elementary school cafeteria poster or a short story. (Allow students to further specify the age group if they like — for some issues, there's a big difference between kindergarteners and sixth graders.)

- Shorten the assignment by asking students to complete a PACT chart for both background texts. For a slightly longer assignment, have them then describe how material from the source text was translated, summarized, edited, and otherwise changed as the mass-market text was written.

- After students have completed the assignment, have them copy the text of the source text and their new text into a website that generates a word cloud or text cloud. Ask them to write a short essay comparing the two clouds: What does each tell them about the type of language used for each text's specific audiences, contexts, and purposes? Were they surprised by what each cloud showed? What types of things were different between the two clouds: Length of words? Variety of words? Abstractness or concreteness? Alternately, you could have students generate the clouds and then share them with one another in small groups or as a class.

- Fact-check work by having students trade sources and new texts. (You could use this activity to guide peer review after a first draft of the new article.) After reading both, ask the fact checkers to answer these questions: What information was dropped in the next text? What terminology was changed? Does the new article honestly represent the material from the source article? Will a general audience be interested in reading this? Why or why not? What might you suggest changing in a subsequent draft?

Scenario 20, Revising a Campus File-Sharing Policy

- To allow students practice in primary research, ask small teams to conduct surveys or interviews with campus residents (other students, faculty, IT staff, etc.). Use that research as background for working on the scenario.

- Anchor the assignment in your local context by having students work with your existing campus policy on file sharing or appropriate use of technology.

- A briefer assignment might include only one of the two assigned documents.

- Provide students with more rhetorical agency by allowing them to take a stance that opposes increased restrictions on file sharing (e.g., by pointing out legal uses or proposing education).

- Ask someone from the IT staff on your campus to visit your class to discuss the impact (legal, technical, and ethical) of file sharing.

- Ask students to do secondary research on laws about file sharing. Have them write a brief report (1,000 to 1,500 words drawing on at least three sources) that analyzes the legal obligations of the university to detect and stop illegal file sharing.

Index of Scenarios and Exercises

Looking for a particular type of assignment in *Changing Writing*? This index will help you choose scenarios and exercises from the text to fit your course goals and outcomes.

Sample Rubric

This rubric provides some sample criteria for evaluating student work. Note that not all elements will be relevant to every assignment. Pick and choose the categories and criteria that are most useful to the pedagogical goals of each assignment. Many of these will need to be adjusted for different text types and purposes. For example, effective prose style in a personal narrative will differ from that in a research paper. You may want to lead a class discussion in which the rubric below is revised to accommodate a specific type of text. For example, texts written for Scenario 10, "Writing a Restaurant Review," could use a modified rubric that included elements drawn from that genre (with more emphasis on sensory details, focus on three to five dishes, a section on ambiance, etc.).

Summary Comments: A short overview summarizing the most important aspects of the critique, highlighting major strengths and weaknesses. If appropriate, provide suggestions about revision strategies.

	Unacceptable	Limited	Adequate	Strong	Outstanding
STRUCTURE					
Genre/Media Choice: Writer chose an appropriate medium and genre for the writing situation.					
Genre/Media Mastery: Writer shows a mastery of the specific genre and media used.					
Effectiveness: The structure provided in the text supports the purpose of the text for its readers.					
Introduction: The introduction situates the reader, bringing them into the text.					
Conclusion: The conclusion summarizes or provides action for the reader to take (as appropriate).					

	Unacceptable	Limited	Adequate	Strong	Outstanding
Detail: The text provides detail where necessary to advance an argument, inform readers, or clarify a situation. Where appropriate, concrete sensory details are provided (including the use of audio and video in new media texts).					
Transitions: The writer provides readers with an effective path from one section of the text to the next. The movement from one section to the next seems logical and / or natural to readers.					

CONTENT

Purpose: The text has a clear purpose (even if that purpose is not specifically highlighted for readers). There are few or no unnecessary parts.					
Argument: The arguments (implicitly or explicitly) made persuade readers to agree with the text's purpose (in thought and / or action).					
Backing: Support is provided for claims made in the text, either through argument or by referring to reliable sources. The text documents external sources according to the conventions of the specific genre.					
Choice of Reference Form: The text makes effective choices among citation, paraphrase, and quotation to support the purpose of the text.					

SURFACE

Prose Style: The word choice and sentence structure are easy to interpret (as appropriate).					
Register or Tone: The text uses an appropriate tone according to the writing situation (formal or informal, casual or distant depending on the specific text type and purpose).					

	Unacceptable	Limited	Adequate	Strong	Outstanding
Grammar: The text adheres to appropriate (for the context and audience) grammatical conventions.					
Spelling and Punctuation: The text adheres to appropriate (for the context and audience) conventions of spelling and punctuation.					
Citation Format: The writer follows appropriate rules for citing information from other sources (dependent on the writing situation), including paraphrase and quotation, formatting of bibliographic information.					
VISUAL DESIGN					
Hierarchy: Elements on the page or screen use hierarchy to imply relative importance.					
Negative Space: Space is used to separate elements or groups of elements on the page or screen.					
Proximity: Groups of elements are grouped for a rhetorical purpose.					
Continuity: Viewer's eyes are drawn across the page or screen as necessary across different elements (or groups of elements).					
Figure/Ground: Important elements on the page or screen are foregrounded.					
Color: Appropriate color is used to highlight some elements while subordinating others. The overall color scheme is consistent with the purpose of the text. When appropriate, colors seem to be drawn from the same family (pastel, bright primary, grayscale, etc.).					
Typeface: The choice of typeface supports the text's purpose (including, where appropriate, hierarchy, aesthetics, and function).					

	Unacceptable	Limited	Adequate	Strong	Outstanding

AUDIO

Levels: The audio does not vary in relative loudness without a good reason. The levels are high enough to mask unwanted background noise (e.g., fluorescent light hum, equipment noise, outside sounds).

Distinctness: As appropriate, individual elements are identifiable.

Voices: Individual speakers are easy to identify and intelligible.

Background Sound: Background sound is appropriate to the text. Musical soundtrack, if used, supports the rhetorical purpose of the text.

VIDEO

Framing: Elements on the screen follow effective principles of visual design (see page 45).

Camera Movement: Any zooms, pans, or tracking shots are smooth and natural.

Lighting: The shots include lighting effective for the rhetorical purpose. Important objects on screen are highlighted and/or backlit.

Editing: Edits from one shot to the next seem natural (not unintentionally jarring). Edits exhibit a sense of rhythm that supports the purpose of the text (e.g., fast-paced edits heighten tension).

Transitions: Transitions from one cut to the next support the purpose of the text. Transition effects are not overused or used inappropriately (in most cases, minimal effects are better).

	Unacceptable	Limited	Adequate	Strong	Outstanding
Titling: Any text titles on the screen use a font appropriate to the purpose of the text. Titles are large enough to be legible at viewing distance and stay on screen long enough to be read easily. Visual design guidelines (see page 45) are used to structure the titles effectively.					
Resolution/Format: An appropriate resolution and file format is used (e.g., avoid very high resolution formats if being displayed on lower-resolution equipment; avoid file formats that users might not be able to view).					
WEBSITES					
Chunking: Information is broken into chunks for ease of skimming by web readers. Long texts are broken into shorter pages.					
Hierarchy: Important information is easy to identify while secondary information (e.g., navigation links) is easy to find when necessary.					
Navigation Labels: Navigation links are labeled with appropriate short words ("Home," "Index," etc.).					
Site Architecture: For multipage sites, users have a clear sense of the overall shape of the site and their current location within it.					
Site Identity: The site makes clear who created it (important for discerning reliability).					
Speed: The page loads in a reasonable amount of time for intended users (e.g., DSL users may not be able to view high-resolution video).					

	Unacceptable	Limited	Adequate	Strong	Outstanding
Copyright: Copyright status and remixing/reuse rights are made clear (either traditional copyright or a variant such as Creative Commons). Material on the site does not itself violate copyright. (This is an issue for any text, but violations on the web can be especially costly.)					
Miscellaneous: Guidelines for visual design, audio, and video (see page 46) are followed as appropriate. Materials are dated where necessary. Pages are viewable on intended users' computers (e.g., if users have smaller monitors, large images may not load; if users are on smartphones, small text may not be readable).					

OTHER COMMENTS

Assignment Specific: Any criteria that apply to a specific assignment or genre (e.g., effective subject lines in e-mail).

Off the Map: Issues (positive or negative) that fall outside the scope of the rubric or that you would like to call special attention to.

LaunchPad Solo Contents

In addition to the twenty scenarios referred to throughout this manual, LaunchPad Solo for *Changing Writing* at **bedfordstmartins.com /changing** includes the following tutorials and LearningCurve activities. LearningCurve offers adaptive, game-like quizzes that help students focus on the material they need the most help with. Students receive access to LaunchPad Solo free with purchase of a new book; students who buy used books can purchase access to the media for a reasonable fee.

Tutorials

CRITICAL READING

- Active Reading Strategies
- Reading Visuals: Purpose
- Reading Visuals: Audience

DOCUMENTATION AND WORKING WITH SOURCES

- Do I Need to Cite That?
- How to Cite an Article in MLA Style
- How to Cite a Book in MLA Style
- How to Cite a Database in MLA Style
- How to Cite a Database in APA Style
- How to Cite a Web Site in MLA Style
- How to Cite a Web Site in APA Style

DIGITAL WRITING

- Photo Editing Basics with GIMP
- Audio Recording and Editing with Audacity
- Creating Presentations with PowerPoint and Prezi
- Tracking Sources with Evernote and Zotero
- Cross-Platform Word Processing with CloudOn, Quip, and More
- Building Your Personal Brand with LinkedIn, Twitter, and More

LearningCurve

- Critical Reading
- Topic Sentences and Supporting Details
- Topics and Main Ideas
- Working with Sources (MLA)
- Working with Sources (APA)
- Commas
- Fragments
- Run-ons and Comma Splices
- Active and Passive Voice
- Appropriate Language
- Subject-verb Agreement

For longer research projects, sort out the tasks into a rough schedule. If you have access to dedicated project planning software such as Microsoft Project, OmniPlan, or Basecamp, use that. Project planning software usually includes specialized tools for connecting dependencies and allocating work to different people on a team. But even if you're not working with dedicated project planning tools, you can use a simple calendar or calendar software such as that in Google Calendar, Outlook, or iCal to sort out tasks to different dates. Refer to Chapter 6 for more strategies to help you manage writing projects.

Secondary Research: Finding Resources

Secondary research usually involves direct contact with fewer people than primary research, but it can still be overwhelming. Many people are baffled by the simple problem of knowing where to start. Others invariably take the path of least resistance: a search engine such as Google or Bing. Admittedly, this method can and often does work, but only if you are good at constructing search queries and analyzing the quality of the sources you find.

Web Research

Web research can provide you with excellent information, but it can also provide you with a lot of junk. In fact, for some types of information, it's easier to find junk and relatively difficult to find accurate sources of information. A web resource such as Wikipedia might provide useful background information on popular topics, but it probably won't suffice for most of your research projects. And general-purpose search engines — Google, Yahoo!, Bing, and others — are often much less useful than specialized resources. Searches on audio equipment such as speakers, for example, will frequently include an immense number of hits for stores selling the product, but far fewer hits on objective, informative reviews about the pros and cons of products. In general, you'll want to locate specialized sources for your work. Knowing a little bit about where to start and how to structure your research can go a long way toward getting you to the information you need.

All of that said, general-purpose sites are often very useful starting points, provided you know how to use them to get at more specific, specialized resources.

Library Research

Before the days of the web, libraries were the center of secondary research. But easy access to web-based resources has made the library seem obsolete. This is unfortunate because libraries can still provide

Tips for Web Research

- *Visit your campus library's website for access to online publications.* Libraries are often gateways to not only print but also online content, with access to hundreds of specialized online publications and databases. Nearly every campus library also has a reference desk that you can visit for expert assistance.

- *Use Wikipedia only as a way to find better sources.* Wikipedia can help you understand the basic outlines of a topic, but use it to help you find better, more specialized, and deeper sources. Follow links to other sites. Use specialized terminology gathered from Wikipedia articles to help you craft queries you can enter into Google or Bing searches.

- *When using search engines, combine specific terms with "resources," "news," "index," or related terms to find collections of resources on your topic.* For example, rather than searching on "drug policy," search on "drug policy resources."

- *Locate specialized search engines by adding "search" or "search engine" to your topic at a general search site.* For example, Google "architecture search" or "sports medicine search engine."

- *Learn advanced search engine techniques.* You can do this by searching yourself: Search on a term like "google power user" or "bing advanced searching." Even better would be asking an expert such as a reference librarian for tips.

- *For academic research, start with Google Scholar (scholar.google.com), which indexes content from academic journals, conference proceedings, and scholarly books.* It's often a good starting point when you don't know a field very well. As you start to find results from Google Scholar that seem useful, you can see whether the best sources you find are indexed by another, even more specialized search engine or database.

important resources, both materials to read and advice from expert researchers, that are unavailable on the web. And in some cases, they provide access to web-based information that might otherwise be locked away from general web research strategies.

Sometimes, your best bet is to talk to the pros — libraries have always been about access to information, and librarians have always been experts at locating information in a wide range of areas. Today, librarians know how to find not only print materials in the stacks but also materials in databases, on the web, and in other areas — not to mention research you might do that draws on video or audio, personal interviews, and more. Don't be afraid to ask the reference desk how to get oriented. Also check your campus library's website to see whether any research guides are available. Librarians often compile research guides like the one shown on page 163 to point users to the best journals, databases, and indexes in particular subject areas.

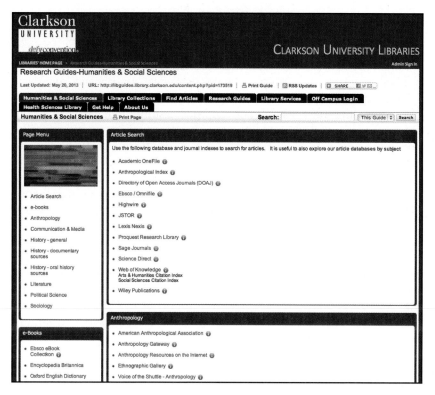

● Research guide for humanities and social sciences at Clarkson University's library website
Clarkson University Libraries screenshot reprinted by permission of Clarkson University Libraries

Another reason to visit the library is that, although an increasing number of publications are available on the web, a huge amount of material remains available only in print. Highly specialized materials and historical documents, to name just two resources, are still sometimes available only in print. Depending on your specific library, you might be able to search its catalog of print materials using its website. In addition, search facilities in library catalogs provide you with tools to hone your search request in more precise ways than are available in most web search engines.

Libraries are also frequently the campus gateway to both specialized databases and expensive web-based publications that aren't available to general users for free, such as professional journal articles (which sometimes cost tens of thousands of dollars per year for access). In some cases, you may have to access those items from one of the library's computers, but check to see whether your library's website allows campus users to log in to see materials that would otherwise be restricted.

Primary Research: Getting Information from People

Sometimes you need to go straight to the source. Primary research includes methods such as feasibility meetings, surveys, interviews, and focus groups. Use your PACT notes to help you figure out what type of primary research will be most useful. For example, assume your purpose is convincing readers that your campus can decrease fuel consumption, pollution, and traffic congestion on campus by reserving one prime parking lot for commuting carpoolers. If you're worried that the logical arguments in your proposal aren't strong enough to convince resistant readers, construct a survey that just asks drivers whether they'd carpool in exchange for better parking (free, closer to campus, or another attractive attribute).

When you're doing primary research, remember to keep your audience and context in mind: Are there going to be people opposed to your purposes? If so, they may discount your primary research, suggesting that it's incomplete, biased, or otherwise unreliable. Think carefully through your research methods and document them, making that documentation part of your argument. Many research projects include appendices that document their research methods at length. For very large research projects, outside agencies are often hired to help the research results seem objective.

Some colleges and universities have regulations about research involving people (surveys, cognitive or behavioral tests, and the like). See the discussion of institutional review boards in the section titled "Being an Ethical Researcher" (p. 171).

Simple Feedback or Feasibility Meetings

Many people spend hours (days or weeks even) working on projects only to find that their ideas won't be implemented. Perhaps the project has already been tried and was unsuccessful. Perhaps regulation prevents its implementation. Perhaps internal politics have put up an insurmountable block. The lesson is that a little bit of feasibility discussion at the start of a project will save you a lot of time.

Assume the campus cycling club you belong to wants to propose a free bike borrowing program for your community. In other communities, a fleet of simple, sturdy bikes is purchased and then simply left at bike stands around town. People borrow the bikes to get from one place to another, dropping them off at the bike stands when they're finished. People get some exercise, and pollution is decreased. The idea seems great on paper, and it's been successful in many communities.

Some quick web (secondary) research, though, unveils a couple of sticking points. Although the bikes have little resale value because they're easily identifiable as community (not personal) bikes, some communities have had problems with the bikes being vandalized. In some communities, opponents of the program protest the cost of the bikes and the upkeep. You find questions about liability: Will the town be liable if someone is hit by a car while riding a community bike? Do you need to also provide helmets? It's not clear that this program is necessarily an automatic win.

Maybe some primary research can help? Why not check with the town council to see what the political (and regulatory and legal) climate is before you spend several weeks writing up a formal proposal? Town officials usually have office hours. Why not call one of the council members and ask to meet with him or her to discuss the idea? You won't be bringing a finished document; you'll just be meeting with the council member to outline the idea, including its strengths and weaknesses, to see what you need to address when you do actually write the proposal.

When you meet, be sure to have some materials prepared (an outline or a list of questions), but don't create anything formal. As you talk about the project, take notes in the same way you'd take notes in a peer-critique session, as described in Chapter 8 on pages 209–11.

Surveys

There are many ways to connect with your future readers outside of class as you plan and create documents: Several sites offer free online surveys that can be used to collect feedback from various groups. Google Drive uses a variation of its spreadsheet document type to support surveys (which it calls forms). Using a special form layout tool in Google, you create a survey that you can then have users take. The results are automatically collected in a Google spreadsheet that you can use for analyzing data (or download for analysis using other programs such as Excel).

Survey design can be complicated because very small differences can sway people toward one answer (often without the survey designer even realizing it). You only have to look at surveys asking people for opinions about politicians to see how much variation there is from one survey to another, each supposedly asking about the same issue but with questions having slightly different wording.

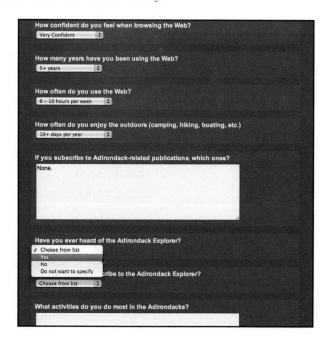

● Google Drive survey from the reader's point of view

● Google Drive survey from the form creator's perspective

Consider this hypothetical but not-out-of-character set of questions dealing with the same topic:

- Do you think welfare recipients should participate in random drug testing to receive benefits?
- Do you think people on welfare should be forced to undergo random drug testing before getting benefits?

The different connotations of a handful of words can be enough to push respondents toward one answer. The first sentence includes several positive-sounding terms ("recipients" and "receive"), while the second includes several negative-sounding terms ("forced" and "undergo").

Interviews

Interviews are excellent ways to get a rich body of information from people. Because you can adjust the questions you ask on the fly, you have more opportunities to let the developing interview change to fit the situation. You can prompt your interviewee to tease out additional information in ways that surveys or forms can't.

Interviews do require extra effort, sometimes a lot of extra effort, so use them only in cases where you need this flexibility and depth. For example, if you're not very familiar with the context, you might use a few interviews as a way to have someone guide you into understanding that context.

Part of the extra effort involved in interviews comes from the need to schedule the interview, prepare for it, and develop questions. You'll probably want to know a little bit about the person you're interviewing before you meet. If you look for information about people online, limit yourself to areas that are obviously public (public Facebook pages, personal web pages, and so on), and don't dig too far unless you're an investigative reporter with very good reasons. People are often surprised (and not in a good way) how much the web knows about them. If you're looking up information about someone you're writing about or will interview, will you be getting more information than they think you should? What will you do if you find information that you think the person would find embarrassing? The best advice is to tread lightly.

Interviews fall along a range from very structured or "closed" to semistructured or "open." Very structured interviews tend to be somewhat like interactive surveys with slightly more flexibility. Semistructured

> **Reflect & Discuss**
>
> Now might be a good time for you to consider your own online presence — you can bet that potential employers are likely to. View your own Facebook page from different profiles. Google your name (including nicknames) and see what you find. Do you need to remove anything from your online profiles? Do you need to change privacy settings?

Tips for Designing Surveys

- *Keep your language neutral and simple.* Look at key nouns, verbs, and adjectives to see whether they lead toward a certain stance.

- *Keep the survey short.* Consider how motivated your users are. Will they be willing to spend 30 minutes filling out your survey? In most cases, no. Test the survey, shooting for 5 minutes or less.

- *Be sure your data will be useful.* If the question is too vague or covers too wide or too narrow a range, it'll be hard to say exactly what the data shows. For example, if you're surveying users of a site designed for web programmers and ask them how many hours a week they use the web, would you offer these choices? 0 hrs   1 hr   2 hrs   3 hrs   4+ hrs

- *Don't ask questions that don't really get at your key issues.* In a survey on opinions about restrictions on smoking in public places, there might be differences in the opinions of Republicans, Democrats, and Independents, but would that information actually be useful for your purpose? Or is your question about political affiliation just taking up space (and people's time)?

- *Never ask the respondent's name unless you have a good reason for doing so.* Doing so may mean some people won't offer honest, open opinions or may not even participate. If you can make your survey anonymous (and verify that no one could identify who filled out a survey), you should do so. This is particularly important

(continued)

Tips for Designing Surveys
(continued)

if you're asking for information that might affect people's reputations or subject them to legal action. A survey that asks, "Have you ever sold illegal drugs?" for example, might lead to inquiries from local or federal law enforcement. Courts could require you to turn over the identities of your survey respondents. So think carefully about sensitive questions and about recording respondents' identities.

- *If you're planning on a large number of respondents (more than 20), use open-ended questions sparingly.* The responses may provide good quotes to use, but it's hard to say something statistically about one user's comment among one hundred responses. It's always good to offer a "Do you have any other comments?" field at the end of surveys, but if

your goal is to gather objective, statistical data, it's going to be hard to work with free-form comments.

- *Contrary to the above point, if you think your audience will be moved by concrete stories and comments, definitely include at least one free-form, open-ended question.* Although a simple "Any other comments?" field is better than nothing, consider including some directed questions to focus people a little: "What are the most promising aspects of this program?" or "What features should be changed?"

- *Before sending out your survey, test it by having a classmate or a friend fill it out.* Testing the survey can reveal questions that participants might not understand or other problems that you didn't anticipate.

interviews provide a more spacious and adaptable environment in which you and another person construct a shared understanding of something. So you need to provide some structure but also some unfilled space that your interviewee can fill. Some types of questions can be so closed that they don't provide space:

> *Do you like living here?*

will likely be met with a simple "yes" or "no." But something like

> *What parts of living here do you like?*

will allow a person space to talk a little more. And you could follow up with

> *Are there aspects you don't like?*

which lets them acknowledge that the situation can be complex rather than simply black and white.

Of course, a single interview will often contain a mix of closed and open questions. You might need to find out your interviewee's name (a closed question). Or if you're interviewing, say, 10 people, you might want to be able to give a percentage of people who agreed or disagreed

Tips for Conducting Useful Interviews

- *If it's not already clear to your interviewee, explain who you are and why you want to do this interview.* Tell the interviewee why his input is valuable to you (and, if it is, to him).

- *Allow time for questions.* Stop and say, "Before I go on, do you have any questions or comments?"

- *Don't go into an interview without plans.* At the very least, have a concrete list of topics you want to cover.

- *Have some method for taking notes, like a recorder or a laptop computer — the most reliable method is still a notebook and a pen.* Besides making sure you have data after the interview, taking notes shows your interviewee that her input is important.

- *If there will be some follow-up step after the interview, make sure you let the interviewee know what it will be.* If you'll be quoting the interviewee in a final text, you may want to ask whether you can give him a draft of your text so he can verify the comments. Even if his direct involvement won't be required, telling the interviewee where his information will be used helps him place his input into the overall process.

- *Thank the person you're meeting with before leaving.* Consider following up later with an additional thank-you e-mail or even a card.

with a position, in which case you might force them to choose one side or another with a closed question. But you could also then follow up with an open question that allows people to provide more detail you can use to flesh out your text.

Focus Groups

Focus group meetings allow you to invite representatives from a community into a meeting where you ask them to discuss, among themselves, a set of questions or issues while you take notes or video-record. Most commonly used by marketers to test how potential customers feel about products in development, focus groups are also used in a much wider range of contexts, including website usability, product design, sociology, and political science.

Focus groups can be useful for early exploration of a topic because the participants can reveal ideas or opinions you might not have thought of on your own. Comments from one person can spark ideas from other participants. New information can be teased out as people criticize other ideas and defend their own.

You may occasionally need to step in to manage the group because the strengths of the focus group format are also sometimes its weaknesses. At the end of a lengthy, lively discussion you might realize the group has just spent 20 minutes talking about a slightly related but

Tips for Running Focus Groups

- *Meet in a comfortable space where all the participants will be able to see and hear one another well.* If possible, a small meeting room with conference tables and chairs will work best.

- *Open the meeting by welcoming the participants, thanking them for their support, and briefly explaining what they'll be doing (including how long the meeting will take).*

- *Allow participants to express feelings and opinions.* Ask concrete, open-ended questions that will lead to rich responses. For example, rather than asking, "Do you recycle?" (which might just lead to a room of yes and no votes), you might ask, "What things prevent people from recycling?"

- *Ask people to respond to things such as mockup ads or websites, scenarios, pictures, or stories.* For example, to see whether your planned website is going to attract the audiences you're after, you might ask, "Describe the kind of person who would enjoy using this website."

- *Concentrate on working through the script without rushing.* Don't be too quick to step in when discussion falls silent.

- *If you're working on a team, have at least one other team member take careful notes during the discussion.* If possible, video- or audio-record the discussion for later reference.

- *Do not post or share video or audio recordings without explicit, signed permission of all focus group members.* Erase the recordings once your project has been graded. And see the notes on page 172 about institutional review boards for human subjects research.

- *Conclude the meeting by thanking participants for taking part, telling them that their input is very useful for your project.*

- *Use your PACT chart to decide how to process the material you get from the focus group.* If you had a complex goal such as understanding what prevented people from recycling, you might have to do some "content analysis," going through your notes or recordings and marking each word that was a barrier of some type: "messy," "smelly," "time-consuming," and so on. Think about what changes you'll need to make in your PACT chart based on the responses.

ultimately useless topic for your purposes. Some participants may feel afraid to voice their opinions if they're not in line with the majority of others', especially if one person in the majority is very vocal or well liked by others. In some cases, participants just get excited about a specific position or way of thinking, and everyone agrees because he or she's caught up in the discussion, not pausing to think about other positions or opinions. Finally, sometimes productive debate can quickly become angry, unproductive bickering.

To help the group stay focused, you'll need to act as the moderator (if you're working as part of a team, select one person to act as the moderator). The moderator runs the meeting, asks questions if responses aren't clear or are too brief to be useful, and generally keeps discussion going. If things are going south, the moderator can step in to smooth things over or move on to the next topic. The moderator should not dominate discussion, however — he or she should step in only as much as necessary.

You should also develop a script. The script can simply be a numbered list of major questions or topics or it can be a word-for-word account of everything the moderator should say and do. Usually it's something in the middle, formatted like an outline. This is a way to make sure you cover all of the main points. Some elements might be written out word for word, such as direct questions you're asking users. (Even the change of one word, such as "can" versus "must," could dramatically change responses.) If you're running multiple focus groups, the script also provides some consistency from one group to the next. Work with your PACT chart to help you come up with topics and questions to include in your script. Where are there gaps in what you know? What assumptions do you think you need to test?

After you have developed a script, you will need to invite four to seven participants, representing a diverse mix of people who represent the eventual audience for your text. A group this size has a large enough critical mass to support diverse discussions, but it's not so large that people don't get a chance to speak. You'll need to think carefully about who should be in the group. You'll want diverse members who represent the population that you're interested in. For example, a focus group discussing possible ads for a video game about Formula 1 racing probably wouldn't include participants older than 50.

The invitation to the focus group should outline the topics that will be covered, why you're seeking members' participation, the location and time, and how long the focus group is likely to take. If you're going to be collecting any personal or confidential data — names, for example — or will be videotaping, be sure to let people know ahead of time.

Being an Ethical Researcher

As you do research, you should periodically step back and ask yourself a simple question: *Am I being honest?* Like many ethical questions, this one is deceptively simple. Many researchers, with the best of original intentions, become so enmeshed in their work that they lose sight of larger issues such as bias, risks to people they involve in their research, and plagiarism.

Avoiding Bias

If you search only for material that supports your point, you may inadvertently miss important counterarguments — information that pro-

Reflect & Discuss

Can you think of any reasons that a focus group for a racing video game might include participants older than 50? Are there aspects of the context, audience, or purpose that might make their opinions useful?

Tips for Avoiding Bias in Research

- *Track down and carefully consider contrasting or opposing views or sources of information.* Do they seem valid? Why or why not? If you disagree with a source, does that color your opinions about its objectivity?

- *Think carefully about your readers' interests or leanings and explore what information they need to make informed decisions about this topic.*

- *Make sure your sources are credible.* Does the text seem to be professionally written, with appropriate grammar and style? Or does it seem sloppy or poorly constructed? Who publishes it? Can you find out information about the publication's reputation (for example, by searching to see what other people say about the author, publication, or publisher)? If the publication seems to have a bias, can you balance that with other sources? Be sure to note any biases when presenting the information to readers.

- *Don't use stale information.* It's not a problem to use older resources if you think you need to (such as a quotation that makes a point eloquently), but check with more current sources to make sure the older information is still accurate. You may also want to back up the older source with the newer one to let your audience know the situation hasn't changed.

Reflect & Discuss

What ethical issues are missing from the Tip Box above? What situations might those issues occur in?

vides important and valid criticisms of your main point. And if your readers do not already have information about those counterarguments, you'll effectively be hiding weaknesses in your argument that your readers have an ethical right to know about. If your readers *do* already know about those counterarguments (or can easily discover them with a little of their own research), they'll consider you an unfairly biased researcher and doubt the validity of your arguments.

Don't confuse bias with a viewpoint: Every text has a viewpoint, in some cases more than one. Being aware of different viewpoints is very important to understanding how texts operate. If you know the viewpoint of a text (or yourself), you can think critically about what things that specific viewpoint might not be able to see, allowing you to take up other viewpoints to improve your picture. It's not possible to ever cover every viewpoint, and things change over time. So usually your goal is to understand viewpoints, not to try to arrive at some universal, timeless truth.

Checking on Regulations about Research Involving People

Before you do any primary research involving people — surveys, interviews, experiments, or anything where you're intervening in someone's life to get information about or from him or her — your instructor (or you) should contact your school's institutional review board (IRB). IRBs are responsible for making sure researchers interact with subjects in ethical ways. At some schools, class-based research that will not be published is not subject to review by that board, but at some schools it is. IRB members can help you see ways you might be putting your subjects at risk without knowing it. For example, asking people about illegal behavior such as recreational drug use can put them at legal risk. Even a seemingly innocuous question about how much someone likes or dislikes a roommate might have serious repercussions if that data is leaked. IRB members can help you rephrase a question or refocus your research methods so you're still getting the information you need without harming your subjects. And as mentioned above, do some secondary research before conducting primary research simply to make sure the information you need isn't already out there.

Working with Sources

Working with sources during research includes two primary activities:

1. Tracking information about sources
2. Taking notes

Both of these are relatively straightforward, but you need to plan a strategy ahead of time and stick with it throughout the project. If you wait until you're well into the research project (or worse, if you've already written the paper), getting the necessary information can be a nightmare or even impossible.

Tracking Information about Sources

In most texts you write in school, you're expected to clearly identify what material you developed on your own and what material you obtained from other sources. When you do research, you'll want to keep track of bibliographic information about the texts you're reading so that you can cite them if you use them later. Citing (or documenting) sources correctly is important for three reasons:

1. It helps your instructor identify what parts of the text you wrote yourself and how well you researched.
2. It allows your readers to go back to your sources if they want to find out more information about the topics you're working with.
3. It helps readers decide whether your text will be useful for their needs. Professionals often refer first to a text's works cited section to assess what works the book or article is based on.

Tracking bibliographic information about your sources can also help you return to those sources later in your writing process. You might need to check the accuracy of a quote or paraphrase or dig back into the source for more material.

There's a wide range of methods for tracking your sources. You'll need to develop one that fits your own research practices and projects. A simple method might include something as straightforward as keeping all of your source material in a single word-processing file. For small projects that include only a handful of sources, you might just enter the source material, where you got it (so you or your readers can locate it later), and a date of access. More complex systems described below capture source material of many types (including things like video and audio), the forms of copyright that apply, and more. Your system will likely be somewhere in the middle.

FIGURING OUT WHAT INFORMATION TO TRACK Here are the key things to track in sources:

- The material itself (with notes or with physical or digital copies)
- Some sort of address for locating the information (URL, author and titlc info, and so on)
- The date you accessed the material (especially important for online sources because they can change or even disappear)
- Anything else specified in the style guide you're using (such as the MLA style guide often required in writing classes)
- Any licensing agreements or fees involved

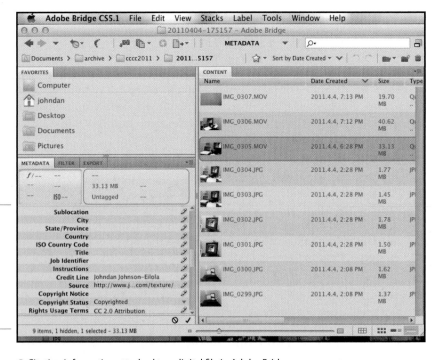

Copyright and other attribution information attached to source files

● Citation information attached to a digital file in Adobe Bridge
Adobe product screenshot reprinted with permission from Adobe Systems Incorporated

Exactly what you track will depend on your purposes and the type of text you are creating. For example, a traditional research paper for a first-year composition class will normally require you to provide full bibliographic information at the end of the paper, so you'll want to capture everything required by your style guide as you do the research. But an informal, oral progress report might require only informal references to your sources. Multimedia texts might contain primary material (such as audio or video you've shot yourself) and secondary material that you might have to cite, credit, or pay fees on to legally use (depending on the licensing agreement and the context you're creating your text in).

In some cases, you might record additional notes in the file you're using to track citation information. For example, you might add the words "pro" or "con" to information about sources depending on whether those sources supported a specific position. Or you might attach citation information directly to your notes and texts. Programs like Adobe Bridge (shown on page 174) and Aperture allow you to attach such information directly to pieces of digital media so the citation information stays with the project.

In other cases, you might create a spreadsheet of citation information. If you know what style guide you're following, you can create columns for each type of information you need to track. If you're not sure what style guide you're using, this general list would be a good starting point:

- Date accessed
- Time accessed
- Full title of source
- Author of source
- Date published
- URL or physical location
- Publisher
- Publisher's city
- Journal or book title
- Mentions of related sources you want to track down
- Comments about how you think you can use the source

As mentioned earlier, information you actually include will depend on the type of text and the style guide you're following, so as you work you may need to add categories or columns. If you're new to using that specific style guide, you'll probably want to refer to the style guide as you research to make sure you don't overlook necessary elements.

More complex research projects, with complex or large numbers of research sources, may require a correspondingly complex approach to tracking sources. Refer to Chapter 6 for more strategies for managing information.

As you develop a plan for what information to track, you'll need to also consider the medium of the source. There's an awful lot of overlap among what types of information you track, and for the sake of simplicity we're going to look at traditional physical sources and online sources. But you'll need to be flexible when you research since sometimes your context will suggest adapting different methods depending on your own needs.

TRACKING MATERIAL FROM PHYSICAL SOURCES Tracking sources of physical material involves making decisions about how to capture material. Are you going to make photocopies or are you going to retype or scan material into your computer? Some smartphone apps like Genius Scan and Evernote support using the phone's camera as a scanner. With a little bit of practice, they work pretty well.

If you're making photocopies, be sure to use well-labeled folders to hold information. If you're retyping or scanning, set up either a file to hold source material (for very small projects) or a directory on your computer (be sure to use file organization and naming techniques described on p. 147). Whatever system you use, be sure to include the tracking information you'll need to be able to cite the source later. You might also consider using a bibliographic tracking program (see p. 179), which asks you to collect a slightly larger amount of information and then, as a last step, converts the raw data into the correct format for a number of citation styles. Some programs even integrate directly with word processors.

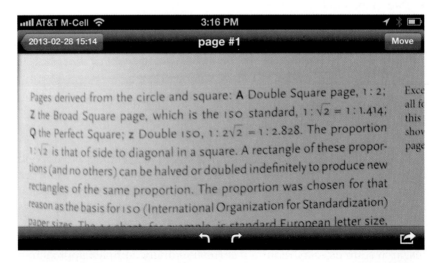

● Genius Scan iPhone App

Applications like Evernote and Zotero help you assemble a database of bibliographic information, which you can then access from within your word processor to insert references and even generate a "Works Cited" section for your essay in the style required by your instructor.

TRACKING MATERIAL FROM ONLINE SOURCES In many cases, you'll be tracking material from online sources. The simplest system involves bookmarking the URLs for web pages using your web browser's built-in bookmark system. As with other types of information, you'll probably want to create at least one folder in the bookmark system to hold URLs for the specific project you're working on.

If you're working on multiple computers, you can share your bookmark system among them by exporting your bookmarks from your web browser at the end of each work session and then importing them at the start of the next session. This method is a little clumsy but it can work, especially if you store the exported bookmarks on the web in a service such as Dropbox so they're readily accessible for importing during your next research session.

Working simply with bookmarks, though, does not resolve the issue of how to maintain access to materials that may disappear or move behind a pay-per-view wall. If this is a concern, consider archiving the web page either by using the archive function in your web browser (usually under the File menu) or by printing the page to disk. Mac OS X, for example, has a "Print to PDF" option in the print dialogue box of every application.

You can then store these files on your hard drive using methods described for file naming and directory structure in Chapter 6 (see p. 147). When you archive web pages, be sure that the URL and date/time are printed in the header or footer — these can usually be set in the Print dialogue box of most browsers. You may need to provide this information when citing your sources.

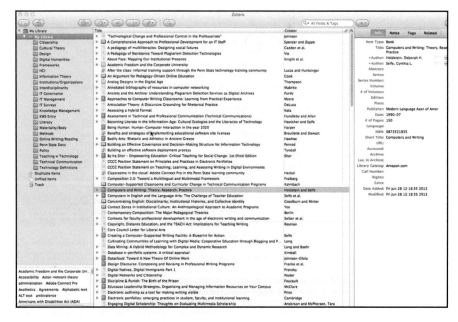

● Tracking bibliographic information in Zotero

Reprinted by permission of the Roy Rosenzweig Center for History and New Media, George Mason University

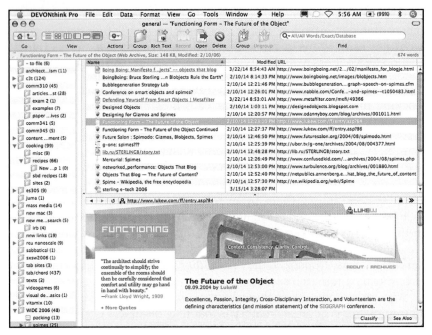

● DEVONthink Pro Database. The bottom pane shows a source grabbed from a website, and the top pane shows titles, URLs, and dates of sources being tracked for research.

© DEVON Technologies, LLC. Reprinted by permission.

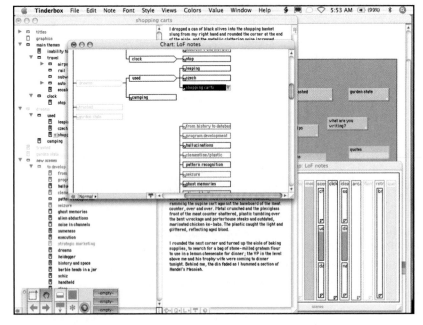

● Tinderbox knowledge maps. Each window on the screen shows a different visualization of the same information.

You would be better off, though, with a dedicated program to manage your bookmarks. A free web-based social bookmarking or web discovery system such as StumbleUpon lets you store your bookmarks online, so they're accessible from any computer. As an added bonus, social bookmarking systems allow you to search for sites that others have bookmarked on specific topics (if someone else has bookmarked it, the site is more likely to be useful). And other programs such as Evernote, Tinderbox, or DEVONthink provide advanced systems for managing information of all types, from bookmarks to Word documents to graphics files. They also allow you to create connections among the various pieces of information while you do research. For example, Tinderbox allows you to create different types of "knowledge maps" that visualize information (see p. 178).

DEVONthink offers advanced searching functions that index your information. The program analyzes the information that you enter and uses artificial intelligence techniques to find relationships between pieces of information that you hadn't noticed before. Tinderbox and DEVONthink are commercial products (both offer free trials); Evernote has a free basic version and a more powerful commercial version.

If you choose a robust system for tracking online sources, you may discover it also works very well for tracking all of your sources, including not just websites but quotes from print journals and even planning notes for the paper itself. The programs referred to above, including Evernote, Tinderbox, and DEVONthink, also offer the flexibility for tracking and working with many types of information.

Taking Notes

At some point, in addition to coming up with systems of naming files, bookmarking sites, and archiving pages, you'll need to *write* something as you do research. You'll want to summarize what you're finding and reading (so you can avoid having to reread a complete source to locate key information) or make connections among various sources to support a main point or to evaluate competing points. You may want to critique a position taken in a source so you'll remember to note that critique if you use the source in a paper (noting, for example, that the source has a nonobvious bias because its author has hidden connections to the topic, such as backing by a political group).

These sorts of things — material that's not completely obvious at first glance — are good examples of why taking notes is a crucial part of research. If you don't take research notes, you'll lose a lot of the important information you identify as you work. And that information needs to be easy to get to when you start drafting papers. Your overall project usually isn't simply *finding* information but *adding* to it: making connections, comparisons, critiques, summaries, and analyses.

At its most basic level, your research notes should track your process of gathering and thinking through the information you gather.

Even a basic research diary can be immensely useful when it's time to use your sources.

In many cases, you'll be interested in only a small portion of a larger text that you're using. You could photocopy or scan the section (if it's in print) or save it to disk (in PDF or web archive format, depending on your operating system and browser). You could also use sticky notes to tag the start of the section you're interested in. If you're working with photocopies or printouts or if you own the text, you can also highlight a section or write a note in the margin noting important features.

Remember that if you remove a text from its own context by saving or copying only a portion, you'll need to add enough information to be able to cite it correctly if you use it in your final text. And remember that cutting and pasting information is helpful when taking notes, but it can also be dangerous. If the source of the text is accidentally removed from the text itself, you might forget that you didn't write it. After reading your draft three or four or five times, the copied text might start to sound so familiar you think you wrote it — a mistake that might result in plagiarism on your part. This danger is a good reason to cite things as you go. When you paste in a quote or type in a paraphrase from a source, add the full citation at the same time; don't wait until later.

Using Sources: Quotations, Paraphrases, and Citations

If you want to actually *use* a source text in what you're writing, you'll need to decide how to use it. You can quote directly from the source or paraphrase the information you want to share with your readers. Part of that decision will be based on your PACT notes and careful thought about what form will be most effective. Very busy readers (or readers who are not very motivated) will probably not be willing to read lengthy, word-for-word quotations. But more motivated readers may be willing to spend time with the quotations you've selected, especially if they're eloquently or powerfully stated. And if the main point of your text is directly related to source texts, such as a biography, you'll likely want to provide some quoted material. It's difficult to imagine a biography of Abraham Lincoln, for example, that did not quote from at least a few of his speeches.

Quoting Sources

When you're taking exact words from your sources — even short, distinctive phrases — you will need to mark them off somehow so that readers know the author of the text isn't you. The most common method for marking a quotation is with quotation marks. Here's a passage from a paper about architecture after 9/11:

In his article "The Fiasco at Ground Zero," Michael J. Lewis writes "[a]rchitecture is distinguished from all other arts by its absolute dependence on the client. Composers have their patrons . . . , but only the architect cannot begin work at all until a client knocks at his door" (10–11).

Notice how the writer frames the quotation to lead readers into it carefully. She provides the title of the article as well as the author's name, Michael J. Lewis. Page numbers on which the quote is found are cited in parentheses after the quotation mark but before the period, in accordance with MLA style.

Because this writer embedded the quotation within her own sentence, she had to change the capital "A" in Lewis's quotation to a lowercase "a." When you make a surface-level change like this, put the change in square brackets to signal the alteration to readers. The use of ". . ." is a sign of another change — it indicates that some text was deleted from the original passage. If you use this technique, be sure that your change does not radically affect the meaning of the text. Do not, for example, change "I do not accept the charges brought against me" to "I . . . accept the charges brought against me."

For relatively short quotations, you can simply use quotation marks in your text to surround the quoted material. But for longer quotations, it might not be easy for readers to remember where the quotation starts and ends. In this case, you'll use what's called a block quotation that sets the quotation off in its own paragraph (or multiple paragraphs if you're quoting multiple paragraphs).

For example, if you were writing an article on Internet activism in which you wanted to quote a long section from Lawrence Lessig's memorial to Aaron Swartz from Creative Commons' website, you'd set it off as a block quote:

> Notices and memorials of the death of Aaron Swartz spread like wildfire among tech luminaries. One of Aaron's mentors, Lawrence Lessig, posted this message on the Creative Commons website:
>
>> It is with incredible sadness that I write to tell you that yesterday, Aaron Swartz took his life. Aaron was one of the early architects of Creative Commons. As a teenager, he helped design the code layer to our licenses, and helped build the movement that has carried us so far. Before Creative Commons, he had coauthored RSS. After Creative Commons, he co-founded Reddit, liberated tons of government data, helped build a free public library at Archive.org, and has done incredibly important work to reform and make good our political system. ("Remembering")
>
> As Lessig notes, Swartz participated in a wide range of web initiatives. From Creative Commons to Archive.org, Swartz's contributions to web activism were characteristic of his unique blend of fervor, optimism, and pragmatism.

Notice that block quotes generally do not actually use quotation marks: The indent is considered enough of a signal. The citation appears at the end of the block, but the end punctuation comes *before* the citation. Because the quote came from a web page without page numbers, an abbreviated title is used instead of page numbers in the citation.

Paraphrasing Text

In a lot of cases you won't want to provide a full quotation, either because several sources all made the same general point (and repeating them is unnecessary) or because the quotation is so long you don't think readers will want to read all of it. In those cases, you'll paraphrase your text while making it clear that the ideas are not your original ideas but ones you got from another source. The Internet activism paper from the previous example might include your own paraphrase rather than a direct quotation:

> Creative Commons posted a heartfelt eulogy to Aaron Swartz, who was highly influential in projects including not only Creative Commons but also the RSS standard, Reddit, and Anti-SOPA activism ("Remembering").

Paraphrases are not set off by quotes or by indentation; they are simply inserted into your own text in your own words but marked with a citation. The general guideline on creating a paraphrase is to avoid using words from the original source except for things like proper nouns, titles, labels, and similar material. So it's not necessary to quote the term "Creative Commons" or "Reddit," but you'd need to use quotations for a distinctive phrase. For the source above, something like "liberated tons of government data" would need to include quotation marks.

Creating a Works Cited Section

You might have noticed that the in-text citations above contain only a partial fragment of the information readers would need to locate the original source. Full information is usually located in a section at the end of your text titled "Works Cited," "Bibliography," or something similar. The specifics vary from one style guide to the next, but the works cited section is usually organized in alphabetical order by authors' last names. Here's a short section of the works cited for an academic essay using MLA format:

> Works Cited
>
> Adams, John. *Hallelujah Junction: Composing an American Life*. New York: Farrar, 2008. Print.
>
> Braun, William R. "Concerts and Recitals—New York City." *Opera News* 1 Dec. 2002: 97–98. Print.
>
> Conrad, Peter. "Voices of the Dead." *New Statesman* 7 Oct. 2002: 39–40. Print.
>
> "Daniel Libeskind's Original Freedom Tower Design." Online image. *Gotham Gazette: New York City News and Policy* 29 Apr. 2009. Web.

The specifics of the works cited section depend on which style guide is being used. In MLA style, the works cited section is arranged alphabetically by authors' last names.

The indenting used in this style is called hanging indent. In most cases, readers using a works cited section are searching for a specific entry; the hanging indent is a visual design feature that helps the eye scan from one entry to the next until the reader finds the right entry.

Knowing When to Stop Researching

The thing about information is that there's always *more*. A lot more. In fact, continuing to do research beyond a reasonable point can become a way to procrastinate. If writing seems challenging to you, it's easy to while away your hours accumulating huge amounts of data and meticulously organizing and tracking that information. But at some point, you need to actually start writing.

So how do you decide when to stop research and start writing? Refer back to your overall writing plans—not just your research plans, but your purpose. Do you have enough information to support the purpose, to convince the reader to agree? Have you done an ethical job of exploring the issues (so that you're not just taking the first idea regardless of its accuracy or objectivity, but honestly representing what's out there)? If so, it's often useful to begin drafting your text, or at least a subsection of it. During the drafting process, you might decide that you need additional research to back up or explain a point—you can always go back and do more.

In some contexts, deadlines can be enough to force you to wind up your research. You need to leave yourself adequate time to draft, to get feedback, and to revise. If those deadlines mean that there are gaps in your research, at the very least you can identify those gaps for readers up front and offer to conduct additional research if they think it's necessary.

Finally, keep in mind the fact that your research is not your primary goal: Your research should support the changes you want to make with your writing. You'll likely discover that it's useful to begin writing before your research is fully completed. Writing can be helpful in sorting information out in your head, exploring connections and coherence in your arguments. Simply accumulating a huge pile of data delays making those connections and developments. As you begin the writing process, you'll frequently discover that you're missing key information. Starting the writing process can be an important part of your research activities by identifying new research areas that you need to return to.

Putting your research to work in a draft document is also necessary for getting feedback from other people: instructors, peer-review team members, or even the people you're writing your documents for. You can't simply give them a stack of photocopied articles or a list of URLs; you need to organize and frame the information in a text so that they can see how the information supports the changes you want your writing to make.

Text for Analysis

RESEARCH PAPER
LINNEA SNYDER, "Memorializing September 11, 2001"

The research paper on the following pages was written by Linnea Snyder for a first-year writing course. In the paper, Snyder discusses the controversy over different 9/11 memorial projects. Snyder draws on a wide range of sources including books, music recordings, websites, and magazine articles to show the complexities of the process of memorializing the victims of September 11, 2001.

As you read the paper, note the ways that Snyder uses her sources to support her argument that one form of memorial (music) was more successful than another (architecture).

- When and why does Snyder use direct quotation?
- When and why does Snyder paraphrase?
- How does Snyder introduce sources? How does she frame them for readers? How does she connect them to her own argument?

Snyder 1

Linnea Snyder

WR 150 O9

Prof. Bozek

April 30, 20—

Memorializing September 11, 2001

Choosing the right way to commemorate a special event
is not easy. Choosing the right way to commemorate a
traumatic terrorist attack is even harder. September 11, 2001,
left people around the world shocked and devastated. As time
passed, it was clear that memorials needed to be created for
those who lost their lives in the attacks in order to remember
them and in order for their families, friends, and the general
public to move on from the tragedy. Two important and
interesting memorials came about in the months and years
following 9/11: composer John Adams's opus *On the
Transmigration of Souls* and architect Daniel Libeskind's
Freedom Tower. Although the objectives of these memorials
were the same—to relieve the pain of September 11th—they
were received in opposite manners. One is a piece of
music—something to listen to, absorb, and then move away
from—while the other is a building: something that will be
present for many generations. The political implications,
over-the-top tone, and permanent quality of Libeskind's tower
caused it to be more negatively received by the public, and
ultimately rejected, while Adams's *On the Transmigration of
Souls* was appreciated for its temporary quality and theme of
healing.

Synder states her
thesis.

Snyder 2

After the Twin Towers collapsed on September 11th, there was much debate about what to do with the spot where these icons once stood (Michael J. Lewis points out the irony that "their obliteration as emblems of American identity inadvertently gave them that [iconic] status" [10]). Mayor Rudy Giuliani called for Ground Zero to be left as it was and in that way be made into a memorial for the victims. Others, including Larry Silverstein, who has a lease on the land, wanted commercial buildings rebuilt immediately to start generating money once again. And then there were those who called for a significant building to be built and to have a proper memorial structure for those who died (Goldberger).

Finally, in the fall of 2002, the Lower Manhattan Development Corporation, or LMDC, decided to launch an architectural competition to determine which building design might replace the World Trade Center. After much debate, Daniel Libeskind, an architect of international acclaim who has designed buildings all around the world, was announced as the winner. This decision came partly as a surprise given the fact that the public, in general, much preferred the design of Lord Foster, another entrant in the competition. Libeskind's design was chosen mainly because it was the favorite design of Alexander Garvin, the vice president of the LMDC, and Governor Pataki (Goldberger 157), not because it meant something to the New York community. Michael J. Lewis reflected the public's opinion of this decision when he wrote, "there is rarely a great building without a great client,"

Snyder 3

followed by the biting line "neither, alas, has emerged at
Ground Zero" (11). The fact that public opinion was not taken
into consideration shows the amount of political influence that
took place over the rebuilding near the Ground Zero site. This
influence lessened the majority's say in what would be most
appropriate and ultimately laid the foundation for a memorial
that focused more on remembrance than healing.

Adams, on the other hand, had no competition for the
task of composing his September 11th memorial. He was
commissioned directly by the New York Philharmonic in early
2002 to write a piece of music commemorating the September
11th attacks for the Philharmonic's first concert of the 2002–
2003 season in late September. Adams was reluctant to take on
the commission, saying that "[o]rchestra music is by definition
a public art form, and I had a great difficulty imagining
anything 'commemorating' 9/11 that would not be an
embarrassment" (263). Adams is well known as a composer
who sees every side of a situation. He is famous for portraying
all characters in his operas as somewhat sympathetic,
regardless of their roles in history—characters such as
J. Robert Oppenheimer, Richard Nixon, and Mao-Tse Tung.
David Schiff, another composer, felt that the Philharmonic
made a brave choice in choosing Adams to write this piece of
music, saying they "may have feared that he would exploit the
commission to make a musical case for al Qaeda" (2).

Even though Adams's ability to show controversial
perspectives of an event cast initial questions about whether he

Snyder brings in
another composer—
an expert, in other
words—to support
Adams.

Snyder 4

could create a suitable memorial, in other ways he seemed like the perfect fit to write this piece of American tragedy. Many critics and fellow composers would consider Adams to be the composer laureate of the United States if such a title existed. In an article published in the *San Francisco Chronicle*, Joshua Kosman describes Adams's music as nationalistic and appealing to a wide variety of audiences. Adams's music about American politics and important events, along with his status as a proud New Englander, establish him as "the exemplary American composer" (May 59–60). When it came down to it, his renown in the culture of American classical music mattered more than peoples' skepticism, a benefit of the doubt that ultimately would not be extended to Libeskind and his Freedom Tower design.

    Adams finally accepted the Philharmonic's commission because he felt it was his duty as a friend to many New Yorkers. He said, "After 9/11, some people gave blood, some people wrote books; everybody was moved to do whatever possible, and writing music was, for me, the obvious possibility" (May 64). When he began composing, Adams had concerns about the proper tone for his piece, stemming from his disapproval of the way the media had treated the September 11th attacks. He stated in an interview that "the one thing that I was really concerned about was that I not write a piece that yanked or tugged the heart-strings," because of his disgust with the intense and overly emotional media coverage that dragged on over weeks and months (May 196–97). Adams decided to name his piece *On the*

Snyder 5

Transmigration of Souls, calling it a "memory space" because within the music, there is a place where "you can go and be alone with your thoughts and emotions" (May 365). *On the Transmigration of Souls* ended up being twenty-five minutes long and is written for orchestra, adult chorus, and children's chorus.

Some of the most interesting parts of Adams's work are the electronic noises and prerecorded voices that he incorporated into the piece. The opus begins with city noises: footsteps, distant car horns and sirens, the quiet murmuring of people passing, transporting the audience out of the concert hall and back onto the streets from which they have just come. The chorus then quietly begins to hum and a prerecorded boy's voice repeats the word "missing." As the music progresses, other prerecorded voices list names of the victims and the adult chorus sings lines from obituaries and missing posters. At the same time, the children's chorus sings the line "It was a beautiful day" (Conrad 40). There is one false climax in the music about halfway through the piece, but instead of resolving it, Adams goes on to have the chorus sing some of the most emotionally intense lines in the piece, including "I wanted to dig him out. I know just where he is. . . ." There is finally a second climax and this one ends with the chorus singing the words "light," "day," "sky," and finally, "I love you" (Gates). The music then fades out as the city noises fade back in, signifying a return to regular city life. This return to normalcy completes the cathartic process this "memory space"

Snyder here could cite either Conrad's discussion of Adams's work or Adams's work directly if she has a published copy of the music.

Snyder 6

is intended to have by taking the listener through the trauma of destruction, back into everyday life.

Daniel Libeskind's design for Ground Zero (see Fig. 1) did not feature this idea of a return to normalcy that influenced Adams's piece, but instead focused on memorialization, a kind of "freezing in time" of the event itself. Similarly to Adams, however, Libeskind often described his building site as a space and used phrases such as "space is a spiritual entity, a soul, like a person" when selling his design to the public (Goldberger 120). Libeskind was referring not to a "memory space" like Adams's but to the literal space in the city that the World Trade Center left: the space that he would have to fill with this new building.

Libeskind infused symbolism into the space, making sure that every part of his design had some sort of meaning. He designed the tower so that through its crystalline exterior, the foundations and "footprints" of the original World Trade Center next door would be visible, keeping the memory of what had originally stood there alive. Libeskind then designed an off-center spire

Fig 1. Daniel Libeskind's original design for the Freedom Tower (2002). AP Photo/Lower Manhattan Development Corp/File

Snyder is following a chronological, parallel progression of both Adams's and Libeskind's work, stage by stage.

Snyder 7

intended to mimic the shape of the Statue of Liberty. Once added to the building, the spire would make the height of the structure 1,776 feet to correspond to the year the United States became independent from Britain. Inside the spire would be what Libeskind called "Gardens of the World": hanging plants and flowers from around the world. According to Michael J. Lewis, this multiculturalism disturbed many people because they believed the focus should be on the patriotism of America itself and also because of the severe xenophobia many Americans developed after September 11th (11–12). The overly symbolic elements of the design were problematic, but the idea of the building itself also was controversial. Because the Freedom Tower was to stand permanently at Ground Zero, its mere existence would call to mind the events of 9/11. If the only part of the tragedy memorialized in a design is the drama and heightened emotions of the event, the focus is centered more around remembering than on the final step of moving on.

Adams's work, on the other hand, does call to mind the attacks, but additionally reminds us that we're not in permanent mourning and that, while things don't exactly return to the way they were before, things do return to a state of relative regularity. Adams's intention not to make his piece too poignant proved fruitful in the end and, as proof of his piece's success and acclaim, Adams won the Pulitzer Prize for music in 2003 for *On the Transmigration of Souls*. However, when Libeskind, a Polish immigrant who grew up in the

Bronx, gave a speech at the Winter Garden in New York City, some of his first words to the audience were "I arrived by ship to New York as a teenager, an immigrant, and . . . my first sight was the Statue of Liberty. . . . I have never forgotten that sight or what it stands for" (Goldberger 8). Libeskind immediately began to take a different route with his memorial by selling emotion to the audience. It was this overly dramatic approach, apparent in aspects of his design, that caused a questionable acceptance of, if not a negative reaction to, the Freedom Tower. While the emotion that Libeskind put into his design did appeal to some, Libeskind was to hit many walls in trying to make his vision a reality in the years to come.

In general, *On the Transmigration of Souls* was well received by the public. The main complaints that critics had were about the recordings and electronic sounds that Adams used and about the accessibility of the piece. Peter Conrad, a music critic, was unhappy that Adams continued the city noises after the music stopped, saying that he was not brave enough to end the piece with his own music.

Adams, however, explained his decision to let the tape run on because it provides an easy transition for the audience back into everyday life: a life after September 11th.

Additionally, as a memorial, a piece of music performed by the Philharmonic seems like something accessible only to regular concert-goers and not something for the masses of New York suffering from the trauma of the attacks. David Schiff, however, supports Adams's piece, saying that he

Snyder 9

"breaks down the divide between the high-bourgeois culture that created orchestras like the New York Philharmonic in the nineteenth century and the mass culture that took its place in the twentieth" (3). Adams admitted that his piece can be a bit difficult for audiences to listen to at times, but he was pleased with the ultimate outcome (267). Adams described the reactions of many of the victims' families saying: "I don't know what about the piece got to them, but something got to them" (May 200). Because Adams was careful not to heighten the sense of drama in his memorial, the tone of the piece was not as heavy-hitting as Libeskind's tower, and as a result it was more widely accepted as a reflection of how people felt about and chose to relate to the tragedy. Whereas Libeskind's design prompts remembrance and grieving, Adams's evokes remembrance, grieving, *and healing*. It's the additional therapeutic aspect of Adams's work that makes it more successful in its goal of memorializing 9/11 in a constructive way.

The final blow to Libeskind's already flawed design came when a book surfaced that Libeskind had published in 1997, entitled *Fishing from the Pavement*. The book featured surrealistic sketches accompanied by lewd and offensive descriptions of city infrastructure, seemingly in reference to American and Muslim culture. It was considered un-American and too close to the events of September 11th. As Lewis writes, this began to make people think that "[Libeskind's] glib torrent of patriotism came from the same

In this paragraph, Snyder brings together several sources and her own ideas to form a conversation about Adams's work.

Snyder 10

inexhaustible spigot as his surrealistic doggerel and, like it, was not to be taken seriously" (14). As a result, in May 2003, Libeskind was replaced by architect David Childs for the realization of the design of the Freedom Tower, later renamed One World Trade Center. Childs used Libeskind's original design as a base, but he did away with Libeskind's idea of the off-center Gardens of the World spire, replacing it with a large antenna centered on top of the tower (see Fig. 2). He also added windmills that would be used to generate some of the building's electricity. Safety restrictions set up by the New York City Police Department in order to prevent further terrorist attacks required the first ninety feet to be covered in bomb-resistant concrete, replacing what Libeskind had intended to be a heavily windowed area that would allow people inside the tower to gaze out at the Ground Zero site (Lewis 14–15). Many of the aesthetically pleasing aspects of Libeskind's design, which might have redeemed it from its dramatic elements, were stripped out until what remained was much duller and less visually interesting.

Fig 2. David Childs's revised design for the Freedom Tower (2005). LMDC/Zuma/Corbis

Snyder 11

The resulting building, One World Trade Center, was disappointing. What many had hoped would be a final release back to normalcy has turned into just another skyscraper (see Fig. 3). Lewis sums up many New Yorkers' views by saying "[t]hroughout the long, sad process, architects and public alike have looked in vain for designs that matched the pizzazz and punch of the original towers, when they were really looking for something that matched the graphic punch of their collapse" (15). The iconic status of the Twin Towers influenced the reception of the new tower; because of too much pressure and high expectations for the new building, it can never live up to the legacy of what was destroyed, especially if its design melodramatically emphasizes aspects of American patriotism and multiculturalism in the reconstruction.

Perhaps that was the ultimate problem of Libeskind's design, that nothing would satisfy the public when it came to replacing the Twin Towers. But as a memorial, the building was considered to be too over-the-top, too emotional, and too much of a permanent reminder. Erecting a commemorative building in that spot takes the tragedy and

Fig 3. One World Trade Center (2013). Andria Patino/Corbis

Snyder 12

terror of 9/11 and forces the public to remember; anyone in the vicinity of One World Trade Center will think, *this is where it happened,* whether he or she is willing to face it or not. Conversely, a piece of music about 9/11 likely will be encountered only by those seeking out and choosing to listen to it, to face those emotions.

Additionally, the political aspects of Libeskind's design played a large role in the negative reception it got from the public and resulted in his removal from the project. Ultimately, people were more moved by Adams's *On the Transmigration of Souls*—they found it accessible and disturbing, yet cathartic and real. Had Libeskind focused more on the catharsis that the people of New York City needed rather than painful emotionality, perhaps changes would not have been made to his building and it would have been better received by those looking for resolution.

Snyder 13

Works Cited

Adams, John. *Hallelujah Junction: Composing an American Life*. New York: Farrar, 2008. Print.

Braun, William R. "Concerts and Recitals—New York City." *Opera News* 1 Dec. 2002: 97–98. Print.

Conrad, Peter. "Voices of the Dead." *New Statesman* 7 Oct. 2002: 39–40. Print.

"Daniel Libeskind's Original Freedom Tower Design." Online image. *Gotham Gazette: New York City News and Policy* 29 Apr. 2009. Web.

"The Freedom Tower, Again." Online image. *Gotham Gazette: New York City News and Policy* 29 Apr. 2009. Web.

Gates, David. "A Requiem from a Heavyweight." *Newsweek* 29 Sep. 2002: 139. Print.

Goldberger, Paul. *Up from Zero: Politics, Architecture, and the Rebuilding of New York*. New York: Random, 2004. Print.

Lewis, Michael J. "The Fiasco at Ground Zero." *New Criterion* Dec. 2005: 10–15. Print.

May, Thomas, ed. *The John Adams Reader: Essential Writings on an American Composer*. Pompton Plains: Amadeus, 2006. Print.

Schiff, David. "Memory Spaces." *Atlantic Monthly* Apr. 2003: 127–30. Print.

Exercises

1. Find an article (in print or online) that you disagree with (check out websites or magazines aimed at groups holding positions counter to your own). Read through the article and take notes about points you disagree with. Is the source presenting what you consider to be an unfairly biased or incomplete view to score cheap points? Is it honestly attempting to make a logical argument with a balanced view? Find reliable (to your audience) sources backing up your points. Write a short (500-word) letter to the editor of the publication, using some of the resources you found, to change the minds of people who read the original article.

2. Write a short (500-word) defense of the sources you chose for exercise 1. What makes them believable to your audience? What, if any, sources did you decide not to use because you thought your audience would dismiss them out of hand?

3. Find three different citation style guides and review their guidelines for citing online and print sources. Create a practice citation in each style for an article from an online newspaper and an article from a print newspaper. Write a list of the main differences between each citation format and discuss (overall) how the three style guides vary in what they require for online versus print sources. Why do you think they differ?

4. Pull out the notes you've taken for a class. Make copies (scans, photocopies, or printouts) and use annotations to mark the range of types of notes you took (margin comments or highlights in a textbook, handwritten notes, things in a computer file, and so on). Bring them to class to discuss how effective you think they were and what you wish you'd done differently.

5. Pick an issue that you feel conflicted about—one that you're not sure whether you're for or against. Spend several hours locating expert sources arguing for and against. Create an outline and then a first draft of a short (2,000-word) research paper using the style guide most commonly used by experts in this discipline.

Scenario Connections

1. Look at Scenario 6, "Writing a Profile for a Magazine" (p. 280), and think of a person you'd like to interview for this assignment. Develop a list of interview questions that includes a mix of closed and open questions. Which of your questions might you be able to answer through background research before the interview?

2. Scenario 4, "Making Invisible Things Visible: Mapping Data," asks you to find data about a population of your choosing and create a map of that data to

make an argument. Look for research guides on your campus library's website or talk to the reference librarian to get help finding reliable sources of data on your topic. What types of sources did you find? Which ones seem the most useful, and why? Make a list of five possible datasets that you might want to map for this scenario.

3. In Scenario 8, "Drafting a Poster about Online Privacy," you'll need to do some research to help you narrow the topic and understand the context you're working in. Find three relevant sources and develop a system for tracking bibliographic information (using whatever application you like) for each source using material covered on pages 172–78. If you're working with a review team, compare your system to those developed by other people in your team. Do any of them have ideas you can adopt?

4. Scenario 1, "Advocating Voter Registration on Campus" (p. 263), involves convincing students to register to vote. As a full-class activity, create a survey to better understand reasons that students at your school do or don't register to vote. (Review the material on pages 165–68 for advice on constructing and running surveys.) Keep the survey short (4–7 questions) but try to explore a range of areas. Launch the survey by publicizing it on campus by whatever means you think will work best. Discuss the results in class.

Writing with Other People

People write together all the time — in school, in the workplace, and in their communities. We write together because it's a way of dividing up large or complex projects and a way of generating multiple viewpoints.

Unfortunately, in many cases the people writing together gain their strategies for collaborative writing through guesswork, instinct, and hard-won experience. In this chapter, you'll learn methods for working effectively on writing projects with other people, including strategies for assigning responsibilities, setting up schedules, and creating consistency in your texts. Many of these strategies draw on adaptations of the same purpose, audience, context, and text framework you've learned, with your teammates as your audience. You'll also learn strategies for managing inevitable conflict in groups. Finally, we'll briefly look at ways to give useful feedback to your group members.

Strategies for Writing with Other People

Methods for collaborative writing run along a continuum between two methods: divide and conquer and side by side. You might notice that I didn't use the term "versus" here. That's because the two methods are often complementary, with one working well at some points in a project and the other working well at other times.

Divide-and-Conquer Method

You've undoubtedly already used divide and conquer as a method for team-based projects: Take an assignment, split it into parts, and have each person in the team complete some portion of the work. Different people write different sections, take on different research tasks, create different graphics, or work on other tasks. Work goes more quickly because each person has only a small chunk to do. And because there's not as much "communication overhead" (discussions about work), the process goes more quickly.

As a final step, the team (or even just one person) combines all of the individual pieces into a single text. A project that might have taken one person eight hours to write now takes four people a few hours each. These time and resource savings are the divide-and-conquer method's greatest strength. The method distributes workload.

But while this method is very good at getting a project done by portioning out work, it can result in texts that are inconsistent from section to section in tone, in level of development, and in visual style. To readers the final text can seem "choppy" or uneven, like a patchwork quilt rather than a seamless whole, because the team members did not have the same understanding of how to draft the text, did not devote equivalent amounts of work, or did not have similar abilities or styles. From a writer's perspective, the divide-and-conquer method can also mean one person taking on more than his or her fair share of work, either due to mistaken estimates about how long each task would take or because another team member slacked off.

Take Wikipedia as an extreme example of a text written by people with different levels of interest. In an article in the *Guardian* in 2009, Mark Graham analyzed Wikipedia's coverage of geographical regions and noted that the site covers the United States much more

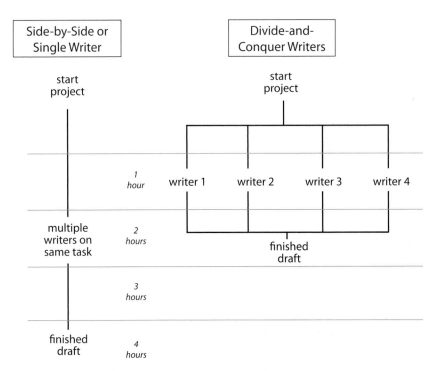

● The divide-and-conquer method typically takes far less time than working alone or side by side

comprehensively than the rest of the world. Users didn't intentionally set out to weight Wikipedia toward the United States; the individual interests and experiences of Wikipedia editors, who lean heavily toward living in the United States, resulted in this imbalance. (Those editors also appear to be science fiction and fantasy buffs: There are many entries written about Middle Earth and Discworld, locations that exist only in fantasy and science fiction novels, than about many real countries.)

Writing Side by Side

At the other end of the continuum is the side-by-side method. Instead of dividing up the project, writers sit down together to work on it at the same time. As you might guess, writing side by side offers, in some ways, a mirror image of divide and conquer: One excels where the other is weak and vice versa. Most notably, writing side by side offers a richer space for sharing diverse opinions as members of a team discuss new ideas and offer opinions. At the early stages of writing (brainstorming and other idea-generation strategies discussed in Chapter 3), the members of an effective team can support each other by creating a dynamic and creative environment.

The same synergy can continue into the process of drafting and revising text. A well-tuned team can gather around a computer, with one person typing while the others contribute words and phrases to the emerging text.

You're probably familiar with some of the drawbacks to writing side by side: The process is time consuming. In order for diverse opinions to emerge, the team has to slow down and evaluate ideas before integrating new ones into the text. In fact, in some cases writing side by side requires more time than a single person sitting down and writing the full text alone.

The side-by-side method also has the slight potential to increase the effects of groupthink: It's easy to get caught up in the excitement of a slightly chaotic but exciting team writing session, agreeing to new ideas quickly because it feels good to get new text on the screen. If team members were sitting separately in their rooms, looking at drafts of a teammate's text with a calmer eye, they might be willing to be more productively critical.

Writing side by side often allows more back-and-forth discussion (but at the expense of efficiency)

Tetra Images/Corbis

Back and Forth: The Middle Ground

The divide-and-conquer and side-by-side methods each have benefits and drawbacks, and there's a middle ground that often proves more reasonable: Two or more writers divide up a project but also remain in communication with each other, sharing drafts, discussing roadblocks and strategies, and providing comments on emerging work. This strategy is not as speedy as the divide-and-conquer method, but it's faster than pure side by side. And it's not as unified as the side-by-side method, but it can lead to a much more coherent vision than divide and conquer.

The back-and-forth method is not necessarily the best approach to every project — sometimes the two more extreme strategies make more sense for specific projects. But you'll likely find yourself relying on this method because it's the best general strategy for most projects.

In this way of working, you'd start the project by discussing broad goals, working through some of the major early stages of writing together before splitting up. You might work through the purpose/audience/context/text framework, coming up with structures for your text while working next to one another, on paper or on the computer. Begin by filling in sections of the PACT chart that are determined by the assignment itself, and then discuss and flesh out the rest using techniques from Chapters 2 and 3. For larger projects, you'll also want to work face to face as you create a schedule, making sure everyone has roughly equivalent workloads and that due dates fit with each team member's individual schedule.

Before you break, make sure you have firm lines of communication set up: What's the best medium for communication? Where will drafts be stored? How will files be named? Can the team meet *before* the final draft, just to check in and make sure everyone is making good progress?

One method for ensuring consistency is to have team members pair up, either passing back and forth a single section or task or working individually but reviewing the other person's work for feedback on a regular basis (every few days or once a week).

The back-and-forth approach is not without its own flaws. As with side-by-side work, the back-and-forth method can be time consuming because of the additional communication and review work involved. It requires more coordination between schedules so that a draft doesn't sit for days waiting for a reviewer to find time to work with it. And if two weak team members are paired up, their portion of the project may flounder without the rest of the team knowing until it's too late. So relying on a back-and-forth strategy sometimes means closely monitoring participation and addressing team problems quickly. Done well, the additional work required for back-and-forth work (compared to the divide-and-conquer method) should pay off in a higher quality text.

	Divide and Conquer Better for	Side by Side Better for	Back and Forth Better for
Project size	Large projects	Small projects (or small sections of larger projects)	Midsized to large projects
Creativity level	Less creative, standard reports; proposals with predictable, standard structure and content	Innovative work (in terms of structure or content)	Any creativity level
Voice/ vision	Projects with predictable, standard structure and content	Projects that are less predictable but still need a unified voice/ vision	Any range of voice/vision
Time	Projects with limited time that require speed over quality	Slower-paced projects	Any except the most time sensitive

Combining Approaches

So which strategy should your team choose? There's no single best strategy; you'll have to decide based on the demands of your project. In reality, you'll often shift strategies at different phases of a project. Brainstorming usually works better with multiple people involved, but writing may be more efficient when only one person is involved at a time. Also, no two teams are alike, so strategies that work well for one team for one type of project might be a disaster for a different team working on the same type of project. The table above is only a starting point; your team should be open to switching gears if your project seems to be off the rails.

Strategies for Managing Collaborative Projects

Most collaborative projects don't run smoothly on their own. Team members have differing abilities, goals, and schedules. They have different ways of working, some of which conflict with each other. Life happens.

Learning how to manage collaborative projects increases the chances that your work will succeed. That doesn't mean bossing your teammates around (although you might have to resort to that occasionally). Good project management is usually a collaborative effort in and of itself. There's not space here to get into a full-blown discussion of managing collaborative projects — whole semesters are often devoted to the topic for management students — but below we'll cover a handful of powerful but simple strategies to get you started. Be sure to also review material from Chapter 6 for more advice on project management.

Build Effective Teams

If you've worked on teams, you've probably worked on both very effective, positive, and fun teams as well as dysfunctional, stressful, and unproductive teams. If you want to increase your odds of being on productive teams, you'll need to get better at helping structure your team and at analyzing what's going on in your team to see where you need to make changes. Even the best teams have rough patches; good teams are good at self-analysis and change.

Like every important aspect of writing, there's no magic wand. In the long run, paying attention to your team's processes and structures is nearly always helpful. (See Tips on pp. 206–07)

Set Up a Schedule

For all but the shortest projects, come up with a reasonable schedule that specifies what work will be done by which person on what date. Leave in some extra time at the end for inevitable complications. You should also leave enough time for a full pass through the whole document by one or more team members. When individual sections are read in isolation, it's easy to miss gaps or inconsistencies. In general, you also normally leave "apparatus" development — tables of contents, introductions, conclusions, cover pages, bibliographies, and so forth — until the end; it's easier to create those things when you have the full document constructed.

If possible, post the schedule in a shared location, such as a networked drive or an online site such as Google Drive or Basecamp. As soon as schedule-related issues come up — a draft isn't completed on time or you realize another section will need to be written — the team should discuss how to adjust the schedule so that the work still gets done on time.

Set Up an Internal Style Guide and Style Sheets

Inconsistencies in style can be very distracting, even confusing, for readers. A text that shifts in tone or format can be difficult to follow. Switching, for example, from casual language ("I'm going to start by discussing existing research on DNA fingerprinting as admissible evidence") to bureaucratic ("One can dependably ascertain a firm link tying gender to said subject's DNA profile") may cause readers to stumble. And because the logical structure of a document is often supported by its visual layout, apparently random changes in font or margin can throw readers off balance.

Tips for Building Effective Teams

- *Formally list team responsibilities.* For smaller projects, that might be as simple as electing a team leader by informal vote and then assigning basic tasks. For larger projects, you may need an informal or even a formal document that spells out in great detail who reports to whom; how much text has to be produced, reviewed, or copyedited each week; and so on. For this class, you'll probably be on the "smaller project" end of the scale.

- *Share contact information.* Include at least two points of contact in case one fails. Agree to check both points on some concrete timeline. (How often depends on the project. For projects that last only a week, daily checking might be necessary.)

- *Talk to each other.* In-team communication is crucial to project success. This is true of nearly every aspect of team writing. Communicate about schedules, drafts, work habits, team meeting times, or any area where there's the potential for drift. If you're going to be late with a draft, give your team a heads-up. Even if you're working side by side (*especially* if you're working side by side), keep engaged with the writing, offering input and productive critique.

- *Deal with problems quickly.* If you see a problem emerging, keep an eye on it to see whether it's a little glitch or a rapidly growing tear in the fabric of your team. If one team member seems to be going off the rails, check with her to see whether something's wrong or check with another team member to see whether he agrees with your assessment. Sometimes merely mentioning the issue—in a productive way—can put a team member back on track. If one team member continues to cause the team

problems, set up a team meeting to discuss the issues. If that's unsuccessful, contact your instructor for advice. Team problems generally get worse if you let them slide.

- *Consider setting aside time at a team meeting for assessing how well each of you is doing.* There are many ways to provide feedback. You can sit around a table, for example, and have each person give a self-assessment, followed by comments from the team about whether everyone else agrees. You could set up a simple survey form in Word, Google Drive, or SurveyMonkey that allows people to give written feedback. (You might want to avoid doing anonymous surveys because they can lead to flame wars rather than constructive critique.)

- *Don't forget issues of context, audience, and purpose as you provide feedback.* Avoid simply venting about a team member's pushiness or lackluster performance. Instead, ask yourself what might motivate that team member. Ask yourself what he or she needs to hear to make behavior changes. The sample PACT chart alongside the Reflect & Discuss box on page 207 represents one writer's notes when trying to decide how to approach a team member who hasn't been participating.

- *Be self-aware.* Check your perceptions to make sure you're not being unfair to your team or mistaken in your assessment. Before firing off an angry e-mail or text message after you're the only person in your five-member team to show up for the 9:30 meeting in the lab, check your notes to make sure the meeting wasn't in another lab or on a different day. Similarly, before you say something angry at the team member sitting behind you text-messaging while you type a draft, ask yourself whether

Tips for Building Effective Teams
(continued)

you've been open to contributions. Maybe you need to stop occasionally to ask for feedback or work more slowly. Maybe you need to consider taking turns at the keyboard to give everyone an opportunity.

- *Document your work and keep records.* Being able to account for your contributions is generally a good work practice for several reasons. First, it's a way for you to look back and reflect on your own role in the team: Where are you contributing? Where are you absent? Second, in the event that the team starts to have problems, it's one way for you to spell out (calmly) what you've been doing. If the team really disintegrates and you have to involve your instructor, it's a way to show what work you've done. Finally, it's very common in the workplace to be required to document your work on a periodic basis (weekly, monthly, quarterly, or yearly); being able to reproduce an accurate report of what you've done will be much easier if you've gotten used to documenting your work as a standard practice.

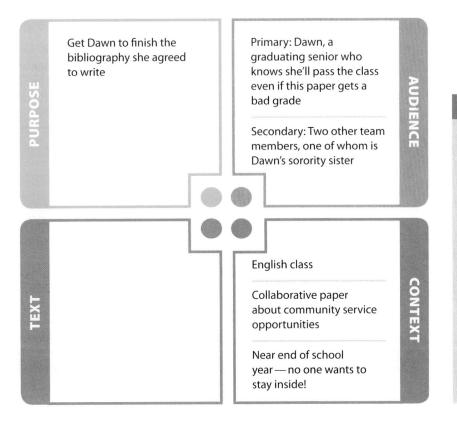

PURPOSE
Get Dawn to finish the bibliography she agreed to write

AUDIENCE
Primary: Dawn, a graduating senior who knows she'll pass the class even if this paper gets a bad grade

Secondary: Two other team members, one of whom is Dawn's sorority sister

TEXT

CONTEXT
English class

Collaborative paper about community service opportunities

Near end of school year — no one wants to stay inside!

Reflect & Discuss

Imagine that you're on a team with Dawn, who has missed a deadline your team agreed on. Fill in the text column in the PACT chart at left. What type of text would convince Dawn to do her work? A face-to-face conversation in a team meeting? A short e-mail? What might the text contain, based on information in the other columns?

Luckily, it's not difficult to avoid those problems from the outset by setting up and maintaining shared style guides and style sheets that team members refer to as they write. Style guides are similar in function (if not size) to the style guide you might use to format research papers; they are basically manuals for how to write and design. Style sheets are groups of settings in a word processor or document design program that automatically format certain types of text in specific ways (body text in one font, size, and style; main headings in another style; and so on).

CREATING STYLE GUIDES   A style guide for your projects, at least in school, will probably be much shorter and less comprehensive than the guide you use for research papers. Style guides developed in organizations are often used in addition to a larger, mass-produced style guides to cover situations that aren't discussed in the larger guides.

In your style guide, you'll specify things such as how to address the reader — are they addressed directly at all? In second person ("you")? Third person ("the user")? Do you, the writer, have a presence ("I"), or are you completely behind the scenes? If possible, find similar texts that readers are used to using in that context. What aspects of their style and format do you need to follow? Refer back to your PACT notes. If you didn't address these issues, add them in.

You can come up with some of these things beforehand, but for short, "one-off" projects, a style guide can be developed by the team over time: Each time you have to make a decision about choosing *a* over *b*, the team should briefly discuss the decision and then update the style guide to reflect that decision. In some cases, you'll have to make a decision while you're writing individually, in which case you can stop and ask the team for feedback before moving on, or you can make a tentative decision yourself and check with the team later.

In most cases, though, style issues emerge once the team starts reading each other's work: You'll notice that something you did in your draft conflicts with what someone else did. At that point, the team can discuss the issue and update the style guide accordingly. On the opposite page is an excerpt from a style guide that records one team's decisions about specific style issues.

It's a good idea to be slightly obsessive about developing, updating, and adhering to a style guide, at least at the start of a project. Your team will develop a sense of how strict or detailed your materials need to be once you start working. It's important to pay attention to style guides at the start because they're difficult to implement once team members have developed their own habits.

Your style guide will also need to include file-naming conventions. At the very least, you should specify how to distinguish one person's document from another's. One good rule of thumb is to at least include

Structure: In general, use relatively short, active sentences with short to moderate complexity.

> *Bad:* "A group of prospective students was taken on a tour of the campus radio station by station staff."
>
> *Bad:* "A good impression of campus was fostered by having station staff, including campus DJs and the station's Program Director, lead prospective students on a tour throughout the station."
>
> *Good:* "Guided by DJs, prospective students toured the campus radio station."

Voice: Use plural first person ("we") not singular ("I").

Word choice: Lose the thesaurus.

> *Bad:* "utilize"
>
> *Good:* "use"

Citation format: Refer to *MLA Handbook*, 7th edition, for issues not covered in our own style guide.

Headings: Use only two levels of headings. Make headings informative and between one and seven words.

Main sections: Include an introductory paragraph that overviews topics covered in that section (and its subsections).

Files: File names must include the specific topic covered in the file (introduction, lit review, etc.), draft number, and your initials. Increment the draft number by .1 for minor revisions and 1.0 for major revisions. Put an underscore between each element.

> *Bad:* draft.docx
>
> *Bad:* intro.docx
>
> *Good:* intro_1.3_jj.docx

● Portion of a style guide for a team project

the team member's initials (check to make sure no two team members have the same initials) along with a word summarizing the content ("budget" or "summary," for example) and a date or version number.

CREATING STYLE SHEETS   Style sheets are, in many ways, even simpler than style guides: A style sheet is a set of formatting rules used by software such as Microsoft Word or Adobe InDesign or by web browsers to format texts consistently. In one way of thinking about it, a style guide is the rulebook, while the style sheet is the implementation of the rules at the level of the text.

Style sheets can usually be exported from one document and imported into another, making them an easy way to make all of the sections to a complex document conform to a single standard.

Style sheets condense all of the formatting decisions in a document — what font, point size, and weight to use for body paragraphs; how much space to put above heading level 1; and so forth — into a single point of control. In the example below, a style called Heading 1 is being applied to a chunk of text in Microsoft Word. You might apply the same Heading 1 style to 10 different headings in the document. If you decided to change how Heading 1 was formatted, instead of carefully locating each occurrence of it in the document and manually changing each one, you can update the style sheet, automatically changing how Heading 1 text looks throughout the document.

Style sheets remove the inevitable inconsistencies caused by manual reformatting. And when your team brings together separate chunks of the document and pastes them into a single file, the style sheet in the single file makes each Heading 1 consistent. You only need to make sure people are using the same style names and applying them consistently (so that one person doesn't use "body text" for default paragraph text while another uses "Normal" as the name for the same thing in a different file). Similarly, you want to make sure that everyone uses a consistent approach to breaking up documents, including things like relying on the same number of heading levels or using bulleted lists for one purpose and numbered lists for another. Those things should be specified in your style guide.

● Configuring styles in Microsoft Word
Used with permission from Microsoft

Share Materials

As the discussion of style guides and style sheets illustrates, writing in a team relies heavily on sharing information. You will also want to share (frequently) the texts that you're writing. You can do this by saving files to a central location (a lab server or a shared website), by e-mailing attachments back and forth, or by meeting somewhere to go over drafts. It's important, especially for medium-sized or larger projects, to schedule in more than a single draft. If your team waits until an hour before the due date to meet and merge their material, you might find out that the sections are wildly inconsistent. If you can compare work at an earlier stage, you can head off any consistency issues while there's still time. With only rare exceptions, good writers plan on multiple (often many) drafts. And, just as important, they get feedback on their drafts from other people.

There are three primary approaches to reading your teammates' drafts. You might share drafts simply to allow people to compare how their material relates to yours in terms of levels of development, tone, and structure. (As you notice issues, flag them for potential inclusion in the style guide.) Or you may do a formal review in which you give your teammates direct feedback on their drafts (and they do likewise for you). Or you might just each take a turn with the full draft, either because team members are getting tired of looking at the same section or because different members contribute different strengths. For example, a person with relatively weak writing ability but a great deal of knowledge about a topic might pass a draft off to someone with lower topical knowledge but great writing ability. (See "Tools for Collaborative Writing" on page 213 for tips on commenting and collaborating with word-processing programs.)

How to Give Feedback

Down deep (and often right up on the surface), most people don't like to be criticized. Giving people feedback, especially if they're not well seasoned in getting constructive criticism, can be a tense process. As a reviewer, part of your job is figuring out how to get the writer to see that you're helping her to improve her text.

You might notice that the process of giving feedback is like the process of writing itself: You're attempting to get a writer (your audience) on your team (the context) to understand how you can help her change something in ways that benefit her and her community (her text and her purpose). On the next page is a PACT chart created for just such a situation. If you look around, you'll notice that the purpose/audience/context/text framework can be applied to nearly any social interaction.

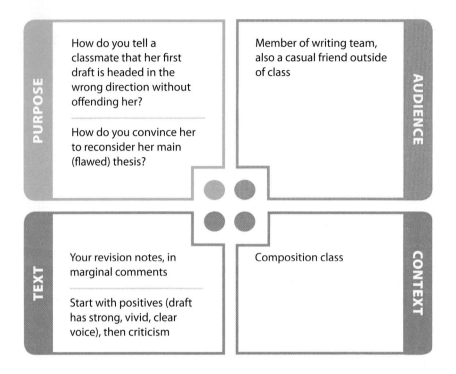

● Summary comment that starts with positives
before turning toward weak areas
Used with permission from Microsoft

So how do you keep a writer from getting defensive? Start with the positive aspects of her text. Starting with the good things puts the writer in a more accepting state of mind. At some point, though, you'll need to shift over to the constructive criticism: "But we can make this stronger if you. . . ."

Teachers and textbooks frequently use the phrase "constructive criticism" to point out that criticism can be a useful thing even though the word "criticism" often has negative connotations. It might be better to think of it as simply "constructive change." Keep your comments constructive by pointing out what needs to change. More important, point out *why* something needs to change. Figuring out the "why" will require you to think about what motivates the writer. Most writers are worried about the eventual readers of their text, so if a passage seems like it will confuse those readers, point that out and say why (for example, because readers will not understand the terminology). Continue to push for constructive change by specifying what that change

Bad Comment	Good Comment
Hard to read »	This paragraph has some very long, wandering sentences. Can you break it up a little?
Looks good to me »	Very well argued: logical progression of points, dealt with counterarguments well, good transitions
Seems a little short »	Can you develop the second example more? Can you explain why voters were unhappy?
I don't agree »	The examples you have aren't enough evidence to convince me of your point here. Do you have census data that might back this up?

might be. The writer will be more likely to take your comments to heart if she sees how the comments can help her achieve her goals.

Although high-level summary comments are useful in framing critiques, you also need to provide concrete, direct comments to help people understand what you're asking them to do. The table above shows a set of vague (and not terribly useful) comments along with some more direct (and useful) alternatives. The specificity of the "good" comments will give writers clearer direction.

Tools for Collaborative Writing

The tools we write with affect how we write. That's true of the writing you do on your own and the writing you do in teams. Other chapters explore some of these tools, including the use of things like whiteboards and sticky notes for brainstorming (Chapter 3, pp. 65–66) and research tools such as search engines and information organizers (Chapter 7, pages 162–63). This section covers some tools with features specifically designed to support collaborative writing (and, to some extent, any writing on which you'll get or give feedback).

Before we turn to software, it's useful to remember that older analog tools are sometimes the right choice in a particular situation. If you're reviewing a printout of a team member's draft in class, for example, writing notes in the margin and tagging important sections with sticky notes is probably the best strategy.

But usually digital tools are preferable for their ease of distribution and quick revision. Most word-processing programs offer a simple commenting feature that allows you to insert comments into a text in a way that makes them stand out visually for the original author. The screenshot at the top left of page 215 shows commenting features in Google Drive.

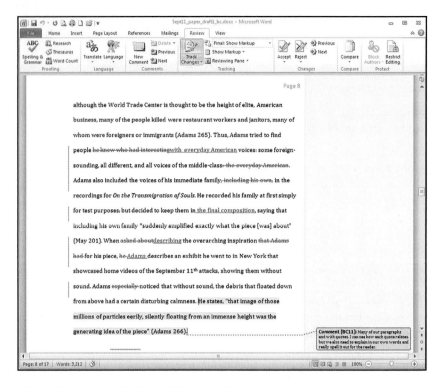

● Track Changes feature in Microsoft Word showing proposed changes from a team member in context

Tracking Changes

If you're working collaboratively on a single document, it's often useful to use a program's built-in Track Changes feature to highlight pending changes made. This allows one team member to make tentative revisions to a document that another (or all) team members can review before accepting the changes into the document.

As you can see in the figure above, the Track Changes feature also includes information about who suggested a change or made a comment, along with other information.

Sharing Access

Web-based writing software often includes facilities for collaborative online editing, such as simple sharing of documents, commenting features, discussion threads, and more. At a basic level, Google Drive allows you to easily share access to text documents, presentations, spreadsheets, and other file types.

Another option for collaboratively editing documents on the web is the use of wiki software. While Wikipedia is the most popular wiki site, the software on which the site runs also provides the underpinnings of

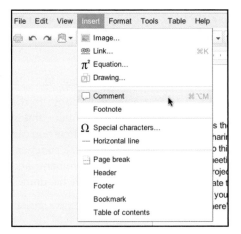

● Comment feature in Google Drive

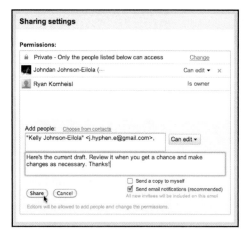

● Sharing document access in Google Drive

● Wikipedia editing project involving two English classes at Towson University

Towson University American Editors Project, http://en.wikipedia.org/wiki/Wikipedia:School_and_University_Projects/Towson_University_American_Editors_Project

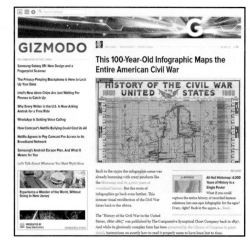

● Some collaborative weblogs, like Gizmodo, feature articles written by individual contributors

Reprinted by permission of Gawker Media Group

thousands of smaller wikis. Wikis are used for all types of collaborative work, ranging from tech support to classroom projects. Writing and editing a wiki will require you to learn some new skills, but the learning curve is fairly shallow and well worth the investment.

Weblogs also offer opportunities for collaboration, especially for collaborative publication. Multiple users in a class or on a "real-world" project can contribute stories to the blog, much like an online magazine. Other weblogs can be used as a place for sharing course materials and other information.

Text for Analysis

DRAFT OF AN ESSAY
Rachel Steinhaus, "Demystifying Frito-Lay"

Student Rachel Steinhaus wrote this draft of a short essay in response to the assignment below. Review the draft and provide the writer with critique notes. The essay has not been revised or edited, so expect to find places where you can make constructive criticisms. Include both marginal comments and a summary comment at the top. Then, form small groups to review all your comments and consider how successful they might be in helping the writer improve her draft.

Advertising Analysis Essay

We've been analyzing the ways that advertising shapes and is shaped by our cultures. For this three- to five-page essay, choose one piece of advertising and discuss how the ad positions viewers in a certain way as well as the ways viewers can resist or oppose that positioning. Use outside sources to back up your arguments.

Your grade will be based equally on four categories:

- Power of arguments: How convincing and logical are your arguments? Have you proved your main point?
- Use of sources: Did you choose an interesting ad? Have you used your sources effectively to make arguments?
- Language use: Is your language clear, strong, and vivid?
- Surface-level polish: Is your text grammatically correct? Did you follow formatting conventions? Did you cite your sources correctly in MLA style?

● Rachel was responding to this assigment

Steinhaus 1

Rachel Steinhaus

ENGL 101

Prof. Choi

October 29, 20—

Demystifying Frito-Lay

All advertisements use a number of different methods in order to tempt the public to buy their product. The advertisers draw on our history, our ideology, and cultural cues which impact how we think and act in relation to the product that is being sold. This ad for Fritos corn chips is no different, using all of these techniques to promote their brand. In this case, the advertisers draw mainly on the desires of the target population to be American and to be healthy.

In this Frito-Lay advertisement, a middle-aged man carries a bushel filled with Fritos chip bags. The man wears work gloves and a baseball cap with an American flag on it. The bushel is stamped with the letters USA. He has a slight smile on his face, which is lighted by the sun, distinguishable by the shadow from his cap. Behind him are two other people, both in flannel shirts, tending to a number of other baskets of Fritos, which sit on a red trailer. There are blue skies with a few white clouds over the cornfield that grows behind the people.

The image conveys the idea of a hardworking, American farmer who has finished a long but satisfying day on the farm. His face and the words at the bottom of the ad tell us that he is proud of the work he does for his country. The caption also tells us that the chips are made from "100% American corn"

Steinhaus 2

and contain 0 grams of transfat. The way in which the Fritos are displayed makes them appear as though the farmer has been harvesting them, like produce, fresh from the field, giving the idea of naturalness.

The rhetoric of this image is two-fold. First and foremost, as in any ad, this ad is trying to persuade the consumer to buy a certain product, in this case Fritos corn chips. In order to motivate you to do this, the ad attempts to elicit a patriotic feeling from the viewer, hoping that by associating their product with American patriotism, you will feel better about purchasing their chips than any other brand. To some extent they want you to feel as though if you are not buying Fritos, you are less American than those who do get the chips. The ad also attempts to take advantage of the idea that natural foods, or those with fewer preservatives and additives, are what is healthiest for the buyer. The company wants the consumer to believe that Fritos chips, represented as coming right out of a cornfield, are more natural and therefore healthier than other chip brands. The rhetoric of this image deals with both the quality of a consumer's food and with her loyalty to her country; it presents both patriotism and food as "natural." The message is that, if you are an American, you should buy Fritos, both because they are "grown" in America by Americans, so you would be supporting your country, and because they are healthy and natural, which is how true Americans eat.

This Fritos advertisement relies on a number of historical debates and topics in order to present its product in

Steinhaus 3

the best light and influence the viewer's desires. The first of these is the debate over immigrant workers, especially illegal immigrants, and their role on American farms. According to Bonnie Erbe, a blogger for *US News and World Report*, a 2009 poll found that seventy-four percent of American voters believe the federal government should be doing more to secure our borders. While some people want to find ways to legalize the status of illegal immigrants, others believe that they, by working for extremely cheap wages, take jobs away from American citizens. With this in mind, the creators of this ad for Fritos largely imply in this ad that their product is made by American farmers and citizens, in hopes of prompting support from the public, drawing on their desire for more American jobs and products. The creators of the advertisement believe that the public is motivated to buy American products, so they hope that by connecting their product with "100% American corn" they can motivate the viewer to buy Fritos.

This advertisement also draws on public concern about the obesity epidemic in America. A Reuters article from January of 2009 states that, at that time, the percentage of obese Americans (34%) had surpassed the percentage of Americans who were overweight (32.7%). With this growing number of obesity cases in America, the public has become obsessed with new diet and exercise regimens in an attempt to combat this trend. Advertising executives, largely aware of this tendency, have attempted to capitalize upon this attitude in American culture by presenting Fritos as a healthy snack.

Steinhaus 4

They make them appear natural, having just been "harvested" from the field by the farmers in the image, and list at the bottom of the image a few details of the chips, insisting that they are made directly from corn and that there are 0 grams of trans fat in their product. By placing this advertisement in *US* magazine, a magazine directed mostly at women, who are more likely to be concerned about their weight, Frito-Lay capitalizes even more profoundly on the cultural aspects of health food that this image relies on.

In a more indirect way, the advertisement is designed to appeal to the viewer's desire to be attractive and successful. Some viewers might be concerned with healthy eating but not able to afford expensive organic foods. Fritos are relatively inexpensive, so by presenting them as a healthy alternative to other, more fatty chips, this ad could inspire lower-income shoppers to buy Fritos, as an attempt to join those who can afford to care about healthy eating. Eating healthy foods also impacts a person's physical appearance, making them (in our culture) more attractive. In this way, the Frito-Lay company motivates consumers to buy their chips with the idea that by doing so, the buyer can be more fit, more attractive, and consequently, can be more successful in the social interactions and the dating world.

Not all viewers would respond to this ad in the way the advertisers intended. Viewers who do not believe that illegal immigration is a problem, who are immigrants themselves, or who do not fit the ad's image of what it means to be patriotic

Steinhaus 5

and American might feel alienated by the ad. Other viewers
might criticize the ad's attempts to portray chips as a natural,
healthy food. They could point out the low nutritional value
versus the relatively high fat and sodium content of each
serving. Nevertheless, by relying on the desires of people to
feel healthy, American, attractive, and successful, Frito-Lay
creates an effective, if manipulative, ad. The ad presents pride
in one's country and the desire to eat healthy foods as natural
rather than cultural phenomena, encouraging consumption of
the product as a way to experience what it is to be a natural,
health-conscious, successful American.

Steinhaus 6

Works Cited

Erbe, Bonnie. "Poll: Immigration Amnesty Is Unpopular

Outside the Beltway, Pols Remain Clueless." *U.S. News

and World Report.* U.S. News & World Report, 16 Apr.

2009. Web. 11 Oct. 2009.

"Obese Americans now outweigh the merely overweight."

Reuters.com. Reuters, 9 Jan. 2009. Web. 11 Oct. 2009.

Exercises

1. Develop, possibly in a team, a list of good characteristics and bad characteristics for a hypothetical team member, focusing on behavior during discussion. (This is an exercise; don't critique actual team members.) Examples might include "interrupts other people" or "texts constantly" or "invites other people to express their opinion." Using that list, create index cards for five fictional people. Make at least one person purely good and one purely bad, with mixes for the others.

   Next, place the index cards face down and shuffle them. Have five people pick up an index card: The card they get is the person they will pretend to be.

   Have the team come up with a shared answer to this question: Are there too many team projects at our school? Take up to 15 minutes to agree on an answer to the question.

   After you arrive at an answer, step back and discuss how well the discussion went. Can you guess what role each person was assigned? What strategies seemed to work best for resolving problems you ran into? Should you have tried other strategies?

   As a group, write a short e-mail to your instructor summarizing the results of your work (including the discussion).

2. Locate a short article, essay, or editorial that you think is poorly written. It doesn't matter whether you disagree or agree with the article, only that you think it suffers from poor grammar, writing style, logic, or rhetoric, or from other things that prevent it from being successful. Copy the text into a word-processing document. Use the commenting features of the software to write a review of the document that you think will convince the writer to want to revise his or her piece as you suggest. You'll need to think about what might motivate

the writer to change as well as how to phrase and structure your advice in a way that doesn't offend him or her so much that your help is rejected.

3. Locate a website that supports collaborative or team projects. Google Drive and Basecamp are two, but there are many choices. Sign up for the service, read through the documentation or watch a video tutorial, and then attempt to complete the following tasks.

   a. Upload several documents in various file formats (not just Word .docx files but other common types such as .pdf or .mov). Consider uploading some open source MS Office alternatives (OpenOffice, NeoOffice, etc.).
   b. Invite another person to join your team or share editing rights to a document.
   c. With your new partner, make changes to the document.

   What are the most important features a website like this needs to provide? How easy was the process? Could you imagine using this to collaboratively write a document? Why or why not?

   With your collaborative partner, give a five-minute presentation that covers the pros and cons of the website and demonstrates key features.

4. Locate a text you wrote for a different class. Remove any comments or grades from your teacher or classmates. Pretend you are your teacher. Before you start reading the document, ask yourself, *OK, Teach, what are my goals here? What did I want the student to learn or demonstrate in this piece of writing?* Make a list of the key characteristics. If this class used a formal grading sheet or rubric, you can use that.

   Then read through the document, thinking of yourself as your teacher, making notes to the writer (you, in other words). As you make these notes, ask yourself, *What am I trying to teach the writer with these comments? How can I help the writer improve? What words will do that?*

   As an alternative, have each member of a team individually comment on copies of the same document. After they're done, read through all of the comments and discuss how they compare. Do people agree on certain points? Disagree? Pick three comments that you agree are useful and three that could use some work. Summarize your discussion and send it, along with the commented files, to your instructor.

5. Why might some of the comments below make you feel defensive or insulted if you received them from a reviewer? Revise the comments to make them less barbed.

   "Your examples don't make any sense."

   "I don't like the font you're using."

   "This has a really stuffy tone to it."

   "I can't follow your logic."

   "Seems fine to me. I can't really think of anything you should change."

   "It's just kind of *blah*."

Scenario Connections

1. In Scenario 17, "Designing a Newsletter for the Zeeland Farmers' Market," you'll need to create a consistent format for body text, headings, figure captions, and running headers or footers. Determine what program you'll be using to create the newsletter and then create a style sheet in that application for the different textual elements you'll use. Review the section on style sheets in this chapter on page 210 and, if necessary, the section on typography from Chapter 5 on pages 118–24.

2. Scenario 2, "Teamwork Problems," asks you to draw on a set of existing texts to make an argument to your teacher about grades for team members. Download these texts from the e-pages into a word processor that provides commenting features similar to those shown in the screenshot on page 214. Make comments in each text about what sections of the text might be useful, how they should be framed in the new text you'll write, and any other information that might be useful to think about as you create the new text. If you're working in a team, come up with a system so that all team members can make and share these comments.

3. If you're working on a team-based version of Scenario 7, "Podcasting Campus Life for Prospective Students," discuss the tips for building effective teams on pages 206–07. Come up with concrete things that your team will do to be effective and document them in a list that you'll revisit on a set schedule (at each meeting, once a week, or on some other schedule). At the end of the project, discuss how well this strategy worked. Were you able to stick to the plan? Did the tips help? Are there other things you think would have helped?

4. In Scenario 10, "Writing a Restaurant Review" (p. 286), you may be writing a collaborative review after your team visits the restaurant. Familiarize yourself with the Track Changes feature of the word processor you'll use. Track the changes made in the draft by each writer as you take turns working on the draft. If your word processor does not track changes, develop a system that shows where each writer has changed the draft (for example, each person can add text in a different color).

5. For any of the scenarios involving team review of each other's work, research and select a system for online exchange of documents. After you've reviewed drafts, discuss the pros and cons of the system you used.

Revising Your Texts

Even talented, experienced writers often have mixed feelings about revising. It's hard work, often frustrating. Sometimes, the text seems to get worse rather than better. The process can feel more like tearing things down rather than building them up. But smart writers also see revising as a second (or third or tenth) chance, part of a complex process in which new strategies are tried out, tweaked, and adjusted on the way to creating an effective, useful text that becomes part of the larger conversation.

The complexity of your revising processes will vary from one text to another, depending on the details of the situation. Small, simple texts may get no revision at all. A short e-mail to your lab partner or a text message to a family member might be a one-shot deal. A novel, a research proposal, or even a short poem might go through many, many revisions, especially if it is considered important.

This chapter covers a range of ways to undertake revision that you can draw on (and modify) as needed when you begin revising your own texts. We'll discuss both how to get other people to give you revision ideas and how to assess your own writing for revision needs. You'll also learn how to make a prioritized revision plan that focuses on the big picture items before you begin fine-tuning.

Reviewing Your Own Texts

Even if you're going to get outside feedback on your texts, you also need the ability to look critically at what you've written yourself. Reviewing can (and should) take place throughout your writing process, from screening initial mind-mapping notes or freewrites to looking at the logical structure you're building into an outline to carefully and critically reading full drafts.

You'll want to review and revise your work before getting outside feedback so that you're giving your reviewers something worth reading. And there will be times when you don't have someone around to provide feedback or the time to get outside feedback. In those cases, you're on your own. Let's consider some strategies for improving your ability to review your own writing.

As Chapter 6 on managing writing projects mentioned, if at all possible give yourself some time away from your text before returning to review it. This time will give you a little "critical distance" that lets you look at your own work with fresh eyes (making it more likely you'll see what the text actually says rather than what you wanted it to say). The steps listed below are one method for reviewing your own work. You can adapt them as necessary to fit your process.

1. Create a duplicate version of your file and add a version number using whatever versioning system you've developed for your drafts. (See Chapter 6, page 147, for a discussion of file names and versioning.)
2. Begin your review by going back to the original assignment as well as any purpose, audience, context, and text materials you completed. Review all of them carefully.
3. Imagine that you are a member of your audience based on what you have in the audience section of your PACT chart.
4. Read through your text carefully, responding to it in ways you think that audience member might.
5. As you discover issues (comments your audience might make, things you notice missing or out of order), insert a comment into your text. You can use the built-in comment feature or just add in text that's formatted differently than the original text (bold, for example). Don't start making actual revisions at this point; that will interrupt the flow of reading. Just make a note and move on.
6. After you've reviewed the text, assess how successful it was at achieving its purpose. Will readers act or think in the way you had hoped? If not, why? What can you do to address the gaps?
7. Read through the assignment and your PACT notes again to help you come up with revision plans. Be sure to read through the "Creating a Revision Plan" section (p. 234) for more advice.

Getting Feedback

In some cases, you'll have a set process for getting feedback. Your instructor may give you a set of instructions to follow in peer-critique teams, or your company may have a cover sheet or online form that you include with your draft. In many cases, your peer-critique team is not actually the audience you identified in your PACT chart. Remind your peers about your audience and the context. Share your PACT chart with them to help them better read and respond.

If you haven't been assigned a review team or paired up with another student to review your text, consider recruiting a reviewer. Ask a friend with good writing skills to help. Or visit your campus's writing center. Trained staff at the writing center can review your text and talk to you about revision strategies. If you do visit the writing center, be sure to bring the assignment description as well as the PACT materials you've developed to help your reviewer better understand your assignment.

Helping Reviewers Help You

If there's not already a process in place for peer critiques or reviews, you'll need to construct one. In some situations, you can hand a draft to someone without much instruction and still get good feedback, but in most cases the reviewer is going to need you to give them some context and instructions about what you'd like them to do. Ask yourself what your goals are, what you need to get the reviewer to do. Ask yourself how you can convince the reviewer to provide those things. You might even want to consider mapping out a quick PACT chart about your reviewers: What things will motivate them? How can you make them feel like their contributions are valuable? Simple things like taking notes while they talk, explicitly thanking them, and asking good clarifying questions can go a long way to making people feel appreciated. And if you're providing them with feedback on their own texts, be sure to be a role model by providing constructive, supportive feedback.

Here's an example: Rachel has drafted a short, personal-reflection essay for her English class that describes the different dialects or types of language she has spoken throughout her life, from the "broken English" spoken by her family in Guyana to the New York City slang she learned later in her life to the Irish and Scottish influences she picked up when visiting family members in those countries.

Rachel needs at least a B on this paper. The original assignment asked her to draw on a course reading as she analyzed how her family used language. She's not sure whether her experiences really connect with those described in the book, so she wants to get feedback from someone else. Rachel asks her roommate Inez to read through the draft. Inez agrees, saying she'll get to it after she washes dishes. Rachel thanks her and e-mails her a copy of the draft.

The next afternoon, Rachel asks Inez whether she had a chance to read the draft. Inez, looking up from her computer, says, "Yeah. Yeah. I liked it." "Anything else?" Rachel asks. "Uh . . . ," Inez says, looking back at her computer. "Your family sounds great. You might want to proofread it — I saw a lot of typos."

Rachel thanks her, trying to keep the annoyance out of her voice. Rachel realizes Inez probably skimmed through it like she was browsing through a magazine article in the dentist's waiting room. She realizes she should have given Inez a little bit more to go on, such as the goal of the assignment or her concerns. She might have asked herself some of the questions shown on the next page.

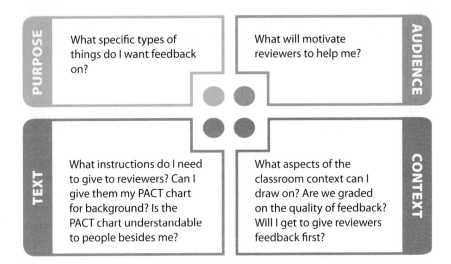

PURPOSE — What specific types of things do I want feedback on?

AUDIENCE — What will motivate reviewers to help me?

TEXT — What instructions do I need to give to reviewers? Can I give them my PACT chart for background? Is the PACT chart understandable to people besides me?

CONTEXT — What aspects of the classroom context can I draw on? Are we graded on the quality of feedback? Will I get to give reviewers feedback first?

The questions here are similar in many ways to the questions you asked yourself while you were working on your primary PACT chart, so it might be useful to refer back to that. First, what did Rachel do to motivate Inez to help her? Not very much: Inez and Rachel are fairly good friends, but Inez didn't know how important the assignment was to Rachel. Rachel also realizes she could have done Inez a favor that would have both given her a little motivation *and* given Inez more time to read the draft: Rachel could have offered to wash the dishes, for example, while Inez read the draft.

Rachel also realizes she didn't give Inez anything to work with: She didn't tell her what the assignment was or what things Rachel was supposed to achieve for a good grade. At the very least, she could have given Inez a rough description or even given her a copy of the short assignment from class, which outlined the goals for the assignment and even how it would be graded. She could have told Inez that at this stage typos weren't important: She wanted feedback on the overall meaning of the essay. Rachel had hoped that Inez would use this unstructured, open-ended approach to give her a wide range of comments — that strategy had worked in her writing class — but in this case it looks like Inez needed a little more structure and direction.

Rachel sits down at her desk, calls up her PACT chart, and begins cleaning it up a little bit so that it'll be easier to understand when she gives it to Inez. She opens up her e-mail program and begins a quick note to Inez:

Inez —

I really appreciated the feedback you gave me on my draft. I've worked on the typos you pointed out. But now I'm stuck and I could use a favor.

I just realized I didn't give you a chance to give me feedback on the big issues: Do the experiences that I discuss really connect with the material from the book that I referred to? Or am I stretching it? If they don't connect, then I have problems.

If you have 20 free minutes, I could really use some feedback on the large-scale issues. Can you meet me at some point tonight or tomorrow at the cafe? I can give you some additional background about the assignment that will help you see my overall goals (and concerns). I'll buy the coffee.

Thanks!

Rachel

Rachel sits back, reads through the e-mail, and presses Send. She starts working on a set of specific questions she'll ask Inez to respond to:

- Primary: Does the material from my life seem similar to the things from the book that I discussed? Could I make those connections stronger?

- For the audience that we talked about, are there parts of my draft that you think they'll disagree with?

- Can you identify the major points that the draft is trying to make?

- Is the language I'm using in the draft appropriate for this audience and this context?

- Do you think my overall strategy will convince this audience?

- Are there any other large-scale things you think I need to work on?

She feels a little more comfortable with this approach. When she checks her e-mail she sees that Inez has replied already to say she'd be glad to help and is free at 8:30 tonight.

Types of Comments: Summary and Marginal

There are many ways to structure a review, but two types of comments are most common: summary and marginal. Summary comments ask reviewers to provide a set of overall notes separate from the text. Marginal comments, as you probably guessed, ask reviewers to insert comments directly in the margins of the text, referring to specific sections or elements of the text. The two types of review are often used together because they complement each other: Summary comments typically deal with the text at a more abstract level, noting how well the overall argument works or whether the examples are useful; marginal comments usually point out very specific things in a text, such as problems with the transition from one section to the next.

The example at the top of page 230 shows a set of marginal comments on the first page of an essay in which the writer analyzes an ad for Fritos.

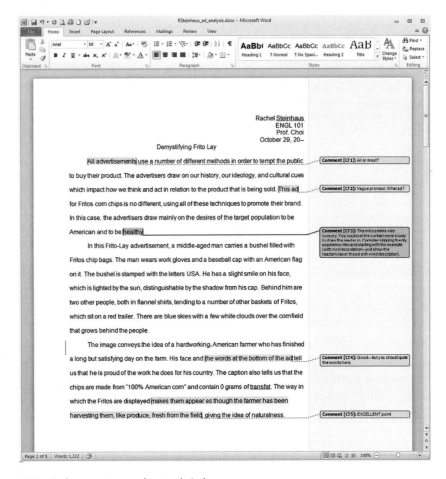

● Marginal comments on a short analytical essay

The comments range in scope from grammatical corrections (a vague pronoun) to a broad suggestion to make a fairly large-scale change to the introduction. Although the writer will end up using most of these suggestions, she'll be best served by considering the large-scale changes first.

The example on page 231 shows a section from a set of summary comments for an essay. In this case, the reviewer is working from a standard reviewing template (sometimes called a rubric) that was provided by an instructor for reviewers to use.

Getting and giving critiques can be stressful. After all, you're usually either telling someone they did something wrong or someone is telling you that you've done something wrong. As you gain more experience getting and giving critiques, you'll start to rethink the negative feelings

Review Sheet for Essay Three

Writer: Steve Armey
Reviewer: Leanne White

Note to Reviewers: Before you start the review, take a few minutes to review the major categories below so you can keep them in mind while you're reading the draft. Since this is a rough draft, you should only be paying attention to major issues: the usability test itself and in the report. After you've read through the draft, fill out the form and provide a rough 1-10 grade in each category. Comments are important.

Once you've completed the review, your review team should meet to discuss your reviews of each other's comments. Email your review comments to the author after your meeting.

Category	Score (1-10)	Comments
Strength of Argument		
Stated argument in clear terms	7	You're making two different arguments: One about wind power and one about technology and progress. I'd pick one (probably wind) and stick with it.
Stated evaluation criteria	8	The criteria are clear but you don't offer much evidence that addresses the criteria. Can you find data?
Considered pros and cons fairly	7	You don't seem to offer any negative aspects. I know wind power is controversial, so there must be some.
Structure		
Provided structural cues	9	Very clear structure.

● Summary comments on a short essay

involved and start to focus on the positive ones: Good critique sessions should feel collaborative, productive, and positive (See the tips on page 232.). Think of them as exercise. You're trading a certain amount of stress for improvement in the long run. They're a way for several people to come together for the purpose of building a successful text.

Interpreting Comments

After you get a review (or finish reviewing your own text), you have to figure out what to do with the comments. This obviously varies depending on the specifics of your writing project, but in general you'll want to spend some time interpreting the comments and using them to create a revision plan.

One of the hardest things to do in reading through review comments is assessing what a comment is worth. Reviewers are certainly not infallible. In general, you can assume readers are giving you their honest

Tips for Getting and Giving Critiques

- *Try not to be defensive.* Even very experienced writers can get defensive during critique sessions. After all, criticism of a text implies criticism of the writer. Making the most of feedback can be difficult if you take constructive criticism as a personal attack on yourself. Remember that it's about making the text better. Getting feedback is one area in which you try to push your ego to the back for a little while and just read or listen. When you push your ego back during a critique session, you're not disengaging. Instead, you're trying to avoid getting defensive.

- *Don't offer explanations unless explicitly asked.* It's surprising how often an in-class critique turns into the writer offering weak rationalizations for why the text is as it is or arguing with the reviewers about what the text *really* means. That's not the writer's job during the critique session: The writer is there to get feedback he or she can use to improve the text. Even if you think the reviewer misinterpreted your text, you should consider the fact that your audience may make the same misinterpretation. Can you somehow revise your text to avoid that mistake?

- *Take notes about the feedback, highlighting key points or jotting down ideas as they come to you while you read or listen to comments.* Taking notes will help you stay engaged while stepping back.

- *Ask questions.* One of the rare exceptions to stepping back is that you can ask the reviewer to offer more details or give you a moment to catch up in note taking.

- *When giving critiques, format your comments so they stand out as separate from the draft.* You can use a word-processing program's marginal commenting features, make your comments a different color or font, or put each of your comments between distinctive characters {{{such as repeated curly brackets}}}.

- *Whenever possible, start critiques with the positive aspects of the text.* Complement writers on effective phrasing, solid structure, strong examples, or some other specific thing they've done well. Even if they haven't completely achieved what they set out to do, you can focus on what they *intended* to do. Then help them fulfill that intention.

opinion, but it's not uncommon for reviewers to read your text while they're distracted or when they're in a hurry. They may not understand what the text is trying to achieve. They may lack the language to describe a problem they've spotted. So you need to *interpret* your reviewers' comments, deciding whether they're worth following. If reviewers ask you, for example, to cut something that you thought was a key element in your draft, step back and ask yourself what led the reviewers to make that suggestion. Is the section extraneous? Or do you need to do something to help readers see that the section is crucial in making a larger point? In other words, you can't simply follow reviewers' suggestions without thinking about them. But you also can't reject reviewers'

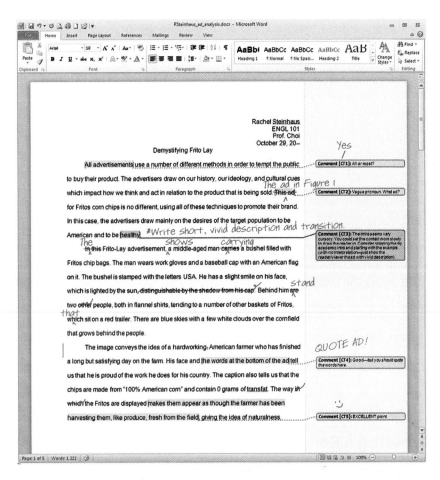

● Revision suggestions from reviewer (in red) with revision plans sketched on printout for reference. Asterisks indicate more important revision plans.

suggestions simply because doing so makes your life easier or because you're feeling defensive.

For simple projects, you might sort through your reviewers' comments by simply circling, putting an asterisk next to, or highlighting the important suggestions, as shown in the example above. If any of reviewers' points is phrased as a question or a vague comment, you may need to add to the note yourself to clarify how that comment should lead to revision.

For larger projects, you may want to take a slightly more formal approach. As you read, write down key points the reviewer is making. You can think of the key points as headings or steps that you'll use when you're creating a revision plan. Translating your reviewer's comments into short key points is especially important if, as with many reviewers, the comments wander or aren't very specific: The key points that you write down should be specific, concrete actions.

For example, suppose a reviewer comments,

> I'm not sure why this example is here. The first example makes your point well enough so a second example just seems to drag on.

In response, you would begin by reading the section the reviewer is referring to and considering why you added that section. You'd look back at your PACT materials to see whether they can shed light on what the example was supposed to do for the reader. Do you need to revise the PACT chart, or is the flaw in your text or even in the reader's interpretation?

After rereading the section, you decide you need two examples to show that your point is valid for two different but common situations. Do you ignore that reviewer's comment? No. You can see that it's not clear what the difference is between the two examples. You also can see that the two examples could be copyedited to tighten and shorten them. So you make a note to use in your revision plan:

> Write transition between two examples to show how they're different. During copyedit, tighten these two examples up. Cut excess words and use more active verbs. Currently a little too loose and dull.

Your next step will be to sort your key revision actions into categories in a revision plan.

Creating a Revision Plan

Lay a foundation for your revision plan by getting out the original assignment and your own notes about the project. It's not uncommon for a writing project to drift away from its original goals as one idea bounces off another during the writing process. Sometimes these tangents are useful, offering new ways of approaching your overall goal. But sometimes these tangents are headed off in the wrong direction, interesting but not addressing the purpose of the assignment. Straying too far may result in an ineffective text or a poor grade. So read through the original assignment and your notes before you get started thinking about revision.

The PACT materials you've developed should be used throughout your drafting and revising processes. They're the anchors that keep your writing from drifting. But also be open to revising the PACT materials themselves. As you're interpreting your critique comments and creating your revision plan, you may (and, ideally, should) learn new things and change your opinions occasionally. You may decide, for example, that the pur-

	Revising Text-centric Documents	Revising Design-centric Texts
Major structural revising »	• Changing the overall structure or sequence • Cutting or moving large sections • Adding new sections • Changing purpose, type of text, or even audience	• Changing format or layout • Resolving potential technical glitches (e.g., making sure software works) • Changing purpose, type of text, or even audience
Midlevel revising »	• Writing or revising transitions • Filling in sections • Working on figures or tables	• Testing different font choices • Continuing to change format or layout • Testing usability
Surface-level revising »	• Tweaking sentences • Checking verb tenses and other grammatical issues • Formatting (type, margins, headings, etc.) • Proofing	• Editing (to tighten video or audio) • Adding transitions (in audio or video) • Compressing (video or code) • Proofing

pose you started with shifts as you learn more about context or your audience during the reviewing and revising processes. Or as you learn how to create a new type of text such as a podcast or Pinterest page, you might discover that your audience is shifting or growing in exciting ways.

As you interpret reviewers' comments and questions and turn those comments into action items, you'll start creating a revision plan by separating the large-scale issues from the small details. The table above shows two approaches to creating revision plans, one for text-centric genres and one for design-centric genres. The table's suggestions represent only a fraction of revising activities.

Revising traditional text-centric texts such as academic essays usually leaves design work until the end. But design-centric genres such as websites, videos, posters, or podcasts will need attention paid to visual aspects early on. Depending on the type of text you're developing, you might use either list (or combine the two). Remember that these two categories are at ends of a spectrum: Even a very conventional text like a memo or an essay can benefit from some attention to things like white space and effective headings to help readers understand the text. The bulleted items are just examples of the type or scale of work that *might* go on at that stage. There are actually many types of work you could do in each stage depending on the project.

Sorting your revision plans into levels allows you to focus on big issues first, the large, structural changes you need to make, followed by increasingly fine-grained revisions. Consider the levels with a construction metaphor:

- Major structural revising: The foundation, load-bearing walls, and roof of the building. The primary structure holds everything up. It doesn't make sense to work on anything else until your foundation and other major structural aspects are relatively solid.

- Midlevel revising: The heating, cooling, electrical, and plumbing systems as well as the interior walls. You need the building enclosed and sitting solidly on the ground to protect these elements. These midlevel aspects must be relatively finalized before you start doing things like painting walls — changing the plumbing, for example, might require you to tear a wall open to get at the pipes.

- Surface-level revising: Paint, carpet, tile, and appliances. Save work on these aspects until the final stages because you don't want changes in any of the earlier phases to affect these more delicate items. It's not impossible to work on major or midlevel aspects at this point, but that will require undoing and then redoing surface-level work.

Major structural revisions will probably be listed as a summary comment or as a list in a separate document, while midlevel and surface-level revisions will likely be marginal comments because they can be tied to specific sections of your draft.

Many writers work in successive phases, working through a draft to make major revisions and then taking a break before coming back to the draft to work on midlevel parts. Only then do they make a last pass in which they pay attention to sentence structure and word choice, adding the polish that distinguishes a pretty good text from an excellent and effective one. More important projects may require multiple passes at each level and a little bit — not too much if possible — of recursion back to earlier levels. For these important texts, you should do major structural revising and then do a full review of the text, ideally with input from others, to make sure that more revisions aren't required at the major structural level.

Your revision plan is just that: a plan. Plans don't always have the results you intended. This is especially true when your revising plans call for a lot of major structural changes because dramatic changes might require a couple of passes to gel into a solid draft.

Making Major Structural Revisions

You'll work first on major revisions. Before you start, save a new copy of the draft with a new file name so you don't lose your comments as you begin revising. Recall what we discussed about "versioning" in Chapter 6: Decide on a strategy for naming new versions and stick to it. If you don't have an automated backup plan, now is a good time to create a backup version as well.

You'll want to be able to refer to both your revision notes and your draft at the same time, so come up with a system for seeing both. If you have dual monitors, open one file on each monitor. If you don't have enough screen real estate, print out (or write by hand) the revision notes so you can refer to them.

In this first pass, if you move text around, the marginal comments will move with the original text. Keep an eye on the marginal comments if you delete material. Ask yourself whether the marginal comments will still be useful in the new draft. If so, cut and paste the comments into a new marginal comment before deleting the original text.

After you've worked through major revisions, read the draft again to see whether the revisions seem to work. If there are still issues, either continue revising or get additional feedback before moving to midlevel and surface-level revisions.

If you're working on a team project, discuss the reviewing and revising process with the team: Do your teammates need to review your changes? If so, pick a system for indicating how you've changed the file. Programs such as Microsoft Word have Track Changes features (see Chapter 8, p. 214). If you're not using a program that tracks changes in a document, you can agree to bold or color any added text and use strikethrough on things deleted.

The process of revising requires you to mentally juggle several things:

- Your current draft
- Your revision notes
- The assignment
- Your future draft

You can't focus on all of those at once, but you'll want to develop a rhythm as you move back and forth among them. You'll probably attend closely to your current draft and revision plan. If you reviewed the original assignment as you wrote your revision plan, your revision notes should do a fairly good job of acting on your current draft to help shape it into something that addresses the assignment or the changes you want to make.

Tips for Surface-Level Revising

- *Pay attention to verbs and sentence structure.* Readers are often more engaged when reading texts that use active verbs ("I filled the pitcher" instead of "The picture was filled") and varied sentence structures and lengths (although this sometimes depends on the genre of a text).

- *Look carefully at elements that are meant to follow a consistent format or approach.* For example, if captions to your figures should be set in Helvetica 12-point bold, look at each caption and make sure it's correct. If a series of podcasts leads off with five seconds of your theme music preceding any voices, make sure it's consistent in every episode. You may want to create automatic or manual style guides to ensure consistency (see Chapter 8, pp. 208–10, for advice on style guides, which can be useful for any complex text, not just collaborative texts).

- *Don't automatically accept changes suggested by your word-processing software.* Using automatic grammar- and style-checking tools is OK, but use them only as warning signs—they're sometimes incorrect. When software flags something, actually look at the text and ask yourself whether there really is a problem.

- *Read your text out loud.* It's surprising how often something that looks OK to you on paper or screen will sound awkward or clumsy when you're speaking it. If it does, ask yourself whether you need to revise your language.

You might not need to. Some texts, especially ceremonial or very formal ones, tend to sound odd or slightly awkward. But it pays to consider such issues carefully.

- *Make several passes through your text to check for different types of errors—for example, grammar first, then spelling, then punctuation.* If you check your spelling but then later catch a grammar error, you might introduce new spelling errors.

- *To check for spelling errors, try reading the text backwards, word by word, from end to beginning.* If you just sit down and read the text from start to finish, you'll sometimes begin skimming (especially if you're already familiar with the text). Reading backwards prevents your mind from "filling in the blanks" as you read sentences, allowing you to focus on one word at a time.

- *Consider asking someone to proofread your text for spelling and grammar issues, either as a favor or in exchange for you doing the same for a text he or she wrote.* Because you're so familiar with your own text it's sometimes hard to see the little details.

- *If you're working with the writing center, do not hand your draft to a staff member and ask him or her to proofread it.* Writing centers can help you learn how to proofread your own texts, but they usually won't act as unpaid proofreaders. Proofreading is a skill that you can learn, so if you're not good at it, ask for some strategies to use.

Surface-Level Revising

Surface-level revising requires you to pay attention to details ranging from things like sentence structure, grammar, and spelling (text-centric aspects) to things like alignment, positioning, and color (design-centric aspects). Both aspects should be considered for nearly every text. As mentioned earlier, even the most text-centric documents have important design aspects and vice versa for design-centric texts.

Although a text might be adequate or even successful with minor problems at the surface level, such problems can distract readers, especially if they're expecting something very polished like a formal research paper or an informational video. A single spelling error in a résumé can be enough to send your application to the recycling bin or trash folder.

How much time and effort you spend on this phase depends on things such as your readers' expectations, the purpose and importance of the text, the genre of text, and more. If your instructor has given you specific things to look at, you'll obviously want to pay attention to those at a minimum. But you should also think about constructing a list of surface-level elements that you know you need to check. This might be as simple as reading slowly to see whether your grammar and spelling are appropriate, but they might be more complicated.

If you don't already have one, it's time to start building up some resources for grammar and style such as a trusted website or a grammar handbook. If you weren't required to buy a handbook for a class, ask your instructor for advice about what guide to use. Most printed handbooks will be reliable on common, basic grammatical issues, but websites often have varying degrees of accuracy. Purdue University's OWL (Online Writing Lab), published on the Internet before the days of the web by faculty and students, is a great starting point: owl.english.purdue.edu/owl/.

Text for Analysis

DRAFT OF A PERSONAL REFLECTION PAPER
Rachel Ramprasad, "My Language"

Student Rachel Ramprasad wrote the draft of the paper below for an assignment that asked her to reflect on her family's heritage in terms of the way they used language. Write a summary comment of at least 200 words that comments on at least three large-scale or major aspects of the essay. One aspect should be a positive comment, but the other two should focus on things the writer should try to change. Then choose one paragraph of the essay to comment on in terms of surface-level issues (style, sentence structure, grammar, and so on).

Ramprasad 1

Everywhere you go you hear a different dialect. Everyone that has traveled knows another dialect, because when you are surrounded by a certain language, you pick up that dialect to adapt to the environment. You don't have to speak a completely different language, but change the way you pronounce words. I for one speak more than one language; all formed by living in different environments. I have an inherited language giving to me by my parents, and 2 types on English from living in two completely different places.

The first language I was taught from my parents was broken English. It is the native language of Guyana, South America the place I am from. Broken English is what you hear Jamaicans speak, but it is not as deep. For example, Instead of saying 'over there' one with the accent would say 'ova dey'. Instead of saying 'boy' one speaking broken English would say 'bye'. I cannot speak broken English anymore, because I was taught how to speak American English from my cousin Anil before I started school. My parents do not speak broken English when talking to me, for they have learned the American English when I was younger from their workplace. So because I haven't spoke broken English since I was 6, and because it is not the language in my household I do not have the dialect anymore. If I try to speak it I'll say the words with the American accent. It is still the language of my inheritance.

My Parents might not speak to me with the broken accent, but when they talk to my family in the Caribbean they speak broken English to them. When I try to speak it to my

Ramprasad 2

family in the Caribbean they just laugh at me for trying. When my dad gets angry he mixes his American English with broken English. My dad has a stronger accent than my mom, so I'll hear my dad speaking broken English most of the time to Caribbean people, more than my mom.

I only spoke broken English with my family before I started elementary school, then I learned how to speak proper American English. I would always get corrected by my cousin because in broken English for example you do not pronounce the th in three, it would be said as 'tree'. He taught me how to speak proper English, and after a short while I spoke proper English when I started elementary school in NYC. The NYC language is more broken English than proper English. The elementary school that I went to had kids from all over the world; every kid spoke English in their inheritance language accent. City kids spoke fast so not every letter in a word would get pronounced. Taking to my friends and other students I started to pick up their accent, and started sounding like them. I picked up the city accent fast because I wanted to sound like my peers. My friends would tease me for saying a certain word differently. For example, I would say 'bottle' pronouncing the two t's, where as my peers would pronounce it as 'botle'. I wanted to fit in, so I became fluent in the city accent fast. The first year of middle school in the city I was introduced to a lot of slang words such as 'mad good'. By the first year of middle school I forgot how to speak proper English; I was now speaking city slang and pronouncing words like 'those' as

Ramprasad 3

'dos'. I spoke this way to everyone, even my family members who didn't have the city accent.

Other than having the city accent, I picked up the foul language, cursing ever so often. However, only my friends and my peers got to hear my foul language. My family members, especially my parents never heard this kind of English coming out of my mouth. At home we were taught to never swear, and I rarely heard it from my parents. I only cursed when I was angry at something or someone. I didn't swear a lot so it never became a habit and accidentally slipped out to the wrong audience. To this day I don't use the foul language everyday, but I do use it expressing emotions.

Going back to the city accent that I had, moving to upstate NY in middle school is when I realized I had the accent. Every one upstate spoke a different dialect of English. Kids used the worlds "like" a lot and emphasized every word, pronouncing every letter. I guess after constantly hanging out with my upstate friends I picked up the upstate dialect quickly without even knowing. I adapted very quickly, because I spoke this way when I just started elementary school before I picked up a city accent. I tend to exaggerate the ending of a word now such as saying guys as 'guyyss'. For the past 6 years, this is the English that I now use everyday talking to everyone. It is my primary language. Like my city accent that I purposely picked up; I didn't mean to have the upstate English. I didn't even realize I was speaking like an upstate New Yorker until I went back to the city and friends pointed it out. I guess being surrounded 24/7 by this accent I

Ramprasad 4

adapted to what I was hearing. I adapted before when I was younger so changing my accent came easy.

Last summer I went to the United Kingdom to visit my family living there. I have family living all over the UK. I visited England, France, Ireland, and Scotland. There, I picked up a bit of the English and Irish accent. I also picked put a few Scottish slang words such as faur meaning where, bevy meaning alcohol and scoosh meaning soda. When I was vacationing in those countries I mimic the people there so I could be less of a foreigner, speaking like them. Since I have relative from the UK when I talk to them on skype or on the phone I try to mimic them.

My surroundings quickly changed my accent. Similar to me, Barcott from the memoir *It Happened on the Way to War* language quickly changed when he was at different surroundings. He had the military language which he spoke only when at boot camp, or talking to his military peers. He had the Swahili accent when talking to African citizens. So they can understand him and from out of respect. He also has the language of his inheritance when talking to everyone else, like the Potsdam students when he came to give a speech. He most likely also has a different language when he socializes with his friends, and when talking to with his daughter. He learned so many different languages so he can blend it, fit right in with his surroundings.

Everyone has more than one dialect either from exposure to other languages through the media or traveling. I have more than one English accent from my inheritance to living in

> Ramprasad 5
>
> different counties. When arguing I will pull out different
>
> accents accidentally. Hearing my accents tells you where
>
> I've been, where I'm from. The way I speak makes me who
>
> I am.

Exercises

1. Track down a short essay you have written and reread it, adding marginal and summary comments. Create a minimum of three major structural-level summary comments and seven mid- and surface-level marginal comments.

2. Locate a short commercial that you've recorded or can watch online. (You'll need to watch it several times.) Assume you've been hired to repurpose the video into a full-page magazine ad for the same audience as the original video. Begin by creating a PACT chart and then create a revision plan: Which of the existing major content elements (images, words, and so on) can you simply copy? Will you have to create any new elements? Come up with at least 10 things you'll need to do and order them into the three levels of revision (major structural, midlevel, and surface-level).

3. Take a draft of an in-progress paper (including the assignment and your PACT charts) to your campus's writing center (either by appointment or during walk-in hours). Ask someone there to help you improve your draft. Revise using the reviewer's feedback and also write a short (500-word) response about the experience: Was the feedback useful? Did you find the process intimidating or welcoming? Will you consider using the writing center again? Why or why not?

4. Trade drafts of a paper (including PACT charts) with a classmate. Make marginal and summary comments on your classmate's draft and trade back. After you've each reviewed the comments you received, write a concrete revision plan for all three levels described above in "Creating a Revision Plan" (pp. 234–36). Then get together with the same classmate to compare notes. Discuss whether the comments each of you made on the drafts are all addressed by your revision plans. Did they miss or misinterpret any comments? Do the revision plans seem like they'll succeed in creating a stronger draft?

5. Create a list of your own strengths and weaknesses as a writer, things that you think you do well and things that you sometimes struggle with. Your list should include at least four strengths and four weaknesses. Put each item

into one of the three levels of revision. In parentheses following or next to each weakness item, list a concrete plan for improving that ability. If you're stumped, consider talking with someone in your campus writing center or searching online for tips in that area.

Scenario Connections

1. Scenario 10, "Writing a Restaurant Review" (p. 286), asks you to visit a local restaurant and review it for an online publication. To help you better understand how restaurant reviews are constructed, locate a review online. Copy the text into a word-processing app and review it using the steps listed on page 226.

2. Scenario 17, "Designing a Newsletter for the Zeeland Farmers' Market," asks you to work with existing texts. These texts will need to be edited for style and length as you integrate them into the newsletter. Review the Tips for Surface-Level Revising on page 232. Choose at least three of the strategies and follow them as you revise the texts. After you've completed the newsletter, write a one-page essay analyzing how well you think your revision strategies worked.

3. In Scenario 20, "Revising a Campus File-Sharing Policy," you'll be revising an existing campus file-sharing policy. As a first step, open or paste the existing policy into a word-processing app and read through it. Given that students are a primary audience for the policy, you can assume your own viewpoint. Make marginal comments noting areas that you disagree or agree with and sections that seem confusing.

4. You'll be taking an existing text written for a specialized audience and repurposing it for a mass market audience in Scenario 19, "Repurposing a Text" (p. 297). Select an article to work with and complete a PACT chart to help you understand the new context, audience, and purpose for the text you'll create. Review the article and create a list of major, midlevel, and surface-level changes you'll need to make (review the table on p. 235 for help).

Publishing Your Texts

In this chapter, you're going to look at ways to reach wider audiences for your texts. In one sense, any time you create a text and send it to another person, you're publishing. But in another sense, the one we'll take up here, "publishing" grapples with a more diffuse and diverse audience: dozens, hundreds, even thousands of people or more.

Revising for Publication

Occasionally, texts that you create for a specific class will be ready for publication without any additional revision. This is especially true for shorter, less formal texts. You may have revised your work for publication for earlier assignments in this class that asked you to create a poster or flyer, a podcast, or other media you put out in the public.

But in many cases a text created for a class will require some additional revision before it can be published, to adapt to the conventions of a new location or even to change the text from one medium to another. Unless the class project was specifically designed to result in a publication, you'll need to gather some examples of similar publications and compare them to your own. Better yet, show your own text and those similar publications to an honest, objective reviewer and ask them questions such as these:

- Does my text read as easily as these other publications?
- Is my writing in the same style and tone? Does it use the same level of vocabulary?
- Does the layout of my text seem to fit the design of these publications? Does my document look as polished? If not, what specifically is off?
- Does my text follow the submission guidelines or other advice in the publications that details what type of texts they're looking for?

If you or your reviewer answers "no" to any of these questions, you'll need to make at least one round of revision before publishing.

In some cases, your revisions will be more like translations, from one type of medium to another. This can entail some work, but you won't be creating the new text from scratch. You'll be using the raw material from your current text to construct something similar, but in the new medium or venue. Consider these options:

- Convert your essay about a local community resource into a three-minute audio piece for local radio.
- Convert your research paper into a "poster" for a professional conference (see the discussion of posters on p. 255).
- Use photos from your photography class to create a picture book at self-publishing sites such as lulu.com or Amazon's CreateSpace. Some of these will also help you publish to iPads, Kindles, or other devices.
- Create a video or audio dramatization of a short story you wrote for airing on local TV or radio.

Publishing Your Own Texts

An important early step in publishing is deciding where your text will be published, posted, or distributed. Refer back to your PACT materials to figure out what medium, genre, and specific site or publication will work best. In many cases, you may have settled on this if you considered questions such as those on page 248 while working on your initial PACT chart and your text.

But you may also have decided that a text you developed for different or more limited purposes (say, an essay you wrote for class) deserves a wider audience. You're already familiar, at least a little, with the various media in which you can publish texts on your own: not only traditional print media such as posters, newsletters, and short zines but also weblogs, video- and audio-sharing sites, podcasts and vcasts, and more. How do you choose which one? Below we'll focus on two main questions to think about when deciding on the medium.

1. What media work best for my audience and purpose?
2. What media are within my ability?

You probably already considered the first question when you began your project, although you may be considering translating work done in one medium into another. The second question may be a new one, particularly if the answers to the first are pushing you to consider new media. The sections below discuss some of the ways you can begin sorting through these issues.

What Media Work Best for My Audience and Purpose?

You'll often have many options for reaching an audience. Think about yourself as an audience in your daily life. How many ways are there to

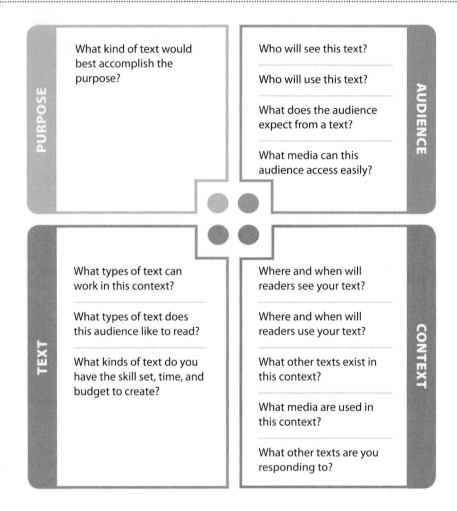

PURPOSE

What kind of text would best accomplish the purpose?

AUDIENCE

Who will see this text?

Who will use this text?

What does the audience expect from a text?

What media can this audience access easily?

TEXT

What types of text can work in this context?

What types of text does this audience like to read?

What kinds of text do you have the skill set, time, and budget to create?

CONTEXT

Where and when will readers see your text?

Where and when will readers use your text?

What other texts exist in this context?

What media are used in this context?

What other texts are you responding to?

reach you? In addition to interacting with corporate mass media such as TV, movies, billboards, and magazines, you probably read a wide range of websites, listen to music, pass bulletin boards on the way to class, read textbooks, watch movies, and read magazines. (Scenario 12, "Analyzing Your Media Diet," and Scenario 13, "A Day in Your Online Life," ask you to think carefully about the media you interact with every day.) You interact with these media for all sorts of purposes, ranging from simple browsing for entertainment to slogging your way through a textbook to finish a class assignment.

When you pick a medium for your own publication, you'll need to think about how your audience interacts with that medium, including how different factors in their own context might affect what they're doing in relation to your text. Will your 2,000-word essay be a good fit for a website? Will your 10-minute podcast be audible when broadcast in a noisy cafeteria?

WHAT MEDIA CAN MY AUDIENCE ACCESS EASILY?   In most cases, your text will be more successful if it's easy for an audience to access. Take the success of viral videos as an example. In the early days of video on the web, access to video had many bottlenecks: Competing video format standards meant that many users would find they didn't have the correct software to play the video on their browser. Bandwidth was limited to the point that images and audio were usually very low quality. And any individual video was usually hosted on only one site. All these aspects tended to limit ease of access, limiting a video's opportunity to go viral.

YouTube, over the course of several years, implemented a series of changes that, along with the growing number of users with broadband, radically improved access to video to the point that videos could spread extremely widely and rapidly. YouTube made it easy to share videos on social media and embed videos on blogs and other sites, decreasing the "friction" required to distribute these texts. As a result, videos are now frequently and widely distributed.

For many of the texts you work on, web publication might seem like a natural move, given the relative ease with which you can set up a weblog or post a video to YouTube or Vimeo. But consider the disadvantages, too. The short story or movie script you've written can be easily uploaded to the web for people to view, but reading habits online differ from reading habits for print: People's eyes tire out while reading long stretches of text online (for many reasons), making it more likely they'll move on before finishing your text.

IS MY AUDIENCE WILLING TO WORK A LITTLE TO GET TO MY TEXT?   Sometimes, your audience's preferred medium won't work for one reason or another, but they might be willing to tolerate a little inconvenience. Copy protection on movies and music rarely makes customers happy, but it's an uneasy compromise between the audience and the companies that own the intellectual property in question. Without copy protection, the industry says, people will freely trade materials rather than buy or rent them. So the audience (or some portion of them) is willing to put up with the inconvenience of copy protection to listen to music or watch movies.

Other texts that are problematic online include things that users want to read without leaving a record. Teens, for example, are less likely to access important information about birth control on a computer located in their family's living room or in a public classroom or library. These are cases in which the audience may be willing to trade a little bit in ease of access for some additional privacy or anonymity.

Sometimes, the effort to get to a text is an intentional part of the process, especially for more creative or artistic texts. Making your audience struggle a little (or a lot) can increase their enjoyment or sense of accomplishment when they finish. And nearly anyone who has spent much time working in photography, video, music, or similar fields knows that web access is often only a watered-down version of experiencing the text in a more appropriate medium: a framed print, a high-quality audio file played through a good stereo system, a film played in a movie theater rather than on a computer screen. Those distinctions aren't always important to everyone, but when they are, they're often very important.

CAN MY AUDIENCE USE THE TEXT IN CONTEXT?   You don't want your text to be the right answer in the wrong place: To be successful, your text has to be useable in the specific time and place that your users need it. Automakers, for example, have begun releasing owners' manuals on media besides print, including DVDs and USB thumb drives. In some cases, the new media provide interactive experiences that weren't possible on paper. But these new media complicate access issues — to access the manual where it's likely to be needed, cars now have to sport LCD displays, USB jacks, and (if audio is necessary) speakers. Starting in 2010, Chrysler announced that it was moving to DVD owners' manuals, even though not all vehicles affected included ways to access that material. Instead, Chrysler included a very short print manual that covered emergencies but assumed users would access the DVD on a home computer. These choices involve tradeoffs.

To take a more local example, look around your dorm hall or in lecture halls. How many of the signs or posters are there as reminders, duplicates of information that's also located in other, less accessible formats? The parking rules listed on the sign shown at left are undoubtedly based on laws written out in printed form somewhere in a government office or website. But because the people the law attempts to control are not likely to have viewed those texts, parking signs remind people of the rules in the context where the rules apply.

Signs are often reminders about regulations

What Media Are Within My Ability?

The question of what media are within your ability is one we raised in Chapter 5 during our discussion of design (see p. 124). The question comes up again here for related reasons: The final step of publication can involve slight (or large) translations of your text from one medium to another, demanding different skills.

In many cases, you'll have a range of options open, even within a single medium. Publishing material on the web, for example, can take many forms: Posting a picture to Instagram or Flickr is something people with only a moderate level of computer skill can accomplish. Creating a custom, interactive website requires a higher degree of technical chops or a budget to hire someone who has those skills.

But there are many options between those two extremes, including weblog-based sites that provide interfaces and templates to users so that they can create a fairly attractive (if slightly generic) site without requiring a lot of direct coding.

WordPress and other self-publishing platforms, including Blogger, Tumblr, Pinterest, and others, offer simple but powerful platforms for creating websites. You can edit posts in a simple, graphical interface like the one shown below without having to know anything about HTML or CSS (let alone the MySQL/PHP database structure that's the foundation of many modern sites).

Tumblr's image-oriented interface, for example, encourages simple uploading of images and reblogging content from other users' Tumblr posts while retaining links to the original posters' Tumblrs.

Different media, even different platforms within the same medium, encourage different types of publications. While Tumblr's interface is

● Editing a post in WordPress's Dashboard

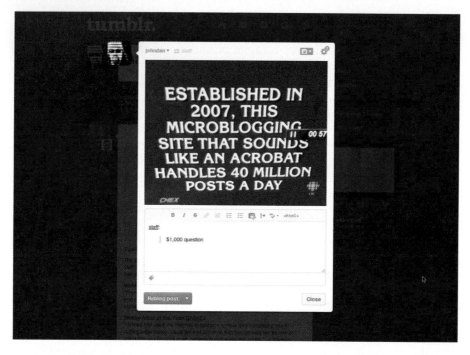

Reblogging a Tumblr post

oriented toward reblogging entries and images, WordPress's interface is slightly more complex, encouraging users to publish a wider range of material.

The number of places to easily publish texts on the web grows with each passing day, so you may want to look around to see whether there are new developments. Here is a partial list to get you started.

- WordPress.com offers very easy setup and free hosting for weblogs. Its features include WYSIWYG tools for creating new, media-rich posts and support for plug-ins that expand capabilities. WordPress .org also offers downloadable versions if you'd like to install Word-Press on your own Linux, OS X, or Windows server for full control of the application.

- Facebook.com is frequently seen as a social site, but it can also be used as a simple publication platform for shorter texts and other media.

- YouTube.com, the extraordinarily popular site for uploading videos, also allows users to post video to YouTube and embed that video into other websites (including weblogs).

- Flickr.com and Picasa.com are two popular websites for sharing photos and videos.

- Instagram.com allows photo sharing and hosting via iPhone and Android apps.

- Twitter.com, the 140-character social media site, allows short texts to be shared among friends and followers. Twitter's Vine app for iPhone and Android takes that focus on brevity to the video world, letting users share looping video clips of up to six seconds.

- Klip and Keek are two video-sharing apps for Android.

- Google.com, once just a search engine, has branched into relatively simple media production and hosting (including spreadsheets, text documents, surveys, or any type of document that can be distributed by sharing a link with other users).

The dramatic increase in power and accessibility of media design environments over the last 20 years has opened up entry-level authoring to most types of publication: In addition to the resources listed above for hosting new media texts, users now have access to many applications that support the production of audio, video, print, 3D design, and more. Commercial applications range from low-priced (or free with a new computer) software such as iMovie for OS X to Adobe Premiere (Windows and OS X) and Final Cut Pro (OS X). And free and open-source options are growing. As with the previous list of applications, applications change rapidly so you should also search the web for new applications.

- Cinefy is a fairly robust video recording, editing, and sharing app for the iPhone (see Chapter 5, p. 126).

- REAPER (www.reaper.fm) is a very powerful audio recording, editing, and mixing application for Windows and OS X.

- Google SketchUp enables web-based 3D modeling and design.

- Apache OpenOffice is an open-source office suite that includes a word processor, a multimedia presentation program, and drawing applications for Windows, OS X, and Linux.

- Blender software for 3D and still animation is also open source and includes a built-in game engine for video-game development.

- Lightworks is an open-source video editor for Windows.

Getting Help Publishing Your Texts

Why would you have someone else publish your texts? In some cases, you may not have the technical expertise to create an effective text in that medium. If you've created a solid draft of a poster, for example, working on the content and general layout, you might recognize that the poster looks only passable, not great. You might hand over the layout to a graphic designer who will take your ideas and bring them to the next level.

In other cases, the forum you want to work in may be access controlled: A newspaper or magazine, for example, doesn't let just anyone publish work within their pages. Some publications accept little or no material from unknown outsiders, while others will consider accepting materials from anyone. You might need help finding publications that will accept submissions from students.

Finding Venues for Student Publications

Submitting your work to an academic journal or online publication is one option. See whether the journal or site you are interested in offers submission guidelines or other advice about what type of texts they expect to see. (The example below shows the submission guidelines for one online publication.) Many academic journals use an editorial board or a set of reviewers to vet all submissions, advising the editor on whether an article should be published. Writers often receive revision feedback from reviewers indicating how an article

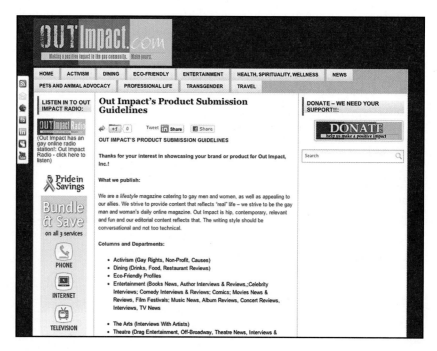

● Guidelines for submitting articles to an online publication
Out Impact's Product Submission Guideline's reprinted by permission of Out Impact

should be changed before it can be published in the journal. Even if the publication decides your material is not a good match for its audience, it often provides detailed revision feedback that can help you improve your work or even suggestions about other places that might publish your work.

Many universities provide venues and assistance for students who want to publish, ranging from student-run newspapers and journals to undergraduate research conferences. Check with the relevant campus department to see whether there are opportunities for you to show your work at poster sessions (like the one shown below), student film showings, or other events.

Professional organizations often recruit members by offering places to publish or present work related to their organizations. Opportunities range from the chance to be part of a panel giving a presentation to authoring a journal article or participating in a poster session at a conference, where students create large displays describing their research and answer questions from attendees. The com-

● Poster session at Clarkson University Summer Symposium on Undergraduate Research Experiences
Clark University Photo

puter science professional organization the Association for Computing Machinery has a division specifically related to supporting student publication. They even provide a limited number of travel scholarships to support trips to regional and national conferences. Similar support for student work can be found in nearly any discipline. Ask a professor in the relevant field whether he or she can help you get connected with a professional organization that might provide support for publishing your work.

Hiring a Technical Expert

You might find yourself in a situation where you'd like to publish material that requires more technical expertise than you possess. For example, you might have written a short essay in your writing class about volunteering for community service that you decide you'd like to air as a public service announcement on a community cable channel. You could purchase a camera and teach yourself basic video editing skills to produce what might turn out to be a very clumsy video with poor audio quality. Or you could find someone who already possesses that expertise

Susan Powers
Associate Director of the Institute for a Sustainable Environment

● A screen shot from student Kimberly Villemaire's documentary *Take It or Leave It,* which was shown at Clarkson University's SURE Spring 2012 Conference (Symposium on Undergraduate Research Experiences)
Courtesy of Kimberly Villemaire

(and equipment) to help you produce a professional video that supports rather than distracts from your purpose. Many campuses have student-run video production groups or even cable television stations that are glad to have someone contribute content. If you're looking for someone to take your content and transform it into a publishable document, you can hire a technical expert or recruit a volunteer.

You'll want to do some background work before taking the next step. If you're going to have someone else prepare your final text, look at other work he's done. He may have a portfolio online; if not, ask him for samples of his work. Is it similar to what you'd like to achieve? Does it seem high quality? Also ask whether you can contact previous clients for recommendations. Previous clients can tell you how happy they were not only with the end product but also with the process of working with the technical expert.

Be sure to get an agreement about the responsibilities of all participants in writing. Specify what work will be done, by what date, and by whom. Will you be paying by the hour or for the whole job? What materials need to be delivered to you? Will you need access to source files?

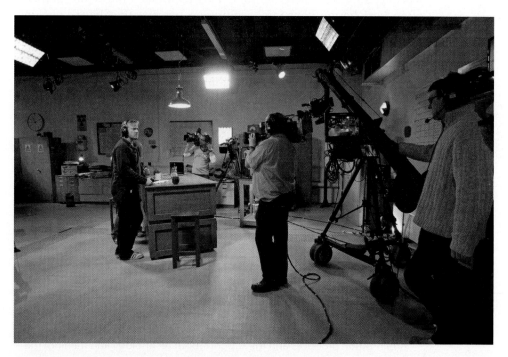

● On the set of the BBC series *Bang Goes the Theory*. Many compuses have TV studios like this one.
marc macdonald/Alamy

Will the technical expert's name need to be formally credited on or in the text? The more complex the work the more complex the written agreement may need to be.

Recruiting a Volunteer

Recruiting a volunteer can be a little more complicated, especially if you're expecting the volunteer to follow orders, effectively acting as your employee but without pay. Still, in some situations you'll be able to recruit a volunteer by offering her different compensation. If she is a student, see whether she can work as an intern or for independent study credit. If you have expertise in areas that might benefit her, you could barter. Are you a strong writer and proofreader? You could offer to help her with a paper she's writing. Be sure that your offer is ethical: Don't offer to simply write a paper for another student — that would be plagiarism, possibly affecting not only the other student's grade but also your academic standing. But it's likely you could give your volunteer feedback on a paper, a cover letter for a job, or something similar; have the other student check with her instructor to be sure.

In some cases, you might form a team to work on a publication. You will probably have less control over a teammate, but team members often work better than simple volunteers because they have a personal stake in the project. You can recruit teammates by spreading the word, posting flyers on announcement boards on campus, sending an e-mail out to a discussion list, or using any method that might reach people interested in your cause might congregate. Depending on your interests, there may already be a local organization you can join. Most campuses have student-run newspapers, radio stations, and even TV studios like the one shown on page 257. Some of these will allow you to work on your own projects, while others have more formal, restricted agendas; but all of them are great places to start learning media production skills and join a community of like-minded people.

Exercises

1. Locate four campus organizations that do some form of media production, including some that produce media as their *primary* activity (campus radio or TV stations, newspapers, or fiction journals) and at least one that produces media as a *secondary* activity (outdoors clubs, athletics teams, and other groups often publish their own web pages or newsletters). Write short descriptions (250 words each/1,000 words total) of the media each organization produces and the support (both technology and training) the organizations offer.

2. Choose a media technology that you are interested in but don't know much about. What tutorials can you find on the web that help you learn how to use

that technology? Use these tutorials (and any other resources you can find) to produce a sample text or publication.

3. Find an online community devoted to producing a certain genre or media. Spend 500 to 1,000 words answering these questions: What resources do they offer to novices? Do they provide a welcoming and supportive environment? Are there special beginner's resources offered, such as mentoring or FAQs?

4. Pick a specific topic or activity and then find at least eight publications that cover the topic. What is the range, in terms of

   - size of publication? (estimate the number of viewers/readers/listeners: hundreds? thousands? more?)
   - publication quality? (professional? amateur? skilled or unskilled production?)
   - tone? (formal? informal?)
   - scope? (very tight focus on topic? or more about "lifestyle"?)

   Format your answers in a simple table, with the title of the publication across the top row and the question topics in the first column on the left.

Title	
Estimated size	
Publication quality	
Tone	
Scope	

5. Pick a website that specializes in user-generated content — YouTube, Flickr, Wordpress.com, or a similar site. Examine published material from five different people on that site. Can you identify their purposes for posting? Their technical abilities? Their creative abilities?

Scenario Connections

1. Scenario 12, "Analyzing Your Media Diet," asks you to keep track of the media you engage with over a 24-hour period and write an essay analyzing those media. You can extend this scenario by publishing your essay. Review the advice in this chapter for publishing your own texts and finding venues for student publications, and find out what opportunities for publication are available in your class or on your campus. Which method of distributing your text do you think will be most successful, and why?

2. Scenario 7, "Podcasting Campus Life for Prospective Students," requires you to record and edit an audio or video podcast. Select a recording technology and an editing application and create a 30-second test audio or video to

make sure you're comfortable working in this environment. Be sure to include at least three separate "edits"—audio or video from three different portions of the recording edited together to make a seamless file.

3. In Scenario 16, "Designing a Website for Doglake Records," you'll be creating the mockup for a website. You can extend that scenario by actually implementing the website. Using a free site such as WordPress.org, explore what design options are within your (growing) abilities. Design the Doglake Records site within that web application.

4. After reviewing the Background Text in Scenario 18, "Creating a Facebook Page for an Organization," complete a PACT chart that highlights concerns, goals, and strategies to keep in mind as you develop your organization's page.

Part 2

Scenarios for Writing

You'll find all the Scenarios in the e-Pages at bedfordstmartins.com/changing. Five Scenarios are included in Part 2. See the inside back cover for details.

Advocating Voter Registration on Campus

Overview

Your Aunt Sheila, always something of a local activist, is asking for your help. To the surprise of, well, no one in your family, she announced that she was running for Congress. She's an underdog in the race, but by only a handful of points. And she's closing the gap. It's late July, and you're just starting to think about returning to campus.

Her request isn't what you'd expected. Surprisingly, she doesn't want you to campaign directly for her. Or maybe not so surprisingly, because she's always been an idealist. She wants you to do something more basic: She simply wants you to get college students to register to vote. "It's the first step in becoming an adult citizen," she says. "I don't care *who* they vote for. I just want them to vote!" She wants your help developing a simple but powerful text that you can distribute or post when you get to campus in early September.

What will the text say? That's what she wants you to figure out. She's not even sure what medium to use. Poster? Web page? Letter to the editor of your campus newspaper? You'll figure that out once you devise a strategy.

Aunt Sheila's enthusiasm has always been hard to resist. You agree to help. In fact, you're even looking forward to the project. She spreads papers out on the table — reports, posters from other voter registration drives, scribbled notes — and opens up her laptop. Together, you start brainstorming ideas. On her computer she calls up a website called "Rock the Vote," run by a nonpartisan group that offers research and resources for encouraging young people to participate in the election process. "I'll e-mail you the URL to this and some other sites so you can use them later."

Strategies

You obviously need to think about content: What will convince your audience to register to vote? Begin expanding your PACT framework and brainstorm some possible approaches.

PURPOSE
Get college students to register to vote

AUDIENCE
Your relatively apathetic fellow students

CONTEXT
Your campus; an upcoming presidential election

TEXT
Your choice

© B. O'Kane/Alamy

Look at other texts with a similar purpose to see what strategies they draw on. You can find texts online or around your campus. You can even look beyond political ads to other texts that seem like they're successful (advertisements for local events, recruiting posters for campus organizations, fund drives, or more).

You should also look for research and other work that's already been done on this issue: Many organizations have looked at how to motivate college-aged students to vote. These sources might give you ideas on potential strategies.

Questions to Keep in Mind

Use the questions below to help you begin constructing your PACT chart. You can begin with the initial chart at the beginning of the scenario.

Why don't students tend to vote? Think hard: You are probably part of the target audience for your text. Ask your roommates or friends this question. Do an informal poll of your classmates. Or do a more organized and formal poll on campus (in the student union or some other location, or via e-mail if that's feasible). You'll need to find out why students don't vote and figure out how to change their minds. You might find that they don't realize how easy it is to vote. You might find that they don't believe that their vote counts. You might find that they're just apathetic. You might find a mix of all these things and more. Whatever you find, you'll need to come up with solutions.

You'll need to do some research (starting with the materials provided in the Background Texts section) to learn what's involved with voter registration in your state. Can students register locally, or do they have to register at their home addresses? What's the closest or most convenient registration location?

As you start to learn more about your context and audience, you'll be able to start thinking about what text to create: Based on what you're finding, what type of text will best achieve your purpose?

Chapter Connections

PRIMARY CONNECTIONS

- Chapter 2: Approaching Writing Situations
- Chapter 3: Starting to Write
- Chapter 5: Designing Visual Texts (if you decide to create a text that includes visual aspects as a major component)

SECONDARY CONNECTIONS

- Chapter 7: Getting Information and Writing from Research
- Chapter 9: Revising Your Texts
- Chapter 10: Publishing Your Texts

Background Texts

NEWS ARTICLE

Josh Higgins, "Student Turnout to Affect November Election"

From *Collegiate Times,* April 11, 2012

This article on student participation in the 2012 presidential election originally appeared in *Collegiate Times,* Virginia Tech's student-run university newspaper.

Molly Reed has never registered to vote.

"I really just didn't do it," the freshman general engineering major said. "It was just because of lack of time, and I didn't feel like doing it."

Reed isn't alone.

In the 2008 presidential elections, 51.1 percent of American citizens between ages 18 and 29 voted, according to a study by the Center for Information and Research on Civic Learning and Engagement, or CIRCLE. While it was a 2.1 percent increase from the 2004 election and the highest turnout since 1992, youth turnout for elections has typically been lower than that of the older population.

The youth vote has increased in the past few years, but the CIRCLE study suggests voter registration laws affect turnout levels on Election Day. And with the 2012 presidential election fast approaching, registering to vote has become a priority for those wishing to cast a ballot on Nov. 6.

Where do students vote?

In Virginia, citizens are required to register 22 days before primary and general elections. But to register, students have to establish their permanent residency and complete registration forms, which has resulted in confusion over whether students should register in Blacksburg or in their hometowns.

"The actual law says a person must have an abode where they rest their head each evening," said Randall Wertz, general registrar for Montgomery County. "Then they have their residency, or where they actually live."

Wertz said students can determine whether they want to register at home or at school, as long as they use what they consider to be their permanent address on the registration form.

"We don't treat students any differently than any other person," Wertz said. "If they tell us in the application that is their primary residence, then that is what we utilize."

Karen Hult, a professor and director of graduate studies in the political science department, confirms students' ability to register at either location.

"I really think it's a student choice," Hult said. "But why would one choose to register here, when they can register back at home? It's an interesting decision."

Hult said some local residents, believing there is an effect on election outcomes from student involvement, do not like students participating in local politics.

"In the town of Blacksburg, I've not seen much evidence of any effect because I don't think there's been much of a turnout," Hult said. "I was very disappointed at the level of apparent mobilization, activity, and interest here in the fall 2011 elections."

Voter registration rules, the CIRCLE study says, can influence turnout rates. According to the study, youth turnout in elections was 14 percentage points higher if Election-Day registration was allowed in the state during presidential elections. In addition, youth turnout was 40 percentage points higher during presidential elections if the states allowed voting by mail.

In Virginia, there are restrictions on absentee voting, and citizens are not allowed to participate in in-person early voting. In addition, Election-Day registration is not allowed.

While voter registration requirements do have an effect on turnout, the issue for college students remains the decision to register at school or in their hometown. If a student decides to vote at school, Wertz said, they should be aware of possible consequences of changing their permanent address.

"Most students who have registered with us consider their address at the university as their permanent address, and that's what they put on the form," Wertz said. "It's a choice of the student. If there are any ramifications for stuff like (tax dependencies and scholarships), we're not interested in those aspects of it. The only thing we're interested in is their permanent address."

The issue with a student changing their permanent address is there's a possibility tax dependencies and scholarships could be affected.

For example, if a student has a scholarship for living in their hometown, and they change their permanent address to their school address for voting purposes, there is a possibility they could lose the scholarship because they are no longer considered residents of their hometown.

Student political involvement

As the 2012 election approaches, political advocacy and voting registration, as well as its impact on college localities, will become prominent issues on college campuses.

Hult said while some local residents are concerned student participation might skew local elections, there could potentially be positive outcomes from student engagement.

"If there were more attention (to local elections and issues), there might be a better way to build bridges between the two communities," Hult said. "Right now, I would guess that many of the town officials would say something like, 'We would like students to be more involved. We would like to work with and talk to students.' But we've not seen persistent evidence of that happening."

Hult said since the 2008 presidential election, she had not seen much involvement from college students locally.

"This is a distinctly unengaged, uninvolved campus, compared to other places I have been," Hult said. "There hasn't been much visible activity on campus."

However, that doesn't mean everyone is politically apathetic.

Tara Dillard, a senior natural resources conservation major, is politically involved.

"I am registered to vote," she said. "I think having the ability to have a say in who is in government is special and important."

Hult said the geography, history, and demographic of the students that attend Virginia Tech could be a factor in campus disengagement in politics.

"This is an engineering school; most students are in this college or the college of science," Hult said. "It seems like those students don't have that perception of things. I think all of that mixes together in a complex way. That makes it very difficult to get that kind of engagement."

Voter turnout in the last election

The 2008 election was different.

"I think it was one of those years you had really riveting candidates, terrific mobilization campaigns, and some issues people cared about a lot," Hult said, "issues like the economy, jobs, and Iraq."

The 2008 election saw one of the highest turnouts in recorded history, according to the CIRCLE study. Young blacks posted the highest turnout rates ever observed for any racial or ethnic group of young Americans since 1972. Almost 55 percent of women between ages 18 and 29 voted in the elections, as well.

In addition, voter turnout of young people with college experience was 62 percent — a visible effect at Tech.

"It was stunning to see the lines of people waiting to go vote various places around town," Hult said. "But we had people at some of the local polling places that stood in line for hours to cast a ballot."

The 2008 election, Hult said, saw a moment in history where candidates, especially on the Democratic side, were able to mobilize youth and minority groups. She said Barack Obama, as the first black president, was able to mobilize the black vote, while Hillary Clinton attracted the woman vote.

In addition, she said Obama's way of dealing with people in a "riveting and persuasive" way played a large role in his ability to galvanize the electorate.

However, one of the greatest influences on the election — especially on the youth vote — was the ability to capitalize on social media sites, like Facebook and Twitter.

"The drive to mobilize and register (the youth vote) and getting them involved in other ways made the difference," Hult said. "I think it's getting them involved in other ways — local service work, registering voters, talking about problems."

The Obama campaign committed a lot of its grassroots effort on engaging and informing citizens through social media, Hult said, giving him an advantage in the race. However, she said he will likely not have that advantage in the upcoming election.

"I think social media will still be important for the president, but it's no longer a new thing," she said. "And all the Republicans are doing a good job with (social media) too. He's still good, but he won't be that much better."

However, she said family members losing jobs during the economic recession also played a role in voter turnout. But she said dissatisfaction with the president's lack of change and boredom with politics might affect the political landscape for 2012.

Voter turnout in the upcoming election

As the 2012 election looms, political scientists question whether this year will see the same youth voter turnout. Hult said while she considers Tech to be an uninvolved campus right now, certain factors might lead to a close race and political activism on campus.

"That's the narrative that should catch on and continue: What are these old people talking about and making decisions that I'm going to have to live with for a very long time," she said.

While it is unclear whether turnout will meet or surpass that of 2008, Hult said a close race in Virginia might rally the party bases into coordinating active campaigns on campus.

"It looks like there's going to be a race (in Virginia) again," she said. "That should mobilize college campuses, and it may be that, once a Republican nominee is selected, that in the fall, I would expect to see a lot more engagement and involvement.

"I would look for the kind of mobilization on college campuses to be similar to 2008 — great use of social media, but especially in states like Virginia, which is up for grabs again."

And with first lady Michelle Obama and Sen. Mark Warner speaking at Tech's commencement in May, there could be a resulting political buzz on campus.

"Both of them understand this is a commencement speech, not a partisan speech," Hult said. "That puts all kinds of constraints on the reaction there might be. What could get people more focused, though, is that kind of reaction (of commencement speaker selection) from students and parents. That sense of opposition might mobilize some Warner and Obama supporters on the one hand, and similarly the opponents on the other hand."

While she said this is one possibility, she expressed that it could also have another effect.

"What it will do is get news cameras on campus and have people asking questions to students and getting them to think hard about what their answers are," Hult said. "And to that extent, it could have a longer term impact, but we'll see how students react."

Hult said often portrayal of politics disengages citizens — even college students.

"I understand not everyone is excited (about politics)," she said. "I also understand people are increasingly becoming disaffected with what we see on cable TV and what we see cast as politics. I have to say I'm disturbed by it. I don't think everything can be reduced to sound bites or just two sides. That can turn people off of politics. I don't think all of politics has to be about conflict, yet that seems like what we want it to be."

While Reed has not registered to vote, she said she plans to change that.

"I plan on doing it," she said. "I just haven't gotten around to it. It really just wasn't at the top of my list of things I needed to get done before college."

HANDBOOK
Rock the Vote, Winning Young Voters: New Media Tactics
From rockthevote.org, June 2008

Rock the Vote is a nonpartisan group that provides research and resources for encouraging young people to participate in the election process. It published this brief handbook on its website in advance of the 2008 presidential election.

ROCK THE VOTE

Winning Young Voters: New Media Tactics
June 2008

New media tactics should be a central part of any campaign targeting young voters, but can be confusing for people more familiar with TV advertising, door-knocks, or campaign rallies.

"New Media Tactics," the second in Rock the Vote's series of "Winning Young Voters" handbooks, shows you the basics of how to use new media – email, the Internet, social networks, and mobile phones – to register young voters and get them to the polls.

In this handbook

> Online voter registration
> Search advertising
> Facebook and other social networks
> Email
> Text messaging

TOP NEW MEDIA TIPS

1. Run your own online voter registration campaign with our free web tool.

2. Buy targeted online advertising, particularly search, to drive online voter registration.

3. Remind your supporters of registration deadlines and Election Day via ads, email, and text messaging.

4. Get personal via social networks.

5. Simple, clear advertisements perform best; test different variations too.

Online Voter Registration

Registering voters on your website or blog is one of the easiest ways to engage people online. And with a tool that Rock the Vote offers, you can do it for free.

Rock the Vote's online voter registration form (shown right) adds a button to your website where visitors can register to vote. Here's how to do it:

- Go to http://www.rockthevote.com/partners and create an account.
- Check your email – you should have a note with the basic HTML code. MySpace requires a special version; get it by logging in to your new partner account (the link is in the email) then click "widget code" and scroll down to the second box.
- Paste the code into a page on your website.

With this tool, anyone can run an online registration campaign – for free. But placing the registration tool on your site is only the beginning. Tips for running a good campaign:

1. **Place the "Register to Vote" button prominently on your website** – up top, in the "Latest News" section, or on your blog.

ROCK THE VOTE

2. **Promote voter registration.** Send emails to your lists telling them to register, blog about registering to vote, and plug registration at events and in newsletters. **Make sure to do these things around registration deadlines or big events – that works best.**

3. Try different types of emails or messaging and use the ones that generate the most voter registrations.

Rock the Vote's system also provides access to the contact information of the people you register. Use it to follow-up with GOTV reminders, volunteer outreach, or fundraising requests.

– Log into http://registertovoteonline.org/site/login/ to download your registration list.

With this same log-in, you can keep an eye on how many people you're registering. If it's fewer than you want, re-evaluate your tactics or give us a call for additional tips.

Search Advertising

Every day millions of people use Google, Yahoo, or MSN search engines. An organization or campaign can use these search engines to register people to vote by purchasing ads that will appear when someone searches for a certain phrase – for example, "election info," "how to vote," "Barack Obama," or "John McCain."

Rock the Vote has found this to be an inexpensive way to register young adults to vote, at less than $2 per registration form download. You can also restrict your search advertising to certain cities or states, making it a handy tool for state or local campaigns. By combining online voter registration with search advertising you can find the people most interested in your organization and register them at low cost.

How To

1. Log in to http://adwords.google.com to create a search advertising campaign on Google (Yahoo and MSN will be similar).
2. Fill out the campaign details and choose the states, cities, or zip codes to target.
3. Create a basic text ad design (see below for examples).
4. Select the list of searches that will trigger your ad, such as "register to vote," "voter form," "election information," or your candidate's name.
5. Set your daily spending limit and the maximum price you're willing to pay for an ad click. A low limit of $20 per day and $1 per click will let you try out search advertising. You can later expand your budget to fully capture your target search traffic.

Tips

- **Keywords:** Keep your keywords focused on voter registration or GOTV-related information. Phrases like "health care" or "politics" are too general to be worth advertising on.

- **Simple ad designs are best.** Use a title like "Register to Vote" or "Online Voter Registration". Put the voter registration deadline in the description if it's soon.

- **Target:** Use geographic targeting so that you only advertise to the people you care about. Include the state or city in your ad to show its relevancy. If advertising in multiple states, create an ad campaign and destination page for each.

- **Design:** Try different variations in your ad designs and keywords, then eliminate ones that perform poorly.

Facebook

Facebook is the most prominent online social network for young adults in the United States. Nearly 21 million adult Americans have Facebook accounts to date, of which 18 million are ages 18 to 29, and one-half of all Facebook users visit the site on a daily basis.

For organizations interested in registering and mobilizing young voters, four Facebook features stand out as the most useful: fan pages, events, groups, and advertising. These features are usually available on other online social networks as well.

Facebook Fan Pages

On Facebook any organization, campaign, or politician can create a fan page, which acts as their central point of contact for the Facebook community. Supporters can then visit the fan page to get the latest content (blog posts, photos, videos, or more) from the campaign in a way that is integrated with Facebook. They can receive message updates from the fan page, alerting them to action items, deadlines, or important events. Facebook users who subscribe to a fan page then display a link to that organization on their profile page. The profile link acts as a recruitment tool for their friends to join the fan page.

How To

1. Create a fan page for your candidate or organization at http://www.facebook/pages/create.php.
2. Fill in the basic contact information, upload your logo, and start a discussion.
3. Publish the page when it is ready for the public. Click the "Share" button (normally on the right side of the page) to invite your supporters that are on Facebook.
4. Make frequent updates with media, events, and other content from the campaign. Contact your subscribers about once a month to keep them activated.

Tips

- **Leverage Email:** Jump start your Facebook campaign by promoting the fan page to your email list, then link to your Facebook events or groups in future emails.

- **Blogs:** Use the Notes application to automatically import blog posts into your fan page.

- **Apps:** Browse through the Facebook Application Directory to find additional Page features.

- **Ads:** Targeted ads can also connect supporters to your Facebook Page.

- For more ideas visit http://www.facebook.com/rockthevote.

Facebook Events

Facebook events are a social RSVP system designed to encourage peer-to-peer interaction and invitations. Supporters can easily invite their friends to campaign events and expand exposure beyond the initial list of invitees. When one person RSVPs for the event all of their friends can see their response, which quickly spreads awareness of the event through a person's social network.

How To

1. Edit your fan page then click the "Events" box to begin creating your event, which will also be linked from your fan page.
2. Enter the event information then send an update to your supporters to invite them all instantly.
3. After the event, upload pictures and videos to continue engaging your supporters.

Tips

- **Use Facebook Events as an earned media and organizing tactic**. Create events for campus appearances, registration deadlines, fundraisers, and Election Day.

- **Respond**: Monitor each event's discussion board and respond to any comments or questions.

- **+1**: Ask attendees to invite other people they know to generate viral growth.

- **Voter Registration**: Include a prominent link to your online voter registration page.

Facebook Groups

Informal online groups of users have proliferated on Facebook and other social networking sites. Many of these groups are related to political issues, popular local candidates, or upcoming elections, and can grow at astonishing speeds due to the viral nature of online social networks. When groups are related to political engagement they represent a prime opportunity to channel new members to online voter registration, and at no cost. Political organizations in particular should create Facebook groups for their key programs and issues as a way to build awareness among young voters. Groups are more limited than fan pages in that they cannot import content from outside sources; they also do not support the event system's RSVP functions.

How To

1. Go to http://www.facebook.com/groups/create.php to begin creating your group.
2. Invite current supporters on Facebook and use the email import feature to add people who aren't on Facebook.
3. Keep the group updated with the latest news for that issue and provide a few different action items for the members.

Tips

- **Voter Registration**: Include a voter registration link so that all the group members are able to vote in November. As a rough estimate expect to get a registration form download for every 100 members.

- **Officers**: One easy way to reward active volunteers is to designate them as "officers" of the group.

- **Messages**: If your group has less than 1,000 members you can send mass updates to sustain interest.

Facebook Advertising

Political advertisers can purchase "Social Ads" on Facebook, which are small advertisements similar to Google's text ads. They can be targeted by demographics (age, gender, education status, relationship status), geography (country, state, city), place of employment, school, and profile keywords. These targeting options make Facebook ads an inexpensive tactic for voter registration, particularly among 18-29 year olds.

How To

1. Go to http://www.facebook.com/ads/create/ to begin creating your ad.
2. Choose the destination page and targeting options.
3. Enter the title (25 characters or less), body text (135 characters or less), and optionally upload a picture (110x80 pixels or smaller).
4. Choose your daily budget and set the amount you are willing to pay for each ad click. A small campaign could start out at $20 per day and a bid of $0.50 per click.

Tips

- **Titles**: Use a clear call to action in the title, such as "Register to Vote" or "Vote on Tuesday."

- **Deadlines Motivate**: Running ads near a registration deadline or close to Election Day can more than double the click-through rate and lower the cost of the ads.

- **Test multiple advertising designs** at the same time and eliminate poor performing designs.

- **Pay Per Click**: Low click-through rates are typical for Facebook advertising: buy your ads on a pay-per-click basis rather than pay-per-impression.

- **Context**: Include the target geography in the text, e.g. "Pennsylvania votes on April 22nd."

- **Track**: If the ad links to your website, include a tracking code in the URL to log the hits sent by the ad.

EXAMPLE FACEBOOK FLYERS

General Registration	New Hampshire GOTV	Pennsylvania Registration
Register to Vote	Vote New Hampshire	PA: Register to Vote
Register to vote using our easy, fast online form - don't miss the deadline. Download your personalized PDF, then print and mail it.	Tuesday, Jan. 8th! The NH presidential primary is this Tuesday, get out and vote! Click for more info from Rock the Vote: polling places, candidates, etc	HAVE YOUR VOICE HEARD! REGISTER BY 3/24. Your vote matters. Register to vote today to make sure it counts. Pennsylvania's deadline is March 24th and Election Day is April 22nd.

Cost Per Registration

A clear, simple registration advertisement on Facebook can generate a form download for $5 - $10 and can be highly targeted. Targeting generally increases the cost per registration and reduces the total number of registrations that will

be generated over a given time period. Other methods of online organizing, such as events, groups or fan pages, generate registrations at no cost other than the time of staff and volunteers.

Examples of Success

- A student created a Facebook group entitled "1,000,000 Strong for Stephen T. Colbert," which reached its membership goal in less than two weeks.[1] The student added an online voter registration link and generated about 4,000 registration form downloads within a week. To date the group has been responsible for over 11,000 registration form downloads, or one download for every 76 group members.

- "Presidential Election 2008," a popular Facebook event for the 2008 general election, has generated 5,300 registration downloads to date. With 600,000 RSVPs, that corresponds to about one download per 112 RSVPs. A smaller event for the Texas primaries generated 500 downloads in January 2008, at rate of one download per 11 RSVPs.

- Academic research on the 2006 election and the 2008 presidential primaries has found a relationship between the number of supporters a candidate has on Facebook and their share of the youth vote. These results, while preliminary, suggest that online social networks can be an effective component of youth outreach for campaigns… provided those supporters are leveraged into offline actions. [2]

- In 2006 the Minnesota DFL campaign successfully used Facebook to find potential supporters in their target geographies, then generated walk and call lists to persuade and mobilize those young people.

Email

Simply emailing your list and asking your members to register to vote is a surprisingly effective and low-cost tactic.

How To

1. Determine the best time in your email outreach schedule for your registration blasts. These can be repeated every 2-3 months without a drop in click-through rate.
2. Design the content of the email. Keep it simple and focused on the registration message so that recipients can quickly understand the email's purpose.
3. Embed a voter registration form in the destination page and include a unique source code for that email so that you can track the number of registration form downloads.

Tips

- **Emails near registration deadlines are effective**, but provide 1-2 weeks leeway to account for people who may be slow to open the email.

- **Trial Runs**: Set aside a portion of the email list (about 20%) as a test group and divide them into a few groups. Send each group a different subject line and see which group has the best response rate. Then use that subject line to email the remaining 80% of the list.

[1] "The Colbert Nation Quickly Colonizes Facebook." New York Times. October 29, 2007.
http://www.nytimes.com/2007/10/29/business/media/29colbert.html
[2] "The Political Impact of Facebook: Evidence from the 2006 Midterm Elections and 2008 Nomination Contest." Williams, C. and G. Gulati. (January 2008). Unpublished Manuscript. http://blogsandwikis.bentley.edu/politechmedia/wp-content/uploads/2008/01/gwdiscourse11jan08.pdf

- **Be Consistent**: The destination page should look similar to the email and be focused solely on the registration form. Set up the page to open the registration form automatically.

- **Authoritative calls to action do best**, so emphasize the candidate or organization's official clout.

Cost Per Registration

Rock the Vote's testing has shown response rates between 0.5% and 5%, depending on 1) email address quality, 2) the prominence of the call to register, and 3) the email's subject line. These response rates correspond to one registration form download for every 20 to 200 emails sent out. At 0.5% response rate an organization with a million person email list can generate about 5,000 voter registration downloads by encouraging their members to register. At $0.05 per email that's $10 per registration form download, which is comparable to traditional registration techniques.

Examples of Success

- Targeting young movers using change of address data from the U.S. Post Office has proven to be a highly effective targeting technique, generating response rates between 1% and 7%. This results in a cost per form download of $2 to $10.

- Targeting unregistered youth using voter file data is more expensive, in part because it is a population less likely to register to vote, but has shown a cost per form download of about $25 from a pilot test (response rate of 1%).

EXAMPLE SUBJECT AND SENDER OPEN RATES

Sender	Subject Line	Open Rate
Rock the Vote	Make them pay attention: Re-Register to Vote	6.6%
Rock the Vote	By law you must re-register to vote.	12.8%
Voter Registration Center	Notice: You must re-register to vote immediately.	16.6%

EXAMPLE REGISTRATION EMAILS

Official Design	Branded Design

www.rockthevote.com

Text Messaging

Text messaging and mobile outreach are growing tactics within the political sphere, particularly for youth mobilization organizations. Rock the Vote's February 2008 poll found that 85% of 18 to 29 year olds own a cell phone, compared to 75% who own a landline phone. Early research has found large impacts from text messages. A 2006 program by Working Assets and the Student PIRGs showed that a text message on Election Day increases the likelihood that a young adult will vote by about three percentage points.[3] In the 2008 primaries Rock the Vote has found that a text message reminder of a state's registration deadline makes a person about four percentage points more likely to turn in their registration form after downloading it online.

How To

1. Collect cell phone numbers on your website, at events, in your email newsletter, and through voter registration. Make sure they opt-in to receive text message reminders from your organization as it is illegal to send unsolicited text messages.
2. Hire a mobile messaging vendor that can manage your list of text message recipients and send out SMS blasts.
3. Send a text message to your mobile list the day before the registration deadline and again on Election Day.
4. Support your other programs, like direct mail or canvassing, with related text messages blast to prep the recipients.
5. Send an update your mobile list with the results of the election.

Tips

- **Mobile Opt-Ins**: Add a custom question to your online voter registration form so that supporters can opt-in to your mobile list – about 10% will do so.

- Organizations can **rent a mobile short code** that lets supporters opt-in to their mobile list at events and respond to text message blasts. For example, you can text "VOTE" to RTVOTE (788683) to join Rock the Vote's mobile street team, which features GOTV reminders, election news, and volunteer opportunities.

- Text messaging can be particularly effective for reaching youth of color as they are more likely to opt-in to a mobile program and have high rates of text messaging.

Conclusion

If the primaries are any indication, two of the defining factors of the 2008 elections will be the increasingly sophisticated use of online organizing tactics and the surge in participation from young voters.

Organizations that leverage new media tactics to register and mobilize young adults can reap significant rewards at the ballot box and on the ground. But rather than replacing traditional campaign efforts, new media tactics should be seen as compliments to established offline tactics such as door-to-door canvassing and phone banking. Combined, new and traditional tactics are essential to a strong campaign.

With a results-oriented mindset, new media opportunities can expand the reach of campaigns to a new generation of Americans that is ready and willing to be engaged.

---

[3] "Mobilizing the Mobiles: How Text Messaging Can Boost Youth Voter Turnout." Dale, A. and A. Strauss. (September 6, 2007). http://www.newvotersproject.org/research/text-messaging/youth-vote-and-text-messaging.pdf

FACT SHEET

Center for Information Research on Civic Learning and Engagement (CIRCLE), Quick Facts — Youth Voting

From civicyouth.org, 2013

Affiliated with Tufts University, CIRCLE conducts studies on civic education and civic engagement among youth. Many of its reports are condensed into fact sheets like the one below and published in the "Quick Facts" area of the group's website.

The 2012 youth vote

- 45% of young people age 18–29 voted in 2012, down from 51% in 2008. Read the detailed analysis of the youth vote here.
- In states with sufficient samples, youth turnout in 2012 was highest in Mississippi (68.1%), Wisconsin (58.0%), Minnesota (57.7%), and Iowa (57.1%). Voter turnout in 2012 was lowest in West Virginia (23.6%), Oklahoma (27.1%), Texas (29.6%), and Arkansas (30.4%). Learn about the youth vote in your state here.
- There were differences in the youth vote by gender and marital status. In 2012, 41.1% of single young men turned out, compared to 48.3% of young single females. In 2012, nearly 52.5% of young married females voted, compared to 48.5% of married men. Find more detailed analysis of the youth vote by gender and marital status here.
- The youth vote varied greatly by gender and race. Young Black and Hispanic women were the strongest supporters of President Obama. Read more on the youth vote by race and gender here.
- Although 60% of U.S. Citizens between the ages of 18–29 have enrolled in college, 71% of young voters have attended college, meaning that college-educated young people were overrepresented among young people who voted. Learn about the youth vote by educational attainment here.
- In 2012, young voters 18–29 chose Barack Obama over Mitt Romney, 60% to 37% — a 23-point margin, according to National Exit Polls. See more information about youth party identification and issue interests here.

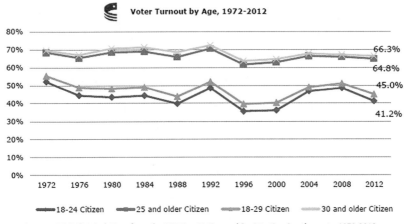

Voter Turnout by Age, 1972-2012

Source: CIRCLE's tabulations from the CPS Nov. Voting and Registration Supplements, 1972-2012

Why youth voting matters

- **Voting is habit-forming:** when young people learn the voting process and vote they are more likely to do so when they are older. If individuals have been motivated to get to the polls once, they are more likely to return. So, getting young people to vote early could be key to raising a new generation of voters.
- **Young people are a major subset of the electorate and their voices matter**:
  - 46 million young people ages 18–29 years old are eligible to vote, while 39 million seniors are eligible to vote
  - Young people (18–29) make up 21% of the voting eligible population in the U.S.
- Involving young people in election-related learning, activities, and discussion can have an **impact on the young person's household**, increasing the likelihood that others in the household will vote. In immigrant communities, young voters may be easier to reach, are more likely to speak English (cutting down translation costs), and may be the most effective messengers within their communities.

And there are **major differences in voter turnout amongst youth subgroups, which may persist as these youth get older if the gaps are not reduced.**

What affects youth voting

- **Contact!** Young people who are contacted by an organization or a campaign are more likely to vote. Additionally, those who discuss an election are more likely to vote in it.
- **Young people who are registered to vote turn out in high numbers**, very close to the rate of older voters. In the 2008 election, 84% of those youth 18–29 who were registered to vote actually cast a ballot. Youth voter registration rates are much lower than older age groups' rates, and as a result, guiding youth through the registration process is one potential step to closing the age-related voting gap.
- **Having information about how, when, and where** to vote can help young people be and feel prepared to vote as well as reduce any level of intimidation they may feel.
- **A state's laws related to voter registration and voting** can have an impact on youth voter turnout. Seven out of the top 10 youth turnout states had some of the more ambitious measures, including Election Day registration, voting by mail (Oregon), or not requiring registration to vote (North Dakota).

In 2008, on average, 59% of young Americans whose home state offered Election Day Registration voted; nine percentage points higher than those who did not live in EDR states. For more on state voting laws see: "Easier Voting Methods Boost Youth Turnout"; How Postregistration Laws Affect the Turnout of Registrants; State Voting Laws and State Election Law Reform and Youth Voter Turnout.

Graph 3: Effect of EDR on Youth Voter Turnout in 2008

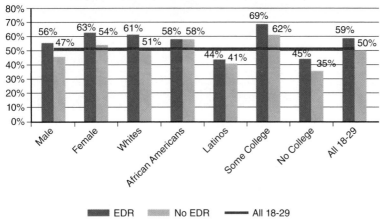

EDR ■ No EDR ■ All 18-29

- **Civic education opportunities** in school have been shown to increase the likelihood that a young person will vote. These opportunities range from social studies classes to simulations of democratic processes and discussion of current issues. Unfortunately, many youth do not have these civic education opportunities, as research has shown that those in more white and/or more affluent schools are more likely to have these opportunities.
- **A young person's home environment** can have a large impact on their engagement. Youth who live in a place where members of their household are engaged and vote are more likely to do so themselves.

What Works in Getting Youth to Vote

- **Registration** is sometimes a larger hurdle than the act of voting itself. Thus showing young people where to get reliable information on registration is helpful.
- **Personalized and interactive contact counts.** The most effective way of getting a new voter is the in-person door-knock by a peer; the least effective is an automated phone call.
  - The medium is more important than the message. Partisan and nonpartisan, negative and positive messages seem to work about the same. The important factor is the degree to which the contact is personalized.
  - Canvassing costs $11 to $14 per new vote, followed closely by phone banks at $10 to $25 per new vote. Robocalls mobilize so few voters that they cost $275 per new vote. (These costs are figured per vote that would not be cast without the mobilizing effort).
- **Begin with the basics: information.** Telling a new voter where to vote, when to vote, and how to use the voting machines increases turnout.
- **Talk to them!** Leaving young voters off contact lists is a costly mistake. Some campaigns still bypass young voters, but research shows they respond cost-effectively when contacted.
- For more information: Young Voter Mobilization Tactics; The Effects of an Election Day Voter Mobilization Campaign Targeting Young Voters by Donald P. Green.

Writing a Profile for a Magazine

● **PURPOSE**

Entertain and inform readers

● **AUDIENCE**

General audience

● **CONTEXT**

Informative or entertainment magazine or newspaper (either national or local)

● **TEXT**

Short (1,000-word) profile piece

© ONOKY-Photononstop/Alamy

Overview

In this scenario, you'll interview someone in order to write an article about him or her for a magazine or newspaper (print or online). The subject of your profile can be anyone. Although you may be most familiar with interviews of celebrities, nearly everyone has interesting stories to tell about their lives and feelings.

The profile piece you write can be humorous, informative, dramatic, touching, or inspiring. It could be all of those things. As part of your preparation, you'll identify a specific publication that sometimes runs articles like this. The destination can be a mass-market magazine such as *The New Yorker*, *Rolling Stone*, *Time*, *FHM*, or *Vogue*. Or it could be a more specialized or narrowly targeted publication such as the left-leaning *Mother Jones* or the music recording–oriented *Tape Op* (each of these publications has a website where you can find examples of profiles). You could also choose to target a local publication such as a school or community newspaper, magazine, or website (all of which often include profiles of local people).

Before the interview, you'll need to do background research on the person you choose to write about so you can create good interview questions or prompts. The background information will also be important for the article, where you can use it to paint a fuller picture of the person for the reader. You'll also need to do research on the publication where you'd like to place your article to get a sense of what types of work it publishes, including issues of rough word count, type of language used, and other factors that might make your article more attractive. The article you write should use the interview as raw material, but it should not simply be a list of questions and answers. Contextualize that raw material with background information, descriptions of the physical surroundings, or other sensory information you gathered.

You may choose to include photos or to lay out your article so that it looks like a professional publication (either print or online). To create something more visually interesting than a simple text document in a word-processing program, use a print page design application such as InDesign or a website design program such as Dreamweaver.

Strategies

Think about people whom you know personally or know of. Who has interesting stories to tell? A grandmother who worked on the line at the Ford plant in 1942 bolting bumpers to cars? Your friend's older sister who's trying to break into the music business in New York? The cook at a diner where you and your friends have eaten at hundreds of times?

Be careful about interviewing people you already know very well — much of your conversation may involve inside jokes and references that your eventual readers will not understand.

Do some background research about the person you're interviewing. This can help you better understand him or her and be useful in coming up with interview questions. The exact process for background research depends on the people involved. Your basic goal is to find out more about the person and his or her history. If the person is involved with an organization, you might start by finding information about the organization — its history, who is involved with it, what its goals are. If you know that the person has interests, hobbies, or other activities, find out what you can about those things.

Talk to other people who know your interviewee — but avoid seeming creepy about it. You may want to avoid doing too much of this sort of "background check" conversation with other people since word about your inquiries may get back to the interviewee, who may feel uncomfortable with people talking about him or her in this manner. See the Tip Box in Chapter 7 for some additional considerations.

Use the information you've gathered from your background research to help you develop questions and topics of discussion for the interview. What questions did your research leave unanswered? What would you like to find out more about?

Your raw notes and recordings from the interview are just that — raw material. You'll be picking and choosing material to create an interesting picture for your own readers or viewers. If you're working on a "creative nonfiction" type of interview, your primary goal is entertainment. Flag the portions of the interview that seem most interesting and entertaining — they could be funny, emotional, inspirational, or suspenseful.

If your goal is entertainment, you'll want to construct the profile like a *story*, with a beginning, middle, and end. You don't want to put the most interesting material at the start (because everything will be downhill after that). Instead, you'll usually want to provide some *glimpses* of what's coming up or some moderately interesting material at the start. You may also decide to provide the general background information in your own words, very quickly, at the start of the piece.

If you choose to lay out your article, look at other profiles on the web or in print magazines. Analyze how designers have used a grid to structure the page, how they've varied font sizes for headings. Do the layouts you see use pictures? Of what? Do they use "pull quotes" (short quotations from the article to generate interest to readers who are skimming)? How is color used?

Questions to Keep in Mind

1. What areas seem to make this person who he or she is? What seems to define him or her?
2. What makes the person interesting?
3. What areas of the person's background seem to have contributed in important ways to his or her life?
4. Look at the interview content from readers' perspective. What will seem to connect the reader to the person you interviewed? What will surprise the reader?
5. If this is a story, what type of story is it? Comedy? Tragedy? A story of human triumph?

Background Text

MAGAZINE ARTICLE
Linell Smith, "The Art of Poetry"
From *Goucher Quarterly,* Winter 2014

Photo by Jim Burger

This article from the *Goucher Quarterly,* the alumni magazine of Goucher College, profiles alumna and artist Jenny O'Grady. As you read the article, note how writer Linell Smith mixes concrete fact—images, rich description, and quotations from O'Grady—with explanatory and narrative text to weave an interesting story about the artist. The annotations highlight some key strategies that are common to profiles like this, but you should also be able to identify additional places where the writer works to engage the reader's interest.

Jenny Huddleston O'Grady '98 writes poems you can undress and poems you can press to your heart. One, written on a shiny fabric eel, can wind around a little finger. Another flutters if you read it out loud. She's even composed a haiku you can wear. Imagine a poem stitched into the skirts of a doll, or hidden in a tiny typewriter, nestled underneath a bird's wing, or etched into the gills of a horseshoe crab. You might say the 37-year-old artist proves how essential poetry is by uncovering the various shapes it can assume.

A quick, vibrant visual description opens the piece.

You might also say she liberates it.

A witty punchline or verbal pun casts a mood.

"Some people really want to see their words in a certain way and in a certain order. They like to control their writing," she observes. "I don't care. I like interactivity. If someone reads the poem wrong, it really doesn't matter to me. If you play around with it, you're still going to get a sense of it."

And, in the process, you might never forget it. Some of these award-winning "poem sculptures" were recently displayed in a gallery in Baltimore's Station North, the city's artistic hub near the Maryland Institute College of Art (MICA). O'Grady's work was part of an exhibition that featured nine artists who were awarded $1,000 "b-grants" last year by the Greater Baltimore Cultural Alliance (GBCA) for artistic excellence and innovation. Her work received an additional $500 grant honoring the late GBCA founder, Nancy Haragan.

Mentions of the artist's accolades from various organizations.

"Jenny O'Grady creates timeless fabric sculptures that incorporate poems reminiscent of her favorite books or memories," says Emily Russell, a MICA graduate student who helped curate the show. "She combines traditional art forms like poetry, sewing, and bookbinding in a nontraditional way, and I think that is why her work is so unique and fun."

Quote from a fellow artist continues to praise O'Grady's work.

It's also a tribute to what this artist and writer can accomplish in the cracks between her job as marketing director for the University of Maryland, Baltimore County (UMBC), and her home life with her husband, T.J. O'Grady '99, and their 5-year-old son, Max.

In addition to her handmade literary works, O'Grady founded and edits *The Light Ekphrastic*, a quarterly online journal that pairs writers and visual artists to create new pieces based on one another's work. The four-year-old journal hosted its first non-virtual exhibition at a Baltimore-area gallery last year.

During the work week she turns out innovative, attention-grabbing pieces for the alumni relations and development department of UMBC, and, until last year, taught book arts and electronic publishing at the University of Baltimore.

Growing up in a family of artists—her sister went to MICA, her mother began an art appreciation program at her elementary school—O'Grady says she never considered herself particularly artistic. "Super shy," she longed to become a community newspaper reporter like her mother, who worked for a weekly in Denton, Md.

The writer adds some history, showing how the artist developed over time.

She did. And you might say that several years of reporting, combined with the perspective of an Eastern Shore farm girl, helped mold her fresh, outsider's vision.

A diet of liberal arts at Goucher, she says, also proved invaluable. "It helped me to not only write clearly but to understand context—to understand enough of history, and of what has happened before me, to write convincingly," she says. An English major, she also served as editor of *The Quindecim*.

After graduation, O'Grady worked for *The Evening Sun* in Hanover, Pa., and then for *The Maryland Gazette*. Covering fires and town meetings, she also learned how to capture the flavor of local feature stories about "ballroom" boxing or an unusual piglet raised on cans of chocolate Ensure. Along the way, she sharpened her visual skills by taking night courses in photography, graphic design, and drawing.

She enrolled in the University of Baltimore in 2002 and graduated with her M.F.A. in creative writing and publishing arts four years later. By that time she was working at UMBC, where she began persuading artist and writer friends not to allow their day jobs to constrain them. "I like to consider myself an artistic nag," she says. "I work with a lot of graphic designers who love to paint or draw but don't feel like they have time. So I said, 'Well, what if I gave you each a poem? Would the guilt of that get you going? Would the inspiration of that get you going?'"

The next step was designing a website, *The Light Ekphrastic*, to display their work. Ekphrasis is a rhetorical device in which an artist in one medium tries to relate to the work of another artist by defining and describing its essence and form. A painting can describe a sculpture, a poem can portray a picture, and vice versa. "It's reactive, a jumping-off point," O'Grady says.

As a young girl she relished "choose your own adventure" books in which readers made choices that determine how the story develops. Now she's passing on the pleasures of reading interactively to young Max. Perhaps her most child-friendly poem is "Homing." The plump cloth bird that carries her words also captures the spirit of the O'Gradys' 2009 trip to South Korea to adopt their son.

"It's based on the idea of migration," she says. "I wanted to write a poem that you could read backward and forward like the trip, and I wanted you to be able to turn it over in your hands. Then I realized that a bird's wings would make really cool pages."

Constructed in stolen moments during her maternity leave, the poem is made completely of fabric, with hand-embroidered text. The feathers, or "pages," fasten to the body of the bird with red buttons. When opened, they reveal the poem that reads forward and backward, depending on which side of the bird you're on:

north says
it is time
all that you own
tucked neatly within
homing
south says

south says
it is time
all that you own
tucked neatly within
homing
north says

Photo courtesy of Jenny O'Grady

Sometimes O'Grady is drawn to troubling subjects. Take, for instance, her award-winning trio of poem dolls, each based on a character from Gunter Grass' dark novel *The Tin Drum*.

"I've tried to make the physical experience of reading each poem doll mirror an aspect of the doll's character, and also somewhat intrusive—as each poem touches on private, uncomfortable moments of their lives. You must lift a skirt, or unzip a dress, or unbutton suspenders to read their stories," she explains on her website, www.kineticprose.com.

You can also consider such work—constructed from eyelet-driven hinges, recycled paper bags, Shrinky Dinks, and Mod Podge—as a marriage between literary inspiration and the do-it-yourself world of Michaels crafts. It's got a roll-up-your-sleeves magic.

When O'Grady teaches bookmaking, she works hard to demystify the challenge posed by the blank page. "A lot of people write, write, write, but they are not makers," she says. "I try to force them in the same way that a live drawing class forces you out of your comfort zone. Sometimes I make my students rip up part of their book so that they don't feel like it's such a sacred thing. They can destroy it," she points out. "And then they can make another one."

10 Writing a Restaurant Review

Entertainment and/or informational

People in your hometown

Hometown magazine or website

Short restaurant review (about 1,500 words) with three photos

© Angela Hampton Picture Library/Alamy

Overview

A friend from high school e-mailed you yesterday to ask if you'd be a part of a new project she's involved with. She's landed an internship at a small newsmagazine published in your hometown. It's a standard "this is our community" type of publication that includes news about current events, stories about community members and organizations, and more. Like many small magazines, it's been struggling to cope with the migration of readers from print to the web. Market research has told the publication that a core group of dedicated readers like to read in print, but also that many readers would prefer online material. So the magazine has begun a small website, actually more of a weblog, that will hold a mix of stories repurposed from print as well as contributions from people in the community.

This is where you come in: Your friend wants you to provide some content for the online publication. She's interested in getting community members like you to write reviews of local restaurants. The magazine can provide a small amount of financial compensation, but most of your motivation is to help out your friend. You're the first person she's asked, so you get to pick the restaurant yourself. The only restriction she has is that the magazine doesn't want reviews of national chain restaurants. (Chain restaurants pride themselves on consistency; unless something is seriously wrong, one Big Mac is like any other Big Mac.)

The review needs to be around 1,500 words and include at least three pictures. You can decide what pictures to take — dishes served at the restaurant or the restaurant itself (inside or outside).

Her excitement about the project is infectious; even though your schedule is pretty busy, you agree to write something.

Strategies

Read other professionally written restaurant reviews to get a feel for their structure and content. You can usually find good sample reviews in local newspapers or magazines; one example is provided in the

286

Background Text section. Avoid reading only reviews from websites such as Yelp or TripAdvisor, which tend to be very short and very uneven in terms of quality.

People have one main reason to read a review of a restaurant: to decide whether to eat there. So your goal will be to give readers a sense of what your experience was like. Obviously you'll want to describe the taste and smell of the food being served, but experiences also rely on sight, touch, and sound. Consider an elegant restaurant that had jarringly loud music blaring while couples attempted to eat an expensive gourmet dinner. Would the sound affect their experience? Probably.

Try to pick a restaurant that will provide something interesting to write about — and read about. Before trying out a new restaurant, many people will seek out opinions from people who've already eaten there to help make decisions about which restaurants are worth a visit, not only in terms of food but also in terms of atmosphere, quality of service, and more. Restaurant reviews are a popular source for gathering these opinions and observations.

When you're taking pictures, keep in mind the other diners and the restaurant staff. Many people object to their pictures being taken during what they consider a relatively private experience. It's become relatively common for people to take pictures of their own meals, but you should do so without calling a lot of attention to yourself — turn off the flash on your camera or smartphone if possible. Exterior shots of a building are usually noncontroversial, but you should ask permission before taking a lot of pictures inside, particularly if you're taking pictures that show people prominently in the foreground.

Consider taking other people with you so that you have more than one main dish to sample. If you go to the restaurant with a group of three or four people, you can order a range of appetizers, entrees, and desserts that you can all share so you have a wider range of experiences. You can also ask your friends for their thoughts about the experience.

Take notes as you eat and be sure to record your impressions of all senses as discussed above.

Questions to Keep in Mind

1. What makes you decide to eat at a restaurant? Think about some recent very good (or very bad) restaurant experiences. Was there one primary aspect involved? Or was it a range of things?
2. What features do you commonly see in restaurant reviews? Do reviews tend to describe the experience in chronological order? Do they give readers an easy-to-scan summary? What structure do they tend to follow?

Chapter Connections

PRIMARY CONNECTIONS

- Chapter 2: Approaching Writing Situations
- Chapter 4: Structuring Your Texts
- Chapter 9: Revising Your Texts

SECONDARY CONNECTIONS

- Chapter 5: Designing Visual Texts
- Chapter 7: Getting Information and Writing from Research (if you decide to interview any of the staff or fellow diners)
- Chapter 10: Publishing Your Texts

3. Does the restaurant you've chosen to review have clear goals in mind for diners? Is it trying to be a fun experience or a calm, quiet one? Does it have a gimmick? Or is it fitting within a specific genre? How well does it achieve those goals? (Tip: Don't review a restaurant that specializes in food you know you don't like.)

4. What pictures show key aspects of the restaurant in terms of diners' experiences? If the restaurant appears to be based on "comfort foods," are the plates loaded with large portions? If the restaurant offers elegant dining, does it offer cloth napkins and nice silverware? What can you show readers that will help them understand the experience they're likely to have?

Background Text

RESTAURANT REVIEW

Alice Levitt, "Taste Test: Review of Maple City Diner in St. Albans"
From *Seven Days,* April 10, 2013

Alice Levitt is a reporter who covers dining and restaurants for *Seven Days,* an independent weekly newspaper in Burlington, Vermont.

This image has a strong, inviting impact on viewers: sweet baked goods, attractively plated and a face for viewers to keep in mind as they read.

Maple City Diner chef-owner Marcus Hamblett
Matthewthorsen.com

Some of Vermont's oldest operational restaurants are diners. Berlin's Wayside Restaurant & Bakery opened in 1918, while Burlington favorite Henry's Diner has been slinging hearty breakfasts since 1925. It could be said that along with maple syrup and cheddar cheese, diners are the backbone of Green Mountain food culture.

Maple City Diner in St. Albans serves all of the classics, but it's only been open for a month. Another thing that sets it apart? The eatery is owned by chef Marcus Hamblett.

Locals may know him as chef and owner of One Federal, also in St. Albans; previously, the New England Culinary Institute graduate worked as a chef-instructor at his alma mater. As he has proved at beloved, all-American One Federal, Hamblett has the chops to create dishes that transcend the comfort-food classics that inspire them. He does so with not just a deft hand in the kitchen, but a green thumb.

Hamblett's own small farm supplies much of the produce used in the from-scratch cooking at One Federal.

With this talented chef in charge of the menu at Maple City, as well, the diner has the potential to be both a place to eat a delicious meal and an important example of true Vermont roots cooking. A little more than a month after opening, Maple City is on its way to realizing this potential but isn't there quite yet.

The space that previously housed Athena's Diner is now decorated with maple-related paraphernalia — vintage photos of locals working their sugar bushes, ads for maple products, and antique taps and other sugaring equipment. A small counter provides an authentic diner experience, but I preferred the exceptionally cushy booths, where the only thing less than comfortable was the temperature. I ate with my coat on, and noticed that other diners did so, as well. With the warm months coming, this shouldn't be a problem much longer, and hopefully the thermostat will be fixed before next winter.

While breakfast is served all day, at my first, evening visit, I ordered from the dinner menu. A bowl of parsnip-maple soup was an obvious choice to ring in the maple season and recognize the diner's theme. Perhaps I should have saved it for dessert. It was delicious but overly sweet, a shock to my palate so early in the meal. A little less maple or a little more salt and acid would have made it a better starter.

As a fan of One Federal's homemade, crunchy chicken fingers, I was excited to try the tenders at Maple City. However, the three small pieces were neither made from scratch nor particularly tasty, and only 50 cents less than those served at the other restaurant.

The salad that comes with every dinner entrée is a taste of One Federal. The same impressively balanced maple vinaigrette perfected at the other restaurant is available at Maple City, among a selection of homemade dressings. Unfortunately, the portion of fresh mixed greens, cucumbers, cherry tomatoes, and onions was small.

The meal improved when our entrées arrived. The eponymously named Maple City burger had personality plus: Cooked exactly to my requested medium, the meat was juicy and slathered in just enough maple syrup to make it flavorful without being too sweet. Bacon and cheddar cheese were good

The review opens with a context- and purpose-setting comment. It explains why diners are important.

For the audience reading this review, the "farm-to-table" approach will be an important feature.

Here, the reviewer announces a clear opinion: This is a promising restaurant even if it does have some current problems.

The "promising, but . . ." theme is repeated throughout the review.

Sometimes, reviews draw on storytelling techniques. Here, you can almost envision a come-from-behind victory forming.

complements to the thinnish patty and syrup, as was the sturdy-but-fluffy roll on which it was all served. The hand-cut fries that came on the side, however, could have used another minute or two of cooking for additional crispness.

The roast-turkey dinner might have time-traveled from one of those Vermont diners of a hundred years ago, with a tweak or two. Over exceptionally creamy mashed potatoes, two thick slices of turkey were succulent, salty, and fork-tender. The delectably thick, pale gravy tasted more like a fine-dining cream sauce than thickened pan drippings. Stuffing was flavored with sage and presented in pebble-like chunks. But while there was plenty of turkey, gravy, potatoes, and stuffing, the sides of cranberry sauce and creamy coleslaw, served in plastic cups, were skimpy, leaving the dish off balance.

The reviewer relies heavily on describing sensory data: images, tastes, textures. These help connect the reader with the reviewer's experience.

There were no complaints whatsoever when it was time for dessert. The pastry case at Maple City Diner is a thing to behold. Giant cubes of bread pudding, extra-large éclairs, and chocolate-drizzled peanut-butter pies were all tempting. So was a pan of biscuits soaking in maple syrup and labeled "ragmuffins." Baker Jill Lanpher and NECI intern Eva Fiske deserve heaps of praise for all of the old-time treats that are far better than great-grandma used to make.

Reviews are often written as first-person narratives: "Here is what I experienced, in the order I experienced it." (Another common storytelling technique, maybe the oldest one around)

I just had to try the maple cinnamon buns that Hamblett has touted proudly. And he's right to brag. While sticky-sweet, the bun didn't overwhelm, perhaps due to its soft, buttery dough, and the giant dessert was easily enough for two. That pastry is the reason St. Albans will never need a Cinnabon. Why visit a franchise that can't compare to the real (local) thing?

Cupcakes were also impressive in both size and flavor. The Black Forest's firm, chocolaty cake hid a delightful secret — after a couple of bites, a mass of sweet cherries oozed out of the cupcake's center. A tall topping of sugary buttercream frosting complemented the seductive synthesis of chocolate and cherries.

Reviewers sometimes (but not always) interview a staff member. This allows the reviewer to discuss the history of the restaurant, its goals, and its plans for the future.

According to manager and One Federal alum Kim Smith, the addition of a second cooler will make room for grab-and-go savory eats. Fingers crossed, she'll be able to fit some extra sweets in there, too. Perhaps it will house the bacon doughnuts that are scheduled to debut soon? Those weren't yet available on my second visit to Maple City, so I tried a different bacon treat.

The bacon waffle is serious stuff. Bits of rashers protrude from inside a fluffy waffle with a lightly crisped jacket. The pork continues through the center of the tender pastry, leaving just enough grease to flavor the mildly sweet dough with a hint of smoke.

Although many reviews are written based on one visit, this reviewer returned several times in order to sample a wide range.

The day I tried the waffle, the maple cream on top didn't live up to its name. What looked like a plain pat of butter also tasted like one. No matter how hard I concentrated, I couldn't detect a hint of sap. Luckily, syrup is provided by request at no extra charge, and a slathering of it combined with the bacon amped up the Vermont flavors of the dish.

Another breakfast entrée, the Vermont Skillet, was cooked — and served — in a small cast-iron pan filled with green apples, bacon, hash browns, and onions. The only detractor here was the onions. Described as caramelized, they were merely browned, and their potent crunch nearly overwhelmed the dish's other flavors and textures.

As long as I avoided the too-thick allium, this dish was fine. A layer of cheddar on top paired especially well with the over-easy eggs that sauced the contents of the skillet with their creamy wash of yolk.

The chef's way with gravies, demonstrated in the turkey dinner, was evident at breakfast, too. The biscuits and gravy plate was composed of four petite, buttery pieces of quick bread drenched in a delectably creamy white sauce that was studded with slices of skinny breakfast sausage. While the gravy itself was a success, the presence of links promised an extra-meaty taste that wasn't delivered — the sausages simply weren't sufficiently seasoned. A homemade, sage-and-pepper-filled version might have been a better fit than the outsourced maple links.

This contrast between in-house and outsourced ingredients is the source of many of Maple City's imperfections. Smith says that Hamblett has increased the size of his farm to supply the diner with fresh, local produce this spring and summer. With this expansion, more of the food at Maple City will be made from scratch. And when that happens, there's no reason the diner shouldn't attain sweet success.

Maple City Diner, 17 Swanton Road, St. Albans

14 Designing Cover Art for Digital Music

● **PURPOSE**

Secure a loan and attract customers for a new record label

● **AUDIENCE**

Complex: Music buyers, a bank loan officer, and a record label owner

● **CONTEXT**

A new record company

● **TEXT**

Three iTunes cover art options (1,400 x 1,400 pixels) and a presentation

© Image Source/Alamy

Overview

You've managed to land a summer consulting job as a graphic designer. You're part of a small team at the firm and are getting ready to start your first assignment. Your supervisor explains to your team that a friend of a friend needs some design work. Unfortunately, the potential client doesn't have a lot of money, so as a favor (but against his better judgment, you can tell) your supervisor agreed that your team would do some initial work for free ("on spec," as designers say) and pitch some designs to the client. If the client likes what she sees, she'll hire you.

Your team meets with the client, Renee Swetland, to discuss the project. Renee is trying to secure a startup loan for her new record label. Renee explains that she wants to show the bank an album or iTunes cover for a band on the label — she wants it to look professional and interesting, the sort of thing that will seem marketable.

She doesn't actually have any bands on the label yet, so she'd like you to create an album cover for a fictional band. For the purposes of the scenario, you can choose whatever genre of music you want. She asks your team to begin by doing some research of what iTunes cover art looks like for other albums in that genre. She doesn't want you to simply copy all of those aspects, but she says it should look like it belongs in that genre. "Sometimes being strikingly different is a good thing," she says, "but it's also dangerous, so if you depart from the genre, you'll need to make a good case for doing that."

"Can you come up with three possible designs? You can present them to me and I'll give you feedback to help you create a single, final version. I'd also really appreciate it if you could show me the results of your research — some key examples of covers you looked at and a list of the key characteristics you think covers in that genre need to have."

Renee finishes by explaining that the artwork should be designed in a format compatible with the iTunes store — 1,400 x 1,400 pixels in JPG or PNG format.

In addition to the three different cover art options, Renee wants you to create a brief presentation (in Power-Point, Prezi, or another program) to present to her and a couple of her employees. They'll decide based on this presentation and the designs whether they'd like to hire you to work on a final cover art design.

> ### Chapter Connections
>
> **PRIMARY CONNECTIONS**
> - Chapter 1: Building a Framework for Reading and Writing
> - Chapter 5: Designing Visual Texts
>
> **SECONDARY CONNECTIONS**
> - Chapter 2: Approaching Writing Situations
> - Chapter 6: Managing Writing Projects

Your presentation should include four to six album covers from the genre you picked, a list of the important characteristics of that genre, and your three designs. As you show the three designs during your presentation, be sure you discuss the strengths of each, including how that design meets the characteristics you identified as well as any other design features you think work well.

Strategies

Your PACT charts are where you'll start doing marketing research. You'll need three PACT charts, one for each design you'll create, but they will probably share some aspects.

Use a website that sells music (for example, iTunes, Amazon, or CD Baby) to find examples from the genre you picked. You could also look at music label websites or your own music library.

As you look at other album covers in the genre, make notes about similarities you see. Fans of genres generally like consistency. As with other types of genres, people process what they see and hear based on expectations they have from other texts in the same genre. As with much work within a genre, the designer needs to navigate a solution that is interesting and innovative while still responding to the elements of that genre.

Like all rules, the one about consistency can be broken if you're very careful. The album art of Nine Inch Nails' *Hesitation Marks* uses a very subdued type and a warm color palette, two features that seem at odds with the stereotypically stark, dark imagery one might associate with an industrial-rock band. But the artwork continues a consistent theme used in the visual identity of the group, a low-key detachment from which convulsive sounds periodically emerge. In this case, departing from genre has been a smart design strategy.

Questions to Keep in Mind

1. Given what you know about the genre you're working in, does your band have a specific look and feel in terms of typography? Logo? Color?
2. What would a good band name be in this genre?
3. What would be a good album title?
4. Does the album title suggest a certain theme or look?

Background Texts

ALBUM COVER
Jimi Hendrix, People, Hell and Angels

Although he died in 1970, Jimi Hendrix remains one of rock's music icons. Designers of the cover art for this posthumous album put the musician in the forefront, using black-and-white photography to give the image a classic feel. The cover art works today because it's a look back at a historical figure — rock album cover art in the 1960s had a very different look.

AP Photo/Legacy

ALBUM COVER
Nine Inch Nails, *Hesitation Marks*

As discussed in the Overview section, this Nine Inch Nails album art adopts a low-key, no-drama approach that's consistent with the carefully crafted image the band has used since its founding.

AP Photo/Columbia Records/Dayve Ward

ALBUM COVER
Thirty Seconds to Mars, Love Lust Faith + Dreams

Thirty Seconds to Mars meticulously crafts all aspects of their work — songs, music videos, and cover art. In this album art, the colored dots suggest careful ordering, but the principle behind the choice of the specific color for each dot remains a mystery to the viewer. The color and size of the text suggest that it's low in the hierarchy of elements, but the use of all caps sends the opposite signal. The overall image is one of tension.

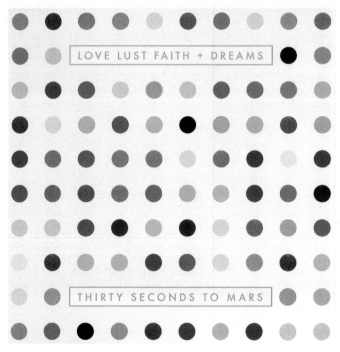

AP Photo/Virgin/EMI

Repurposing a Text

Overview

You've been working at *Perspex*, an online magazine with a self-consciously intellectual and cultural viewpoint (more popular examples of this genre would be *The New Yorker*, *The Atlantic*, or *Slate*). You like working for *Perspex* because you generally get to pick your own projects. You've had the most luck in "translating" existing work, often collaborating with an academic researcher to remake a specialized or highly technical article he or she has written into a more accessible and entertaining form.

You've just published a string of articles on topics ranging from the acoustics of the Metropolitan Opera House to the science of creating compelling television commercials. After a couple of days off, you're ready to head into a new project. You begin by going to an academic library site and browsing recent academic journal issues to find an article that you can translate into something a wider audience would find entertaining. You'll need to take the original (very specialized) content from the article and rewrite it in a style and structure that will be interesting to a nonspecialist audience.

You'll produce a short (around 1,500-word) article or essay for a general, educated audience. The language should be simple and accessible but not oversimplified. You may want to review articles at some of the publications mentioned earlier and think about them in comparison to both specialized academic papers as well as informational news articles. Your article or essay will be somewhere between the two.

Because this genre is also visual, you'll need to locate three to five images to illustrate key points or even just emotions connected to your topic. Because your budget for images is pretty low (actually, it's $0), you'll want to locate Creative Commons or similar images that you can use both legally and for free.

A note on copyright and plagiarism: Copyright law allows limited use of works in the classroom, so you're within your rights to create a text based on an academic article provided you do not publish it (in print, on the web, and so forth) and share it only in the classroom. Although it

© Greg Vignal/Alamy

PURPOSE

Entertainment

AUDIENCE

Mass, college-educated audience

CONTEXT

A web-based magazine

TEXT

Magazine article (online), around 1,500 words + images

should be obvious to your instructor that you created your new text based on someone else's existing text, you should add a note to your draft that lists the author and source of the original text. (Who knows? Ten years from now when you're a wealthy CEO or politician, some journalist may dig through your discarded hard drive, find this essay, and declare that you plagiarized this text. Scandalous! Better safe than sorry.)

Strategies

Pick either a topic or a discipline that you're already interested in and start your search there.

Many specialized academic articles are interested in contributing to knowledge in the discipline. But articles such as the one you're writing are about intellectual stimulation and entertainment. As you read the articles, think about people beyond that original, specialized audience. What are the implications of the work for readers in the wider world? What aspects might interest them? Entertain them? Frighten them?

As you're looking for images to use, think about both the specific content of the article as well as adjectives or emotions it suggests. An article about climate change, for example, might use images of polar bears or icebergs, but it might also use creative images such as a snow shovel, a beach pail full of sand, or even a composite image including a snowball and fire.

Questions to Keep in Mind

1. As you skim specialized articles, create a PACT chart to consider important issues, such as: What about this topic will interest your audience? What within their context can be connected to the article? What does your text need to do to grab your audience's interest?
2. Find some examples of online magazines of the sort you're writing for. What specialized topics are they translating?
3. How do articles in these online magazines treat technical terms? Do they use technical terms and explain them, or do they avoid technical terms altogether?
4. Do academics or researchers show up in these articles? If so, how are they portrayed? Are they quoted or just "shown"?

Background Texts

ARTICLE FOR A TECHNICAL AUDIENCE
Rafi Shaik and Ramakrishna Wusirika, "Machine
Learning Approaches Distinguish Multiple Stress
Conditions Using Stress-Responsive Genes and Identify
Candidate Genes for Broad Resistance in Rice"
From *Plant Physiology,* January 2014

Rafi Shaik and Ramakrishna Wusirika, biologists at Michigan Technological
University, wrote this article for an audience of plant biologists. The full article
is not reproduced here, but the abstract and introduction will give you a sense
of the writers' tone and sentence structure. The writers provide background on
the purpose and significance of their research, use technical and scientific terms
that are appropriate for an audience of fellow biologists, and incorporate sources
from their scientific field.

Abstract

Abiotic and biotic stress responses are traditionally thought to be regulated by
discrete signaling mechanisms. Recent experimental evidence revealed a more
complex picture where these mechanisms are highly entangled and can have
synergistic and antagonistic effects on each other. In this study, we identified
shared stress-responsive genes between abiotic and biotic stresses in rice (*Oryza
sativa*) by performing meta-analyses of microarray studies. About 70% of the
1,377 common differentially expressed genes showed conserved expression
status, and the majority of the rest were down-regulated in abiotic stresses and
up-regulated in biotic stresses. Using dimension reduction techniques, principal
component analysis, and partial least squares discriminant analysis, we were able
to segregate abiotic and biotic stresses into separate entities. The supervised
machine learning model, recursive-support vector machine, could classify
abiotic and biotic stresses with 100% accuracy using a subset of differentially
expressed genes. Furthermore, using a random forests decision tree model, eight
out of 10 stress conditions were classified with high accuracy. Comparison of
genes contributing most to the accurate classification by partial least squares
discriminant analysis, recursive-support vector machine, and random forests
revealed 196 common genes with a dynamic range of expression levels in
multiple stresses. Functional enrichment and coexpression network analysis
revealed the different roles of transcription factors and genes responding to
phytohormones or modulating hormone levels in the regulation of stress responses.
We envisage the top-ranked genes identified in this study, which highly discriminate
abiotic and biotic stresses, as key components to further our understanding of the
inherently complex nature of multiple stress responses in plants.

Introduction

The need to breed robust and high-productivity crops is more important than ever due to increasingly adverse environmental conditions and scarce natural resources. Food productivity has to be raised by as much as 70% to 100% to meet the nutritional needs of the growing population, which is expected to rise to 9 billion by 2050 (Godfray et al., 2010; Lutz and Samir, 2010). Rice (*Oryza sativa*) is both a major food crop and a model organism that shares extensive synteny and collinearity with other grasses. Thus, the development of rice that can sustain a wide variety of adverse conditions is vital to meet the imminent global energy demands.

A broad range of stress factors divided into two major categories, namely abiotic stresses encompassing a variety of unfavorable environmental conditions, such as drought, submergence, salinity, heavy metal contamination or nutrient deficiency, and biotic stresses caused by infectious living organisms, such as bacteria, viruses, fungi, or nematodes, negatively affect the productivity and survival of plants. Advancements in whole-genome transcriptome analysis techniques like microarrays and RNA sequencing have revolutionized the identification of changes in gene expression in plants under stress, making it possible now to chart out individual stress-specific biomolecular networks and signaling pathways. However, in field conditions, plants are often subjected to multiple stresses simultaneously, requiring efficient molecular mechanisms to perceive a multitude of signals and to elicit a tailored response (Sharma et al., 2013). Increasing evidence from experimental studies suggests that the cross talk between individual stress response signaling pathways via key regulatory molecules, resulting in the dynamic modulation of downstream effectors, is at the heart of multiple stress tolerance. A number of studies have identified many genes, especially transcription factors (TFs) and hormone response factors, that play a central role in multiple stresses and manifest a signature expression specific to the stress condition. For example, abscisic acid (ABA) response factors are up-regulated in the majority of abiotic stresses, activating an oxidative response to protect cells from reactive oxygen species damage, but were found to be down-regulated in a number of biotic conditions, possibly suppressed by immune response molecules (Cao et al., 2011).

The wide range of abiotic and biotic stress factors and their numerous combinations in natural conditions generate a customized stress response. This suggests that the identification and characterization of key genes and their coexpression partners, which show an expression profile that discriminates abiotic and biotic stress responses, would increase our understanding of plant stress response manyfold and provide targets for genetic manipulation to improve their stress tolerance. The availability of multiple genome-wide transcriptome data sets for the same stress condition provides an opportunity to identify, compare, and contrast the stress-specific gene expression profile of one stress condition with other stresses. Meta-analysis combining similar studies provides a robust statistical framework to reevaluate original findings, improve sensitivity with increased sample size, and test new hypotheses. Meta-analysis of microarray studies is widely used, especially in clinical research, to improve statistical robustness and detect weak signals (Liu et al., 2013; Rung and Brazma, 2013). For instance, thousands of samples belonging to hundreds of cancer types were combined, which provided new insights into the general and specific transcriptional patterns of tumors (Lukk et al., 2010).

Microarray studies are burdened with a high dimensionality of feature space, also called the "curse of dimensionality" (i.e. the availability of very many variables [genes] for very few observations [samples]). Machine learning algorithms (supervised and unsupervised), such as principal component analysis (PCA), decision trees, and support vector machines (SVM), provide a way to efficiently classify two or more classes of data. Further feature selection procedures like recursive-support vector machines (R-SVM) provide means to identify the top features contributing most to the accuracy of classification.

In this study, we performed a meta-analysis of stress response studies in rice using publicly available microarray gene expression data conducted on a single platform (AffymetrixRiceArray). Meta-analysis of abiotic and biotic stresses was performed separately to identify differentially expressed genes (DEGs) involved in multiple stress conditions. The lists of abiotic and biotic DEGs were then compared to identify common genes with conserved and nonconserved gene expression (i.e., whether up-regulated, down-regulated, or oppositely regulated in both the categories), revealing the broad patterns of their involvement in the stress response. In order to test the efficiency of identified common DEGs in the classification of abiotic and biotic stresses as well as individual stresses within abiotic and biotic stresses, we systematically investigated various classification and machine learning techniques, including PCA, partial least squares discriminant analysis (PLS-DA), SVM, and random forest (RF). We characterized the shared DEGs through functional enrichment analysis of gene ontologies, metabolic pathways, TF families, and microRNAs (miRNAs) targeting them. We also analyzed the correlation of coexpression between the common DEGs to find sets of genes showing high coexpression and identify hub genes that show the greatest number of edges over a very high cutoff value.

Literature Cited

Cao FY, Yoshioka K, Desveaux D (2011) The roles of ABA in plant pathogen interactions. J Plant Res **124**: 489–499

Godfray HC, Beddington JR, Crute IR, Haddad L, Lawrence D, Muir JF, Pretty J, Robinson S, Thomas SM, Toulmin C (2010) Food security: the challenge of feeding 9 billion people. Science **327**: 812–818

Liu Z, Xie M, Yao Z, Niu Y, Bu Y, Gao C (2013) Three meta-analyses define a set of commonly overexpressed genes from microarray datasets on astrocytomas. Mol Neurobiol **47**: 325–336

Lukk M, Kapushesky M, Nikkilä J, Parkinson H, Goncalves A, Huber W, Ukkonen E, Brazma A (2010) A global map of human gene expression. Nat Biotechnol **28**: 322–324

Lutz W, Samir KC (2010) Dimensions of global population projections: what do we know about future population trends and structures? Philos Trans R Soc Lond B Biol Sci **365**: 2779–2791

Rung J, Brazma A (2013) Reuse of public genome-wide gene expression data. Nat Rev Genet **14**: 89–99

Sharma R, De Vleesschauwer D, Sharma MK, Ronald PC (2013) Recent advances in dissecting stress-regulatory crosstalk in rice. Mol Plant **6**: 250–260

ARTICLE FOR A GENERAL AUDIENCE

Marcia Goodrich, "Scientists ID Genes That Could Lead to Tough, Disease-Resistant Varieties of Rice"

From *Michigan Tech News,* March 31, 2014

This article reports on the research done by Rafi Shaik and Ramakrishna Wusirika. It was published on *Michigan Tech News,* a Michigan Technological University website that reports on campus news and the accomplishments of members of the campus community.

A dramatic opening grabs readers' attention.

The drama develops quickly because news articles get right to the point. This paragraph describes a problem and poses a solution.

The researchers are introduced as key figures in the narrative.

The article briefly summarizes, in a non-technical way, what the researchers did.

As the Earth's human population marches toward 9 billion, the need for hardy new varieties of grain crops has never been greater.

It won't be enough to yield record harvests under perfect conditions. In an era of climate change, pollution and the global spread of pathogens, these new grains must also be able to handle stress. Now, researchers at Michigan Technological University have identified a set of genes that could be key to the development of the next generation of super rice.

A meta-data analysis by biologist Ramakrishna Wusirika and PhD student Rafi Shaik has uncovered more than 1,000 genes in rice that appear to play key roles in managing its response to two different kinds of stress: biotic, generally caused by infectious organisms like bacteria; and abiotic, caused by environmental agents, like nutrient deficiency, flood, and salinity.

Traditionally, scientists have believed that different sets of genes regulated plants' responses to biotic and abiotic stress. However, Wusirika and Shaik discovered that 1,377 of the approximately 3,800 genes involved in rice's stress response played a role in both types stress. "These are the genes we think are involved in the cross talk between biotic and abiotic stresses," said Wusirika.

About 70 percent of those "master" genes are co-expressive — they turn on under both kinds of stress. Typically, the others turn on for biotic stress and turn off for abiotic stress.

The scientists looked at the genes' response to five abiotic stresses — drought, heavy metal contamination, salt, cold, and nutrient deprivation — and five biotic stresses — bacteria, fungus, insect predation, weed competition, and nematodes. A total of 196 genes showed a wide range of expressions to these stresses.

The article explains the significance of the research.

The conclusion links to the technical paper.

"The top genes are likely candidates for developing a rice variety with broad stress-range tolerance," Wusirika said.

Next, they would like to test their findings. "We want to do experimental analysis to see if five or 10 of the genes work as predicted," he said.

Their study is described in the paper "Machine Learning Approaches Distinguish Multiple Stress Conditions Using Stress-Responsive Genes and Identify Candidate Genes for Broad Resistance in Rice," published in the January edition of *Plant Physiology.*

Acknowledgments (continued from page iv)

Loretta Graziano Breuning. "Your Neurochemical Self," *Psychology Today*, June 6, 2011. Copyright © 2011 Sussex Publishers, LLC. Reprinted by permission from Psychology Today Magazine.

Center for Information Research on Civic Learning and Engagement (CIRCLE). Quick Facts--Youth Voting. Reprinted by permission of CIRCLE.

Creative Commons. Text from the "About" page of the Creative Commons website. Licensed under Creative Commons Attribution 3.0 license, http://creativecommons.org/licenses/by/3.0/deed.en_US.

Jennifer Egan. Excerpt from *A Visit from the Goon Squad* by Jennifer Egan, p. 199. Copyright © 2010 by Jennifer Egan. Used by permission of Alfred A. Knopf, an imprint of the Knopf Doubleday Publishing Group, a division of Random House LLC. All rights reserved.

Matthew Futterman. "John Madden's Missed Tackles." *The Wall Street Journal*, May 20, 2013. Reprinted by permission.

Marcia Goodrich."Scientists ID Genes that Could Lead to Tough, Disease-Resistant Varieties of Rice" from *Michigan Tech News* site, March 31, 2014. Reprinted by permission of Michigan Technological University.

Josh Higgins. "Student Turnout to Affect November Election," *Collegiate Times*, April 11, 2012. Reprinted by permission.

Thomas H. Holmes and Richard H. Rahe. "The Social Readjustment Rating Scale" from Thomas H. Holmes and Richard H. Rahe, *Journal of Psychosomatic Research*, Volume 11, Issue 2, August 1967, p. 213-218, Copyright © 1967 Elsevier Science Inc. All rights reserved. Reprinted by permission.

Inked Magazine. Excerpt from "Mo Coppoletta's tattoo shop, The Family Business," *Inked*, June/July 2012, p. 22. Reprinted by permission of *Inked* Magazine.

Jumasarchive. Jumasarchive grant proposal reprinted by permission of Johndan Johnson-Eilola, Ph.D.

Holly Kruse. Excerpt from "'An Organization of Impersonal Relations': The Internet and Networked Markets," *First Monday*, Vol. 12 No. 11, Nov. 5, 2007. Reprinted by permission of the author.

Anne Lamott, "Shitty First Drafts." Excerpt from *Bird By Bird: Some Instructions On Writing And Life* by Anne Lamott, copyright © 1994 by Anne Lamott. Used by permission of Pantheon Books, an imprint of the Knopf Doubleday Publishing Group, a division of Random House LLC. All rights reserved.

Alice Levitt. "Taste Test: Review of Maple City Diner in St. Albans," April 10, 2013. Reprinted by permission of Seven Days Newspaper.

Courtney E. Martin. "Wal-Mart v. Dukes Ruling Is Out of Sync with 21st-Century Sex Discrimination," *The Christian Science Monitor*, June 22, 2011. Reprinted by permission of the author.

The Morning News blog. Essays page. Reprinted by permission of The Morning News.

Mike Prior. Letter to the Editor - "Wind energy is important jobs provider," *Des Moines Register*, February 3, 2014. Reprinted by permission.

Rock the Vote. "Winning Young Voters: New Media Tactics," June 2008. Reprinted by permission of Rock the Vote.

Rafi Shaik and Ramakrishna Wusirika. "Machine Learning Approaches Distinguish Multiple Stress Conditions Using Stress-Responsive Genes and Identify Candidate Genes for Broad Resistance in Rice," *Plant Physiology* 164(1): 481–495. Copyright © 2014 American Society of Plant Biologists. All rights reserved. Reprinted by permission.

Linell Smith. From "The Art of Poetry" by Linell Smith, *Goucher Quarterly* Winter 2014 issue, pp. 16-21. Reprinted by permission.

Gina Trapani. "Geek to Live: Organizing 'My Documents,'" Lifehacker.com, February 22, 2006. Reprinted by permission of Gawker Media Group.

David Foster Wallace. From *This Is Water* by David Foster Wallace. Copyright © 2009 by David Foster Wallace Literary Trust. By permission of Little, Brown and Company. All rights reserved.

Brad Williams. "Build Your Own (Inexpensive) QRD/BBC Diffusors," *Tape Op*, No. 83, p. 16. Reprinted by permission of Brad Williams.

Lisa Kalner Williams. "Four Twitter Etiquette Tips to Use Right Away," from SierraTierra.com, August 12, 2013. Reprinted by permission of the author.

Index

Missing something? To access the online material that accompanies this text, visit **bedfordstmartins.com/changing**. Students who do not buy a new book can purchase access at this site.

Inside LaunchPad Solo for *Changing Writing*

Scenarios

1. Advocating Voter Registration on Campus
2. Teamwork Problems
3. Arguing for a Handwritten Letter? Or E-mail?
4. Making Invisible Things Visible: Mapping Data
5. Creating a Parody Ad
6. Writing a Profile for a Magazine
7. Podcasting Campus Life for Prospective Students
8. Drafting a Poster about Online Privacy
9. Educating Users about E-mail Scams
10. Writing a Restaurant Review
11. A Story from Your Digital Life
12. Analyzing Your Media Diet
13. A Day in Your Online Life
14. Designing Cover Art for Digital Music
15. Designing an Organization's Graphic Identity
16. Designing a Website for Doglake Records
17. Designing a Newsletter for the Zeeland Farmers' Market
18. Creating a Facebook Page for an Organization
19. Repurposing a Text
20. Revising a Campus File-Sharing Policy

Digital Writing Tutorials

Photo Editing Basics with GIMP

Audio Recording and Editing with Audacity

Creating Presentations with PowerPoint and Prezi

Tracking Sources with Evernote and Zotero

Building Your Professional Brand with LinkedIn, Twitter, and More

Cross-Platform Word Processing with CloudOn, Quip, and More